KU-709-431

WITHDRAWN

FROM ALL SIDES

MEMORIES OF WORLD WAR II

FROM ALL SIDES

MEMORIES OF WORLD WAR II

COMPILED BY BOB WILLEY

ALAN SUTTON

ALAN SUTTON PUBLISHING
BRUNSWICK ROAD · GLOUCESTER · UK

ALAN SUTTON PUBLISHING INC
WOLFEBORO · NEW HAMPSHIRE · USA

First published 1989

British Library Cataloguing in Publication Data

From all sides : memories of World War II.
1. World War
I. Willey, Bob
940.53

ISBN 0 86299 678 3

Library of Congress Cataloging in Publication Data
applied for

Cover design by Martin Latham

Typesetting and origination by
Alan Sutton Publishing Limited.
Printed in Great Britain
by The Guernsey Press Company Ltd.
Guernsey, Channel Islands.

All royalties to

UNICEF

THE TEAM

Left to right. Back: *Bob Willey, David Morgan, Danny McConnachie, Louise Kirby, Joanna Bill*
Middle: *Debbie Cleaveley, Sasha Hughes, Jenny Smith, Lucy Swingler, Laura Jerram, Owen Elias, Lynsey Wright*
Front: *Joanne Stewart, Maude Milton, Paul Creed*
Not in photograph: *Chris Stevens*

INTRODUCTION

Fifty years is a long time in any person's life and it has to be a very strong memory to endure in vivid detail. The day war was declared is obviously one such memory and, together with fifteen senior pupils, I have tried to assemble a range of such recollections to try and understand the feelings of ordinary people, from all sides, caught up in the last war. The detail of that day was one thing, but for many it was just a key to unlocking memories, just as clear, which had lain hidden for years.

To possible contributors our letter, coming as it did so obviously unannounced, must often have prompted the immediate question 'Why me? How did they find my name?' This list of people to approach was always going to be our biggest problem but once started, the contributors themselves caused it to snowball. Where we had begun with a limited number of British names found through military organizations and reference books like *Who's Who*, we found ourselves receiving floods of letters from all over the world. They had heard of us by word of mouth, through letters from other contributors, newsletters, magazines and newspapers from Guernsey to Jerusalem. For foreign contributors the surprise at receiving our letter must have been even greater and in this case the names had been taken, almost at random, from the *International Who's Who*, together with the help of some embassies. In all cases it would appear that our request struck a chord: the young must know what happened.

To receive so many offers was very exciting and, for those of us lucky enough to have been personally untouched by war, it has been fascinating to catch a glimpse of what it meant to our parents' and grandparents' generations. It is strange that war seems to have brought out the worst in so many respects but that, at the same time, it was a period that so many of our contributors saw as showing the best as well; a time of tremendous national spirit, of all pulling together and working for a single goal. Perhaps it is this apparent contradiction which makes the memories of war so vivid to those who took part and so fascinating for those who did not.

From the very beginning it seemed quite wrong for us to try and make any money out of this and so, to reflect the many nationalities who helped us, we have decided that all the proceeds should go to the United Nations Children's Fund UNICEF. It is very appealing to have children helping children who are suffering, and UNICEF does much for children affected by war.

Thanks are due to many people. To Françoise Jones, Elek Tomaszewski and Mark Lorünser for their translations, which meant that our title had real meaning. To Mr Jack Leonard who so generously gave access to his enormous archives of Jewish material. To Derek Twinn who not only provided many of the photographs, but copied all the others from contributors' originals.

The greatest thanks, though, must go to each and every person who so generously gave their time to write for us. This is only a small selection of the hundreds of pieces we received and it is a pity we cannot use every single one. It is important that those who wrote should know that, even though their memories may not be included in this collection, their pieces will be used in schools, here in Britain and in translation abroad, to try to show what war means to the individuals involved and to try to teach that it is not the way to solve any problems between peoples.

Bob Willey
1989

Helga Howes

We lived in Vienna when war broke out. It came as no surprise. When Hitler annexed Austria a year earlier, everybody said that he would bring us war. Since then we had been prepared for war in a practical way. Air raid sirens had been sounded – only experimentally, of course. Gas masks had been issued.

Our block of flats, in common with all other Viennese housing, had a cellar and an attic where each resident had a partitioned area for his or her exclusive use. Attic partitions were made of wood; they had to be left unlocked and the area emptied to allow access should there be incendiary bombs. For us this presented no hardship. Mother used the attic solely for drying the washing during the winter. The cellar was to be used as an air raid shelter. The central corridor was thought to be the most sheltered area; hence the brick partitions could remain intact as they would provide additional protection. Practical advice was given about blackout.

In May 1939 father was called up for a *Waffenübung*, a four-weekly military exercise. In August we had to break short our summer holiday because father received another call-up.

On the day war was declared, mother and I sat by the radio all evening, listening again and again to Mr Chamberlain's message and Hitler's answer. Mother cried. She said that father will now have to stay in the army. The military exercise had turned into reality. Father had served for two years in the First World War, fighting the Italians in the Dolomites. Mother said her generation was unlucky, having to live through two wars within twenty years.

There was some consolation. People said the war could not last long. Modern warfare techniques were quite different from those used in the Great War. Bombs and chemical weapons would soon put an end to it. Earlier that year I saw a newsreel of the war in China in 1937/8, where Japanese aircraft had attacked Chinese cities: explosions turning houses into rubble; people running, terrified; a toddler amongst the debris, injured, crying. These scenes kept flashing through my mind all day. When will the first enemy aircraft hit us? I kept looking at the sky, but all was quiet. I never slept a wink that night, too frightened that I might miss the alarm.

A few years passed before Vienna was bombed. When war broke out, I was thirteen. At the end of the war I had almost passed my teens and felt I had grown old before my time.

PRESIDENT

ERICH HONECKER

OF THE GERMAN DEMOCRATIC REPUBLIC

On 1 September 1939 I was in the penitentiary at Brandenburg-Gorder. By this day, since my arrest on 4 December 1935, the hell of the terror in Prinz Albrecht Strasse and of Adolf Hitler's bodyguard in Berlin-Lichterfelde lay behind me. After my conviction by the Second Senate of the National Court of Justice to ten years' imprisonment in July 1937 I came via the prisons of Berlin-Moabit and Berlin-Plotzensee to the Brandenberg-Gorder penitentiary in a train of the German Reich – likewise fitted out as a prison. The train was filled with prisoners.

This is written only to show that for me the outbreak of the Second World War was no surprise, but confirmation of our view at the time that Hitler meant war and, with that, Germany's downfall. In the summer of 1934 this opinion was represented by me on behalf of a delegation of German Youth in my speech at the World Youth Congress in Paris against war and fascism.

In the trial before the Second Senate of the National Court of Justice the question of peace or war similarly played a great role. With seven other resistance fighters (male and female) I was sentenced in accordance with the petition of the Public Prosecutor of the Reich, because we, it was claimed, had been endeavouring to alienate German youth from Hitler, to change forcibly the constitution of the German Reich and to topple the 'beloved Führer' of the Reich.

On 3 September 1939 – I was working with the doctor in the penitentiary as a 'trusty' – I heard that Great Britain and France had entered the war, as foretold. The invasion of Poland – in Hitler's words 'since this morning shots have been returned' – and the entry of Britain and France into the war shocked me deeply in view of the consequences that this was bound to entail, but at the same time it strengthened my recognition that it was the beginning of the end for Hitler's Germany. At that moment it was clear to me that Hitler and his companions would plunge the German people, the Polish, British and French peoples, indeed all the peoples of the world into a sea of blood and tears.

In the ruins of Berlin, as a member of the so-called 'Death or Glory' squad that had been set up, this became a certainty in my mind when considering the bombing raids which continued day and night.

I am happy that you and your generation have never experienced times of war. May this also be the case in the future. That is also the reason for my determination – as General Secretary of the Central Committee of the Socialist Unity Party of Germany and Chairman of the Council of State of the German Democratic Republic – to act in accordance with the people of the GDR that war never again emanates from German soil, but only peace. This found expression in the Joint Communiqué on the occasion of my Official Visit to the Federal Republic of Germany.

R. Turk

As a young Territorial Army soldier, 3 September 1939 holds many memories for me.

A few days before the Government had called for General Mobilization, so as a member of the Signal Platoon, H.Q. Company, the Fifth Battalion Gloucestershire Regiment, I was mobilized, and with the rest of the lads reported to the Drill Hall.

We sat around all night in the Drill Hall. Some tried to sleep, others played cards, some just talked and laughed the night away. The next day we were medically examined, all passing A1. We were attested and paid our bounty which pleased us all. At the time I was sixteen years of age, so you can imagine what it felt like – a boy of that age being given twenty pounds plus fourteen shillings. I had never had so much money in my pocket; the average wage at that age was only ten shillings.

The only trouble was we could not get out to spend it for we were confined to the Drill Hall. Married men were allowed home at night but single men were not allowed out. We were on standby so we just sat around talking. I remember someone playing a penny whistle and we had a sing-song. That Sunday was a bright and sunny day, the skies were blue and we all sat out in the Drill Square. So began our war, and I remember saying to my pal, 'On this day of all days!', for it was my seventeenth birthday.

We were given two blankets and, with our equipment, marched to a billiards hall down the road. This was to be our home for a few days, so we slept on the floor or under the tables. It did have its advantages though, for next to our billet was a corner shop, the old type of shop that sold everything; you name it they had it, so we were able to spend some of our money. The Monday morning we bought dripping cakes and a bottle of milk and sat outside the Hall watching the people going to work and, of course, making a few ribald remarks to people we knew.

On the Tuesday we were allowed out into the town after four o'clock, so off we went, pockets full of money and not a thought of saving any. It was the first time I had been into a pub and held a pint of beer and, needless to say, we all went back to our billet a little merry to say the least.

On the following Sunday the Battalion were to lay up the colours and so we had to train for the ceremony for a few days. Then we marched through the streets of Gloucester, drums playing, bayonets fixed and colours flying. It was a great feeling. We entered the Cathedral with the sun shining and the colours of the windows standing out and I remember looking along the rows of khaki-clad figures and feeling how great everything was, never thinking that within six months half of these men would be laid to rest in France and a number of them would languish in prisoner of war camps for the duration.

So the Glosters laid their colours in the safe-keeping of the Church until the end of hostilities when they would reclaim them. We then marched back to the billet to an evening meal and a night on the town. The next morning we were roused, breakfasted, paraded in Full Field Marching Order and were marched out of the Drill Yard and embarked on Black and White coaches for, as it was put, 'somewhere in England'. Despite all this secrecy it was amazing to see the wives and girlfriends milling around the coaches shedding a few tears. To us younger ones it seemed so soppy and so we just had a giggle.

So it was that we left Gloucester for a destination unknown – until we asked the coach driver. He knew it was Marlborough in Wiltshire. This was where we were to learn the soldiering trade, and believe me we did it the hard way!

AIR VICE-MARSHAL

ALEX ADAMS

It was eleven o'clock on Sunday 3 September 1939. In Berlin a few of the British Embassy staff gathered in the Chancery. The tension of the last week had given way to the unreason of war and somehow we were relieved. There had been moments difficult to understand during the two days since Hitler ordered the German army to invade Poland on 1 September just before dawn, which they had done despite the British and French guarantee to Poland. The invasion was a fact and we at the British Embassy in Berlin had known for a long time that nothing would stop Hitler going ahead with his plans. Supported by the experience of success in all his previous campaigns there could be no turning back at this stage.

In the Chancery we stopped the clock at 11 a.m. and Geoffrey Harrison, the third secretary, pasted a piece of paper over the glass with a note on it saying that the clock had been stopped purposely and was not to be restarted until Hitler was defeated.

The fate of the British staff at the Embassy we could not foretell. So, with time on my hands, I sat back in one of those comfortable old fashioned red leather chairs that used to adorn many a Chancery in British Embassies throughout the world, in which one inevitably finished up in the horizontal position. My mind took me over the events of the past few days.

I had been appointed to the post of Assistant Air Attaché at the British Embassy in Berlin a year before. By the midsummer of 1939 the French and British attachés were increasingly isolated. For information we were reduced to our own resources. I laughed over one recollection of those days: the Air Ministry in London had been getting little bits of information from secret sources about a new twin-engined fighter said to be in production by Junkers. They wished to know if it was fact or fiction. Paul Stehlin, later to become head of the French air force, was my French opposite number in Berlin. He always had a bright idea, so I asked him how he would find out. He said 'Why not telephone the Junkers factory and ask them?'

The next morning I did just that and it worked. I got the factory on the telephone and asked to speak to the head of Security. I gave a typical German name and said I was speaking from the *Luftfahrtministerium*. I added, 'I have in front of me your latest Junkers magazine. The aeroplane picture on the front cover is described as a twin-engined Junkers 88.' He immediately interrupted: 'God in Heaven, it's still on the secret list.' 'Precisely,' I said, 'perhaps you could look into it and let Security here know.' As I hung up I could imagine the temporary confusion. The existence of the Ju-88 had been confirmed.

Early in August I had spent a few days touring by car in eastern Germany. I wished to check on any movements of Luftwaffe units into that part of the country, which one might expect in preparation for a pre-planned invasion of Poland at the beginning of September. I was duly rewarded by finding that a number of ersatz airfields, previously empty, were now occupied. Outside Landsberg near Schwerin I stopped to ask an airman, of which there were quite a number around, the way into town. He said he was going into Landsberg so I gave him a lift. All aircrew carried the number of their squadron on their shoulder straps. His was a squadron normally stationed near Cologne. So I asked him how long he had been up in east Germany near the Polish frontier. He said, 'We only came here last week and expect to be on manoeuvres for a month', and added that his squadron commander had told them that they were to be prepared for action by the end of the month, but they had to be careful not to repeat that to any strangers. I agreed with him that he should be careful what he said! We arrived in the town and I left him in the square. This and other similar encounters convinced me that the air force preparations for an invasion of Poland were well in hand and they certainly confirmed the premeditated and unprovoked build-up for war.

Towards the end of August Sir Nevile Henderson asked me to have my four-seater Gull aircraft standing by to take important papers from Hitler to Mr Chamberlain, which were expected to include his reply to a final offer of a peaceful settlement of the Polish question. I had all the necessary diplomatic papers and passes prepared and, even after the invasion of Poland had begun on 1 September, I was given by the Luftwaffe a route to fly out west to avoid anti-aircraft defences. However, in the event, Hitler's reply to the British Government was read out to Sir Nevile Henderson in very quick German and with no interpreting, and he was not given a copy for transmission to London. The correspondence had been overtaken by the Second World War. Beyond any lingering doubt it confirmed Hitler's premeditated aggression against the Poles.

Two days previously, after Hitler's war against Poland had been announced, I had taken a taxi to the British Embassy. The driver, a man old enough to have fought in the previous war, looked serious and when I told him my destination he asked, 'I suppose this Polish war means that there will be another war against England before long?' I replied that there was not much room for doubt. In a resigned voice he added, 'That will mean that we will starve again.' Undoubtedly there were many such people who remembered clearly the hardships of the First World War and who were dreading a repetition. Although the masterly propaganda of Dr Goebbels had effectively introduced into the minds of the ordinary Germans the idea that the Nazi way was just, there were many doubters. Indeed on that same day, after Hitler had finished his introduction to war in a tirade over the radio, I saw a number of women crying in the streets. Those stolid Germans were not all screaming joyously for battle.

At midday I was aroused from my seat in the Chancery to be told that the staffs of the French and British Embassies were to be concentrated in the Adlon Hotel, which was nearby in the same block in the centre of Berlin. A few American friends came there to join us. The United States Government had undertaken to look after British interests in Germany. The news of the French and British involvement in the war was slow to get around. Some of us went to the bar for a drink before lunch and we were able to take lunch in the Adlon centre court, mixing freely with the other hotel guests.

With lunch over our confinement took on a new complexion. The German police had been told that we were at war and they came to protect us, although there was no evidence of anybody wishing to do us bodily harm. We were asked to confine ourselves to the first floor where we were given rooms. Our French friends were confined to the second floor and we were not allowed to communicate with them.

Until late in the afternoon we found that we could still use the telephone within the city. Calls were made to our flats and houses and a little later some of our more essential belongings caught up with us. Tommy Troubridge, who was then Naval Attaché and later became the Fifth Sea Lord, managed to have a case of champagne included in his consignment. When the initial flurry of our confinement had died down I retired to my room and was resting on the bed reading, immersed in a tense passage of John Buchan, when there was a knock on the door and the sound of heavy breathing. A burly German entered and I saw in the reflection of the wardrobe mirror that he was carrying an axe. I was off the bed in a flash and gripped the back of a chair with a determination to keep it between the intruder and myself. My voice was a little unsteady when I asked him what he thought he was going to do with the weapon. After all we did not know exactly how a German worker might interpret his Government's intentions now that there was a war between us. He answered simply, 'I have been sent up to open a wooden case'. At once I remembered the champagne and with relief directed him to Captain Troubridge's room; I followed to slake an anxious thirst.

A special train was laid on the next day to take us to Holland under diplomatic privilege. As we left the Adlon Hotel a few people gathered on the street. They were silent. Only as we drew away, headed by the car of the United States chargé d'affaires Mr Kirk, who had with him Sir Nevile Henderson, did I hear a word from the crowd. It was *aufwiedersehen* in a throaty voice from an elderly German who gave a discreet wave of his hand behind the backs of the armed German police.

SIR JOHN COLVILLE

PRIVATE SECRETARY TO BRITISH PRIME MINISTERS 1939–46

Extract from The Fringes of Power, *Hodder & Stoughton, 1985*

I was living with my parents at 66 Eccleston Square when the world almost went to war over Czechoslovakia. It was September 1938, exactly a year after I joined the Foreign Office, that Britain and France stepped back from the brink of the precipice and signed the Munich Agreement with Hitler. Neither Britain nor France was ready for war. The French had a vast army; the British had the world's largest navy; but the Germans already had a powerful air force whereas by then the Royal Air Force had received only two or three operational Spitfires: not even two or three squadrons. The French air force was in a lamentable state.

In those last days of 1938, trenches were dug in Hyde Park, plans were made to evacuate school children, gas masks were prepared for distribution and every young man I knew who was not already a soldier or sailor joined a 'Supplementary Reserve'. However, after the signing of the Munich Agreement Neville Chamberlain assured us that there would be peace in our time; and he really believed it. So I returned to my middle oriental plays in the Foreign Office (my parish, with of course a senior First Secretary in charge, was Turkey and Persia), to be rudely shaken when on 15 March 1939 Hitler, contrary to the solemn promises he had given at Munich, sent his troops to seize Prague and, shortly afterwards, Danzig. On Good Friday Mussolini invaded Albania and Hitler began to make menacing threats to Poland.

On 22 August 1939 came the signature of the Molotov-Ribbentrop non-aggression pact between the Soviet Union and Germany, secretly partitioning Poland and agreeing to hand over the prosperous little Baltic States to Russia. It meant that short of a miracle war was certain.

On 23 August I had been due to sail to New York on my first visit to the USA for a month's holiday in Wyoming where some close Anglo-American friends had rented a ranch. I looked forward with excitement to seeing America; and I had a strong emotional incentive, which had been growing throughout the summer. Hitler put a stop to all that, for all leave was cancelled just before my ship was due to sail, so at the beginning of September 1939 I was waiting at my desk in Whitehall for war to be declared, twenty-four years old, a Third Secretary in the Diplomatic Service of two years' standing and tempted to resign before, on my twenty-fifth birthday, my employment should become a reserved occupation from which there would be no escape while the war lasted.

The British and French governments, rapidly followed by all four of Britain's self-governing Dominions, declared war on Germany on 3 September 1939, as soon as Hitler's forces invaded Poland. He had already recovered the Rhineland, seized Austria and Czechoslovakia and proclaimed that 'Today Germany is ours; tomorrow the whole world'.

It was a warm and bright Sunday morning, on which the early services in all the churches were packed with worshippers, many of whom had not been seen in church for a long time. When, after following their example, I arrived at the Foreign Office I was informed that I had been assigned to the Ministry of Economic Warfare which was in the course of being established in the vacant lecture rooms of the London School of Economics. It was to be a primary instrument in imposing an economic blockade on Germany, a policy which, combined with our control of the seas, many deluded optimists believed would bring Germany rapidly to her knees.

On reporting to this new and bewildering organization I was given an empty desk and nothing whatever to do. I sat contemplating the green leather desk-tops until somebody switched on a wireless set and we listened to Neville Chamberlain announcing we were at war. We knew it was coming, but all the same Chamberlain's broadcast, made with slow, solemn dignity, induced a numbness from which we were rudely revived by the sirens moaning out the war's first air raid warning.

I say we, for there were others sitting equally unemployed in the London School of Economics. It was widely believed that London would be reduced to rubble within minutes of war being declared, as recently depicted to an alarmed populace in the film of H.G. Wells' book, *Things to Come*; and it seemed that this was indeed about to happen. So we scuttled, preserving what semblance of nonchalance we could, to the air raid shelter. There I played bridge with David Eccles, Rufus Smith and another new conscript to the

Ministry. After the first rubber the All Clear sounded, for the sirens had been set off on account of a single unidentified aircraft spotted miles to the east of the Thames estuary.

We returned to our empty desks and at lunchtime, being assured that I should have nothing to do or even to read that day, I went home reflecting that we seemed remarkably ill-prepared for Armageddon. It was a lovely afternoon and so my brother Philip, awaiting his call-up to the Grenadiers, motored me to Trent Park, formerly the home of Sir Philip Sassoon and now owned by his close friend and cousin, Mrs Gubbay. It had an excellent private twelve-hole golf course on which my brother and I peacefully spent the first afternoon of war.

THE RT. HON.

LORD SHAWCROSS

GBE, QC

Although I was of course aware that war had become almost inevitable following the conclusion of the treaty between Nazi Germany and the Soviet Union, I was on the date of the declaration of war preparing my yacht in the Helford river, Cornwall, to take part in a regatta the next day. I listened to the broadcast by the then Prime Minister, subsequently heard that the regatta had been cancelled and informed my Skipper of this fact. He was an old Cornishman who had served me for a long time and his only comment was true to the tradition of Drake. He said: 'Fancy cancelling a regatta for a thing like that.'

Shirley Black

I was in love, in a West End play, and on top of the world refusing, like everyone else, actually to believe it would be war. Ignoring what my brain told me, I actually believed it wouldn't happen. Life was too wonderful.

We were due to lunch with my beloved's parents in Hertfordshire on the Sunday. His father's office, convinced of war, had already moved out there, lock, stock and barrel from the City of London.

Unknown to anyone, we had rented a tiny, very old cottage in the older part of the town, at the other end of the common near the old parish church, and were longing for some time alone together. It wasn't done then, to live with a man before marriage, so we always told my in-laws we would come down on Sunday morning, in time for lunch. They never knew of our Saturday nights and Sunday mornings together just a mile away. My parents were in Ceylon and only too pleased that I had at last made the West End, albeit in a teenage part (I was in fact nineteen). What they didn't know, I decided, wouldn't worry them.

On Saturday night, after final curtain, we took the last Green Line bus. By this time, tiny hammers were going brutally at the back of my mind, tapping out the message that war was inevitable. Even so, I still believed in some eleventh-hour miracle. There had been several of them in the preceding eighteen months or so. We stayed in bed until late on the Sunday. As Geoffrey went to shave in the tiny kitchen, the only room in the cottage with water, we switched on the old wireless set in the lounge. And we heard the solemn news. And then, on wireless, we heard the air raid sirens that, in times to come, we would hear so often when the bombers were in reality on their way to London and our homes. Then we didn't know what the siren was.

But it chilled us. We clung to each other and vowed marriage – something we had never even thought of up to then. As we set out for the other end of town, we went into the church where services were already finished and told the vicar that we would marry there, in his church, as soon as possible. Then we went to the pub to meet my future in-laws.

It was a silent pub. A couple of men threw darts in desultory fashion, their hearts and minds not on the game. Geoff's mother took the news of our marriage very badly, crying through the red eyes that had so often wept that morning. His father, who had been in the First World War, understood but disapproved. Lunch, roast lamb and all the trimmings, was silent. Geoff's sister and her boyfriend had arrived and told us they were both going to join up in the Air Force at once. They did.

We did marry. I was under age and my crackling 'phone call to Colombo got my parents' blank refusal to consent to my marriage. However, the law allowed the officiating clergyman to use his own discretion if parents refused and he was happy to give it. So we married in that lovely church on the edge of the common, a church I still crane my neck to see as an Inter-City train hurtles me north or back again to London. It is still visible despite all the buildings around it, as is the tiny cottage.

Had there been no war, would we have married then? Would I not have pursued my dream of becoming the first woman film director? There was no such thing for women then. They had to be actresses. Even so, I was determined to translate myself from actress to director and believe I might have made it. Much, much later, after I had embarked on journalism, I became the first-ever woman on the editorial staff of the *Financial Times* and, even then, I thought wistfully of the dream that war had taken from me. On the day I first entered the FT building it was greasepaint and hot lights that I could smell, not printer's ink.

On that first Monday night of the Second World War we assembled at a blacked-out theatre. The show did not go on. All over England the theatres went dark and did not light up again behind the blackout screens and curtains until the following February.

Geoff went into the Air Force – but did come back to being an artist and sculptor as before the war. We had two children in fairly quick succession. Bombed at the London home in which I loathed the loneliness of being separated from him, I welcomed the gaping hole in the roof of the rented house that gave me an excuse to take the next train to Blackpool, to be in digs near him with my baby daughter. I followed him to several camps until he was finally posted to Uxbridge so that I bought a London house and brought up my young amid the bombs, doodlebugs, buzz-bombs and other horrors that the Germans threw into the attack.

As an actress I had a great many cosmopolitan and international friends. Some were interned – our concentration camps for aliens seemed awful but, in retrospect, must have been the best in Europe. Actors of great promise got killed, mostly shot from the skies since the glamour of the air force seemed to attract theatrical people. Some, though serving, became starring actors in battledress, making propaganda films for the armed services.

It had something, though. We became a close-knit people, sharing comradeship as well as fear. Our children went to day nurseries while we worked in factories that made anything from signalling lanterns to bombs and we became a classless society, something we had never been in the snobbish '30s. It was in many ways a good time for women. We had a spirit that has gone from our lives, almost a kind of excitement that we were allowed to work, to be useful, to be part of the war effort. We became individuals, not second-class citizens. As the 1914–18 war had emancipated women, so the Second World War gave them final liberation by teaching them that they could work alongside their men, could succeed in their own right.

A famous radio commentator of the time spoke one night of the anti-climax, the almost-boredom, the flatness of peace. He said we had for so many years gone to bed hopeful and woken up thankful. Now we were waking up hopeful and going to bed thankful. It sounds cynical. Yet it contained much truth.

Halina Sledziewska

From the beginning of August 1939 in the whole of Poland one could sense this great tension; something was brewing, war seemed to be imminent. And although everyone in their heart of hearts had the hope that perhaps it would not come to war, the whole community was preparing for such an eventuality. Everybody had to have a gas mask and had to learn how to put it on and how to use it. On every square and in every large garden shelters were dug. These consisted of trenches one and a half yards deep and one yard wide, dug in a zigzag pattern. It was thought at the time that such a trench could form a useful shelter against an air attack. We were soon to learn how naive was our reasoning.

I lived in Warsaw with my mother. I was a Girl Guide. Girl Guides had been for the past year getting ready for a variety of services, so that should a war break out we could undertake various duties with confidence. Some of us would take up nursing duties, some would do catering to ensure that meals would be provided for soldiers at railway stations, others would perform communication services. Some people were storing sugar, flour and other staples.

From 24 August my group were destined for duty at a telephone exchange. In turn, twenty-four hours a day, we were to man the exchange, answer telephone calls informing of German air attacks. As yet though nothing was happening.

During the night into 1 September I was at home sleeping peacefully. Exactly at 6 a.m. we were all woken by a horrible noise – howling sirens and a voice from loud speakers: 'I announce a state of alarm for the City of Warsaw.' The war had begun.

The Germans, without any declaration of war, crossed the Polish border. The first air attack was directed against our capital. One saw the bombers circling over the city. Some, shot by our fighter planes, were falling vertically, smoke billowing from their tails, while the rest bombed our city. Everybody ran down into cellars. The first alarm did not last very long. After half an hour the aeroplane noise ceased and we came out from the cellars. It was a beautiful, warm, sunny day. In our district of the city no damage could be seen. This first strike had been directed against the city centre where a lot of bombs had fallen, destroying houses and killing passers-by.

From that time air strikes were repeated several times a day. After two days we moved to our cousins' home where we thought we would be better. But there was no safe place in Warsaw. Air raids, bombing, burning houses, people dying . . . telephones did not work, houses were without gas and electricity as the distribution networks were damaged.

After about five or six days the Government left Warsaw. The military defence of the city was assigned to General Czuma and the civilian defensive effort was led by the city's President, Stefan Starzynski. From now on his voice could be heard through the loud speakers all through the siege. It was the voice of a man who cared very much about the inhabitants of Warsaw left to their own devices.

A few days later there was no water in our taps. A well was found in a nearby street and this was the only supply of fresh water. Between air raids we would run there with a bucket, but it was not always possible to get any water as the queue was very long.

Life practically stood still, as in these circumstances not much action was possible. As soon as there was an air raid everybody dashed down into the cellar and listened carefully – a plane is coming – it will soon drop a bomb – will it be here – will it be a little further away? It flew away. Another one is approaching – will it drop a bomb on our house? And it was like that all day through.

When the alarm ended we would run out of the cellar, happy to be alive, to see what was happening around us. There is a house that was bombed – we have to see if there are any people there. Do they need any help? There lies a man. His leg is broken. We must carry him to a medical post. And once again there is an air raid. Once again down to the cellar to wait until it is over.

On 17 September terrible news reached us: the Soviet Union had invaded Poland from the East. Our situation now became even worse. The siege of Warsaw lasted for three weeks, until 27 September. There was no way out – deserted Warsaw had to surrender. At last peace and quiet, but it was a very frightening quietness. When I and my mother ventured outside to return to our home the view that faced us was frightful: demolished and still burning houses, dead people . . . We just stood there and started to cry.

And then, in the distance, we suddenly heard loud rhythmic steps: German soldiers were entering our city, proud and happy to take our capital. It took us a long time to get back to our home as there was no transport and many streets were buried in rubble. Our home was there, with all the windows broken, but luckily it had survived the bombing.

JAN DOBRACZYNSKI

On 1 September 1939, the day of the German assault on Poland, I was, as a mobilized military reserve officer, with my unit the 2nd Regiment of Mounted Fusiliers. At the time I was thirty years old. I left my wife in Warsaw. Having finished my education I worked for a few years as a Catholic writer and journalist. I was slowly making a name for myself with two of my books about contemporary Italian and French writers already published. In September two of my novels were due to be published.

My unit was involved in battle at the village of Mokra on 1 and 2 September, where the Wolynska Brigade consisting of four cavalry regiments of 3000 men was facing the Fourth German Armoured Division of 13,000 men and 500 tanks. The ratio of cannon power was 20:1 and of machine guns 6:1 in favour of the German division.

Our brigade stood its ground for two days, destroying about 100 tanks, but by the end of the second day it was decimated. The remnants carried on fighting until the end of September. On 17 September Soviet troops invaded Poland from the east. In the early days of October 1939 organized defence by the Polish forces had ceased.

I was wounded in action but luckily was not taken prisoner of war. In civilian clothes I managed to get to Warsaw and immediately undertook the duties of an officer in the Polish Underground Army, the *Armia Krajowa*. I was an editor of the underground paper *Walka* (*Combat*).

Throughout the five years of German occupation I lived in hiding, under assumed names, away from my family. During the nights, in hideaways, I was writing a novel entitled *Najezdzcy* (*The Invaders*) about the war being waged around me. The manuscript survived and after the war the book was published reaching a total of nearly 300,000 copies. It is still read today.

In 1944 the Warsaw uprising against the Germans erupted. The fighting continued for sixty-three days, but without the necessary help from either the West or the East it was eventually crushed by the Germans. Over 200,000 inhabitants of Warsaw died in the ruins of the city. What had escaped damage during the fighting was eventually burned down by the Germans. The surviving insurgents were taken to German prisoner of war camps. I was amongst them. My wife and daughters got out of Warsaw in just the clothing they were wearing. They lived in poverty, surviving only with the help of kind people.

I returned to Poland in May 1945 after the Allied victory over Germany. Warsaw was in ruins. We had no home, no means to live on as books were not published again until 1947. As a Catholic writer I was out of favour with the marxist rulers. I lost one of my daughters as a result of an illness she contracted during the Warsaw Uprising because I had no means to secure the necessary treatment.

Finally, after many years of toil and financial struggles, I was able to return to my profession as a writer. Although the state would not help me the Catholic community had its own journals and publishers.

Today, years later, I am a Catholic writer and activist. I have written over seventy books many of which have been translated into several languages. I am also a chairman of the Polish Patriotic Movement of National Revival, whose objectives are to unite all Poles through improvement of morality and civic posture.

GROUP CAPTAIN

PETER TOWNSEND

For the airmen of the Luftwaffe and the RAF who in only twelve months' time would vie with one another for supremacy in the air, the summer of 1939 was none the less enjoyable. At Tangmere in Sussex, 43 Squadron was in top form. We were at one with ourselves and our machines. It was the Hurricane, really, which gave us such immense confidence, with its mighty engine, its powerful battery of guns, and its feel of swift, robust strength and the ability to outdo our enemies. Months would go by before the real test of combat, but we believed in the Hurricane. Performance figures – those of the Me.109 and Spitfire were in a few respects superior – did not in the least dismay us. The Hurricane was our faithful charger and we felt supremely sure of it and ourselves.

On the night of 24 August, some of us in 43 Squadron did a sector reconnaissance – it was the last time we should see the friendly lights of Horsham, Brighton and Portsmouth spread out below. Our next flight would be in the inky darkness of the blackout. After 24 August we would practically cease flying, only to wait for the inevitable.

In Fighter Command our particular concern was the 'knock-out blow' the Luftwaffe was expected to deliver as soon as hostilities began. And in the fighter squadrons not one of us doubted that they would. Leave had been stopped. Mobilization of the Auxiliary Air Force and Volunteer Reserve had begun a week before and most of these peacetime pilots were then in uniform.

On 3 September, at Tangmere airfield, I was lying on the grass beside my Hurricane watching flakey white clouds drift across a blue sky, while hovering larks shrilled and voices came to me from pilots and ground crew also lying beside their dispersed aircraft. Never in my life had I experienced so peaceful a scene.

At 11 a.m. Squadron Adjutant John Simpson walked into the hangar and said to Warrant Officer Chitty, 'The balloon goes up at 11.15. That's official.' Seconds later the news reached us.

We all forgathered in the mess where we had listened to Hitler's shrieking voice just a year ago. Our station commander, Fred Sowrey, looked grave. But his presence was reassuring for us who did not know war. Twenty-three years earlier to the very day, Fred Sowrey had been on patrol with Lieutenant Leefe Robinson when Robinson sent a Zeppelin crashing in flames near London. The Zeppelin L32 had fallen to Sowrey's guns, and in May 1918 he was in at the kill of the last German raider to crash on English soil. This veteran of the first generation of airmen was about to see the horror of a second attempt by the Germans to reduce England to her knees by bombing. He steadied us in our ardour to 'get at the Hun'. He told us, 'Don't think a fighter pilot's life is one of endless flying and glory. You will spend nine-tenths of your time sitting on your backsides waiting.'

Macey and Hoskins, two imperturbables in white jackets, served us each a mug of bitter. The swing door by which they entered the ante-room seemed to creak louder as the silence grew and the fateful hour approached.

Then suddenly the radio came alive and the sombre, leaden tones of Prime Minister Neville Chamberlain fell on the silence of the ante-room. 'It is a sad day for all of us . . . Every aim for which I have worked, everything I had hoped for, all the principles in which I believed . . . have fallen down in ruin. I hope to live long enough to see the day when Hitlerism will be destroyed and a free Europe will exist again.' Chamberlain would never live to see that day. Neither would most of us who listened to him. The ebullient Caesar Hull jumped from one foot to another, exclaiming

'Wizard!', and turning to John Simpson, 'Never mind, John, you'll be killed early on.' And he punched him in the back and laughed.

John, however, would come through (like me) by pure luck. But not Caesar, nor Wilkinson, nor 'Wombat' Woods-Scawen in A Flight. Nor Tiger Folkes, Eddy Edmonds, Pat Christie or Joe Sullivan in B Flight. Within twelve months or so these valiant young men and hundreds like them, who cared for nothing more than the joy of flying, would die in the fight to destroy Hitlerism. Not counting the wounded and the burnt, survival was a one-in-five chance.

But no such thoughts troubled us then. As John said, 'It's the war we've been expecting, so we can't grumble.'

As we waited at Tangmere the atmosphere was so tense that in the end we dismissed it as unreal, and relaxed on the grass in the warm sunshine. Like sleek, powerful thoroughbreds our faithful Hurricanes seemed to be more patient than we as they waited for us to jump up into the cockpit and be off.

SIR CRISPIN TICKELL

GCMG, KCVO
BRITISH AMBASSADOR TO THE UNITED NATIONS

I was just nine years old when war was declared. As a child I had long been conscious of the anxieties of my parents, particularly during the summer of 1938. They were strongly against the Munich Agreement, and I remember my grandparents sending indignant telegrams to Mr Neville Chamberlain. The day we went to war came almost as a relief. I was taken into the drawing-room to hear Mr Chamberlain speak on the wireless. I can still recall his tired, dispirited voice. Air raid sirens were tested soon afterwards. There was a sense of anti-climax. My brother and I went out to play in the garden not quite understanding what had happened, but knowing that it would affect all our lives.

JOAN BERNARD

I was a student of Oxford University at home in London on vacation, living with my mother in a top floor flat in central London. We listened to the Prime Minister's announcement that we were at war with Germany. Being very musical I felt that I could cope better with the idea of being at war if I first let off steam by playing a few of the Bach *48 Preludes and Fugues* on the piano.

That done I went out to get civilian gas masks for my mother and myself and asked what I could do to help. I was told 'fill sandbags' and was directed to the former proposed site for the National Theatre, near the Victoria and Albert Museum. I set to work with a spade (it was now late morning) and went on until dusk by which time I was so stiff that I could hardly stand up and my hands were covered in blisters. I wallowed in a hot bath hoping no bombs would fall and then fell into bed weary and worried. What on earth would happen?

Fearing that war was coming, I had discussed with my Oxford College Principal whether or not to return for the final year of my course in the event of war, and had been persuaded by her to do so.

It was a very strange year. Tutors went off to war jobs. Spare time activities took the form of helping to entertain evacuated children, and courses in air raid precautions and first aid.

Finals coincided with Dunkirk. We had two three-hour papers a day for a week. We listened to the news, wrote the first, returned for news and lunch and wrote the second and so on. Day and night evacuated troops were streaming through Oxford to the west. In such a context our exams seemed unreal to say the least.

I had two weeks' vacation and volunteered for the Army and ended up serving for 5½ years. After regimental duties, first in the ranks and then as an officer, I served for 2½ years as an ATS staff officer at HQ Anti-Aircraft Command at Stanmore, Middlesex. In 1944, on the day after D-Day, I became staff officer to the Chief of the Air Defense Division in SHAEF (Supreme Headquarters Allied Expeditionary Force). We went overseas shortly after the liberation of Paris and were stationed in Versailles and Rheims, and were in Rheims when the armistice in Europe was signed there.

Part of the Air Defense Division's job was to coordinate (both between the Allies and between the Services) counter-measures against German V1 and V2 rockets. After the end of hostilities most of the ADD was formed into the Special Projectile Operations Group. We were based at Cuxhaven in Germany and under the operational command of the Joint Chiefs of Staff in Washington. Our job was to work with German prisoners from the captured V1 and V2 Division and with interned scientists, to find out all we could about the making of the V2 rocket, its handling in the field, launching etc., with a view to developing adequate counter-measures to it. There were no complete V2s left; they had launched them as they came off the production line. We scoured the continent for parts and rebuilt about eight. Three of these were successfully launched on an agreed line of fire cleared of aircraft and shipping in the North Sea. This was to prove that we had got the theory right. The third of these was a demonstration launch for senior officers of all three Services of each of the Allies – quite a party! We produced a detailed report for the Joint Chiefs of Staff, the War Office and the Ministry of Supply. Although the original intention behind the operation was defensive, it did also have the effect of saving Britain years in the post-war rocket programme and led ultimately, I suppose, to Arianne. One of our German scientists was Wernher von Braun, who later headed the American space programme.

My contemporaries and I hadn't got started in civilian life before the war, and had had no specific vocational training. There is, I think, a gulf between those who experienced the war and those who did not. The whole of life was heightened. The dangers concentrated the mind and our sets of values powerfully. There was a tremendous sense of service together in a common cause; great concern for others and unselfishness. This applied to all, civilians just as much as the Forces.

I was terribly lucky in my personal experience of war. No one close to me was killed. I met and worked with some marvellous people, many of whom have remained friends ever since.

THE BAILIFF OF JERSEY

SIR PETER CRILL

CBE

I remember very well the outbreak of war. I was fourteen at the time and was half way through a visit which should have taken one month to a doctor's family in Carhaix, Brittany. We had had his son on an exchange for one month previously.

When it looked as if war was imminent after Germany had attacked Poland on 1 September there was some talk about my being sent home. Travel in 1939 over any sort of distance was usually, except for the well off, by rail. Accordingly, on 2 September the sister of the boy with whom I had been staying was detailed to take me to St Malo and put me on the SS *Brittany* for Jersey.

We went down to the railway station at Carhaix where

French reservists who had been called up were boarding the train. Many of them were dressed in the uniform of the First World War and were carrying the helmets and rifles of that period. Several were drunk.

It was the custom in France, at that time, for women of middle-age and upwards to wear black, and the station platforms were full of desolate women, some of whom no doubt remembered the First World War. I was left with the impression that the French soldiers and the people I saw were most reluctant to fight. Of course, I was looking at it through the eyes of a fourteen-year-old and, with hindsight, I was not surprised at the débâcle of 1914. We should not forget, of course, that several French units, I think particularly the Fifth Army, fought extremely hard and enabled the British Expeditionary Force to withdraw to Dunkirk. We arrived at St Malo and, if you have ever been there, you will know that it is a very long walk from the station to the dock, and my guide left me at the town gates and returned to Carhaix. I found that the *Brittany* had not arrived and made myself known to the Southern Railway agent and was put up for the night.

The next day I was having coffee in a café waiting for the arrival of the *Brittany* when I went out into the street to hear the public announcement of the outbreak of war. I returned to the café and a woman in black asked me what the news was. When I told her she burst into tears.

Eventually I got back to Jersey, although the *Brittany* anchored off the Island for a short time and we all wondered if there were any submarines around. In fact, we had been stopped in order that the agricultural inspectors could search the vessel for Colorado beetles.

I remained in the island until November 1944 when, in common with about sixty other Jersey boys over a period of three months, we escaped to France which by that time had been liberated.

PROFESSOR DOCTOR

Kazimierz Kakol

The 25 May 1939 marked a very important point in my life – I passed my matriculation examinations. My personal problems pushed general problems into the background, although the rumblings of the forthcoming storm were increasing in force.

Anxieties of what would happen tomorrow were softened by the general belief that we were in the right and that Poland must say 'No' to the expansion of civilized barbarism. The totalitarian fascism which shielded the face of the Germanic 'Drang nach Osten' both frightened and mobilized. We, the Slavonic *untermenschen*, not racially pure, were determined to say 'No' to the empire of evil, without taking account of the corresponding military strength. The fact that we were not entirely alone brought us a bit of relief. Renewed and enriched alliances with Western democracies, Great Britain and France, reduced the obvious military superiority of Hitler's Germany. The determination of the Polish nation was so great that a government which considered yielding to Hitler's demands would have fallen immediately.

The war was in every mind, on all lips; we had prepared an excellent organization of civil defence; we were making plans, calculating our chances; saying goodbye to our friends and acquaintances called into the Forces; full of emotion while strolling the streets of Warsaw in the blackout – and yet the screaming of alarm sirens, the roar of exploding bombs, froze everyone, shocked and paralysed.

The solemn nature of official announcements invaded one's consciousness, underlining the truth that Poland had become the victim of aggression by an enemy who had insidiously and artfully prepared to strike the first blow. The battleship *Schleswig-Holstein* entered the waters of Gdansk declaring it to be a courtesy visit. The firing of its guns in anger was its contribution to the first morning of the war . . .

Coded radio bulletins carried alarming news of German planes flying over Polish territory. The air defence was insufficiently tight, insufficiently effective; bombs fell about 100 metres from my home hitting a building and splitting it along most of its length. In this building lived my girlfriend Hania, my younger school friend. How is she? Her family? What about the others? I have to help, to rescue – luckily there is always a need to do something. It helps in this situation not to think about the grave news reaching us through radio newsflashes. The German army pushes on relentlessly.

Suddenly on 3 September Great Britain and France declare war on Germany. We walk in large groups to the allied embassies, shouting loudly, full of gratitude and hope. Long live our Allies! Now we can defeat Hitler!

We walk around, school friends – those who have just passed their matriculation exams and those who were yet to face them. We approach officers of 'our' regiment – 'our' as it is stationed in our neighbourhood – the 36th Infantry Regiment. We could be useful, it is necessary to get ready to defend our capital city, the enemy is approaching. A categorical 'No' is the answer. We do not give up. We argue that our fighting ability is very high. Still 'No! No!', and then 'Yes!' We are given weapons, rifles: the nineteenth-century, French 'Lebelle'. Never mind; even with those rifles one can defend Warsaw . . .

The orders which, at three o'clock, aroused our battalion (made up of school youngsters under the command of experienced officers), caused general discontent bordering on insubordination. We are to march east: who is going to defend Warsaw? Here in the city so dear in our hearts we would like to take our manhood examinations in its defence.

We start a hard march towards Brzesc. Enemy aircraft are attacking us all the time; there is no sight of our air force. Recent information is making us nervous. Our allies, French and British, instead of bombing Germany are content to shower the Germans with leaflets intended to show them the error of their actions. The dull roar of heavy artillery is heard from nearly every direction. The glare of fires lights up the skies. In Brzesc we get on to a train. Moving on quickly we get stuck on the railway track which is constantly being bombed. We mend the tracks. The Germans bomb them again. We get stuck for good.

On 17 September terrible news: the Red Army has crossed the Polish border. Only now do I grasp the true meaning of the Ribbentrop-Molotov Pact made in August – the fourth partition of Poland? The battalion assembles and we march to succour fighting Warsaw.

The trail of the march is signposted by blood. Some of my nearest and dearest colleagues perish. Others are left behind in field hospitals. By the time news reaches us that Warsaw has surrendered our battalion has already been incorporated into an operational group, *Polesie*. We wage the last full-scale battle of the Polish Defensive War of 1939, on 5 and 6 October, at Kock. In the thick of battle we attempt to match excellently prepared German troops. No, the Germans did not force us to surrender. It was lack of ammunition . . .

From the battlefield five of us, school friends, set out into the future, long years of military conspiracy, the underground army bearing the name *Armia Krajowa*. We try to make up for our non-participation in the defence of Warsaw by taking part in the fight to free the capital from the Germans in the Warsaw Uprising in 1944. The examination we went through then had very little in common with the matriculation exams of May 1939. After this exam I was the only one left of the five of us.

The fact that I am still alive I treat as a sort of pledge to remain faithful to the ideals of my youth. The fight for truth, denunciation of crime, and punishment of transgressors, has to be carried out in a logical manner. The memory of a past so filled with personal tragedies and the tragedies of nations should be an instrument used in the formation of the future. The fight for the awareness of new generations is carried out in the courts, in the press and in the pages of books. I take part in the very well-known processes against the mass-murderer, organizer of the Holocaust, Adolf Eichmann, and the murderous members of the guards at the concentration camp of Auschwitz-Birkenau; I gather documentation of the guilt of SS General Reinefarth, whose soldiers burned alive wounded Warsaw insurgents, my friends and colleagues. I have the honour of being the Director of the General Commission for the Investigation of Hitler Germany's Crimes in Poland – The Institute of National Remembrance.

I often meet young Poles of the age I happened to be on that memorable 1 September 1939. I do my best to pass on my experiences, to warn them, to guard them. To warn them about the relapses of history. To guard them against a catastrophy which can be forestalled by working together.

I also often meet young Germans. I tell them exactly the same. Our future, the future of Europe, is non-divisible.

M. FUGILL

The outbreak of war found me, a girl from the South Wales mining valleys, working in a LCC hospital in Bow E3 as a senior officer, i.e. Head Maid, in the Nurses' Home. My young man (we didn't have 'boyfriends' then!) was twenty years old and at the end of his time as an apprentice shipwright. His mother was a widow working in the work-house part of Bromley House. My mother was a widow living in South Wales.

I stayed in Bow and was working in the hospital all

through the Blitz until 1945, even though I married in 1943. At the time my room overlooked Bromley-by-Bow station and I remember watching the children of the local schools setting out from the station with their teachers, suitcases, bags and a label attached to their lapels. There was a great sad silence after they left.

On one occasion during the Blitz we had had a bad night and I was in a bus trying to get over to Bexleyheath in Kent. Because of unexploded bombs we were going down unknown streets. Two young boys were on the bus and the conductress said, 'What are you doing back in London? You should have stayed evacuated.' Their reply was: 'Blimey, they're bombing them to buggery down there.' You couldn't give an answer to that, only realize that to them, no matter what, home still seemed safer.

My young man was working on the SS *Rawalpindi* helping with its conversion into an Armed Merchant Cruiser. That was September 1939, and she was to be sunk in the North Atlantic by the pocket battleship *Deutschland* before the year was out. (Mr Ludovic Kennedy's father was Captain of her and sank with his ship.) By October 1939 he was Carpenter's Mate on the SS *Lancashire*, taking Jewish refugees to New York and bringing back war supplies from America – among them, Lockheed bombers. It was a monthly run and he came home at the end of October, November and December. Then he went away and didn't return until June 1942. He had volunteered to join the crew of RMS *Mauritania* in New York. They were not there long before they were away to New Zealand and Australia bringing Anzac troops to this country. There was not enough time to visit home before they were off again. During the Blitz they never knew if their families were still alive. One of his friends, a quartermaster, was unaware of his father's death in the raids on Liverpool for some months after. They were all upset at the lack of communication. One of the prices, I suppose, one paid for war.

I must ask you not to forget we are old now but then we were young and while we lost five to six years of our lives, young lives, some lost all their life. My young man's mother worked in Bromley House until a bad raid destroyed it. Then she worked in a rest centre for bombed-out, homeless people, always sleeping in her own bed at night, never going to a shelter, until the roof blew off and she went over to her mother and sister in Bexleyheath. They had found a house for her for the duration. She found a job in Woolwich Arsenal but had to give it up because she turned yellow and jaundiced. She died later of cancer of the stomach.

My mother's war was being Auntie to London evacuees. The first two were sisters from Shoreditch and they were very happy with my mother. They went to her in 1939, but when I went home on holiday at the end of June 1940 their mother asked me to bring them back with me when my holiday finished. She thought the Germans had given up thoughts of raids. While I was taking them home with me a sailor on the train asked me why I was taking them back to London. I explained that their mother wanted it and he said, 'What a silly woman. She doesn't realize the carnage is about to begin!' How right he was. My mother would have accepted them back if they had gone straight away, but their mother sent a telegram which, in the chaos, took some time to reach my mother, and my mother's reply was too late. I often wondered what happened to them. We never heard any more.

My mother took another little girl about twelve years old. Her mother was evacuated too, living in the next village. My aunt took a family from Dover to stay in her house.

When the Blitz started on 7 September 1940, I had arranged to visit my young man's mother. She lived a few streets away. I think I set off at about 4 p.m. Anyway soon after I started out the air raid warning sounded. I was passing Lusty's timberyard in Bow (they were the makers of Lloyd Loom furniture – a kind of stiffened wickerwork).

City of Westminster
A.R.P
DISTRIBUTION OF GAS MASKS TO WESTMINSTER RESIDENTS
FITTING CENTRES
DISTRIBUTING STAT
SAVINGS DEPARTMENT
FOREIGN EXCHANGE
City of Westminster
AIR RAID PRECAUTIONS
FITTING GAS MASKS
PROVINCIAL BANK
LIMITED
DATE
BLACK-OUT ON
PERIOD
BLACK-OUT OFF
SUN NOV. 3
5·59 P.M.
" 10
5·47 P.M.
13 HRS. 29 MIN.
7·28 A.M.
" 17
5·37 P.M.
13 HRS. 53 MIN.
7·40 A.M.
" 24
5·28 P.M.
14 HRS. 16 MIN.
7·53 A.M.
DEC. 1
5·22 P.M.
14 HRS. 37 MIN.
8·5 A.M.
" 8
5·19 P.M.
14 HRS. 53 MIN.
" 15
5·19 P.M.
" 22
WAR COOKERY LEAFLET 4
CARROTS
Carrots are particularly useful in wartime as they contain protective substances which help us to resist infection and to see better in the blackout. The same protective substances are also present in milk, butter, margarine and cheese, but since supplies of these foods are limited, carrots help to make good the shortage.
There is very little of the "fruit vitamin" in carrots so it is an improvement to sprinkle them with coarsely chopped parsley just before they are put on the table.
The sweetness of carrots makes it possible to use them to replace part of the sugar in puddings and cakes. Suggestions for using them in this way are given on the back page of this leaflet.
Boiled Carrots
Wash and scrape the carrots and if large cut into rings. Cook in a small quantity of boiling salted water in a covered saucepan until tender. Drain and sprinkle with coarsely chopped parsley or the coarsely chopped feathery tops of the carrots.
Carrots Baked Round the Joint
Wash and scrape the carrots, if large cut in halves or quarters lengthwise. Put them in the baking tin round the joint. Cover with margarine paper, until the last 10 minutes. (Baking time approx. 40 minutes.)
Carrots and Sprouts
Scrape and slice carrots. Wash the sprouts in cold salt water and cut across the base of the stalk. Cook together in a small quantity of boiling salted water in a covered saucepan. When tender drain and serve. The addition of a knob of margarine is an improvement.

At home . . .

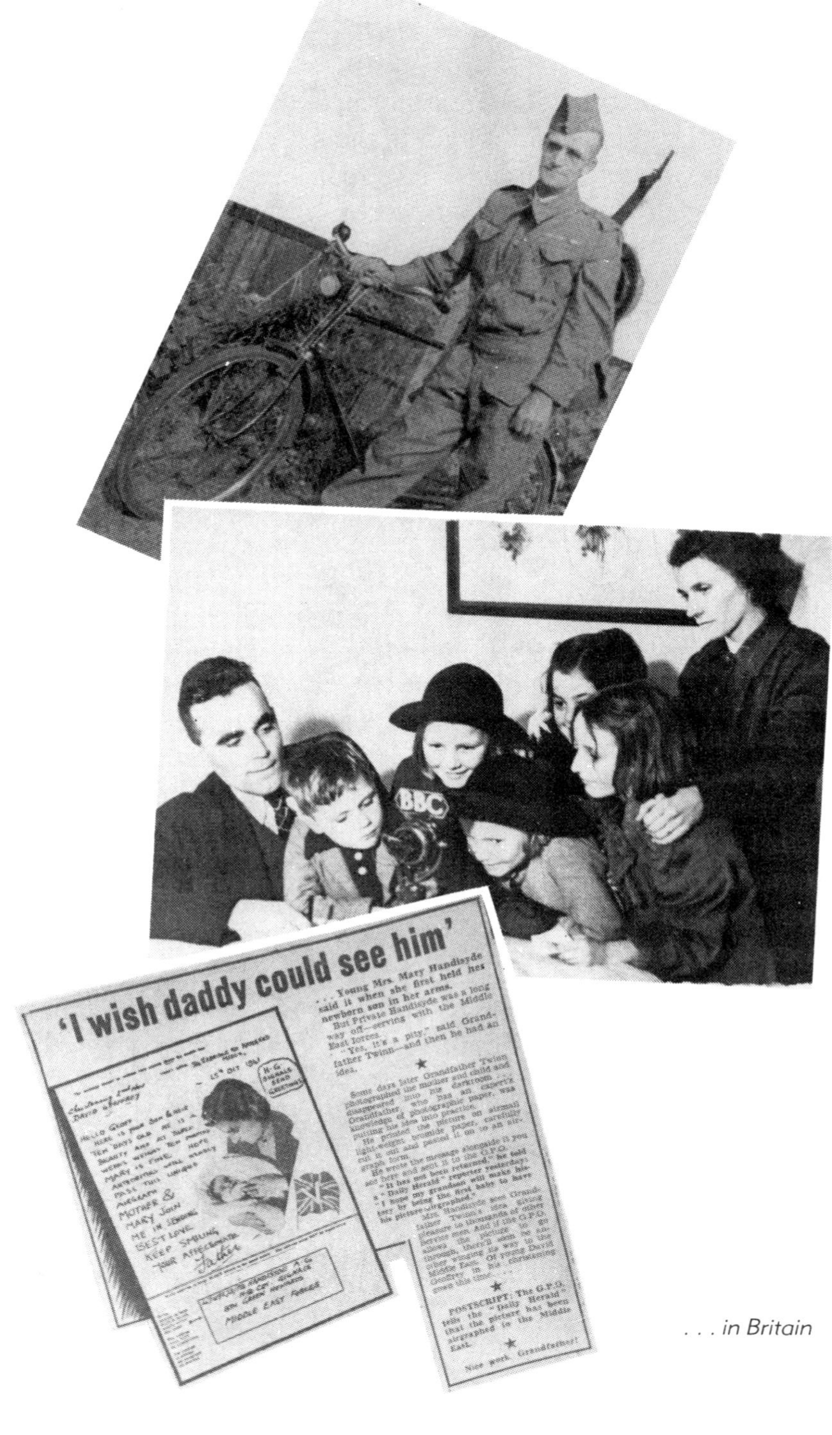

'I wish daddy could see him'

... Young Mrs. Mary Handisyde said it when she first held her newborn son in her arms.

But Private Handisyde was a long way off—serving with the Middle East forces.

"Yes, it's a pity," said Grandfather Twinn—and then he had an idea.

★

Some days later Grandfather Twinn photographed the mother and child and disappeared into his darkroom ...

★

POSTSCRIPT: The G.P.O. tells the "Daily Herald" that the picture has been airgraphed to the Middle East.

★

Nice work, Grandfather!

. . . in Britain

One of the caretakers offered me shelter, but I decided to carry on. I continued until I got to the fire station. Opposite there was concrete shelter and a warden advised me to go in and take shelter as the bombers were overheard. I looked up and saw them still in formation so went into the shelter for a short while. Then I decided to carry on in case my fiancé's mum was on her own, only to discover that she had gone back on duty as soon as the siren went, leaving her little dog. For a while it was quiet and I was on my own. Then the man from the flat downstairs came in; his wife had been evacuated. He was an old sailing ship skipper. He made me a strong mug of tea, buttered some thick slices of bread for me, and with Judy the dog on my lap, I stopped with him. Then the raid began. When the windows went in he took me to the Anderson shelter. When at last it seemed quiet and over I decided to go back to the hospital. There was devastation, and fires everywhere. The only way to the hospital was impassable because Lusty's was on fire. I tried to find another way and met a young sailor who couldn't help me. He was a stranger on a day's leave, but he offered to stay with me until I found a way. We went back to Lusty's but had no luck, there was no way through the fire. Then we met up with a naval officer and he suggested we go through the fire. They both shielded me, one on each side, and we ran through the fire. At the hospital gates we said goodbye and good luck and I never saw them again.

I put on my uniform and went to the Messroom to see if I could help in any way. I stayed there until midnight when we were ordered to the basement. The Messroom was a single storey annexe and was reinforced to give cover. The cooker and the taps were jumping with the force of the explosions. That night we lay on concrete floors with our heads in each other's laps. I was with the probationer nurses.

That was the start of very bad nights of bombing. We organized ourselves somehow with mattresses in the basement and I shared a space with the Office Sister,

Theatre Sister, Housekeeper and senior Messroom maid. The Theatre Sister was another young woman from South Wales who was terrified of the raids when she had nothing to do, but worked in the theatre without fear when it was her turn on duty. We were lucky in our hospital as we had no direct hit and we kept open until mid-1941. One bad night all the windows blew in. Half of Devons Road was devastated. The Maternity ward and other wards had to move down into the basement. I organized young women to carry the babies Welsh-fashion in blankets, until provision could be made for them.

There is a sequel to this. In 1985, my husband and I attended a memorial service at Tower Hill for the merchant seamen lost in the war. A woman was there with a daughter of forty-four. We were talking and I mentioned that I was at St Andrew's Hospital during the Blitz. The woman said that her daughter had been born there during the Blitz, after her husband had been lost at sea. I didn't ask, I did not want to know, but I would like to think the daughter was the little baby I had carried around with me that awful night.

Patricia, one of the girls who worked in the Nurses' Home, lost her life that night. She was visiting two girls who lived off Devons Road and worked with her at the Nurses' Home. She was killed with the brother-in-law of one of them and one of the girls was very badly blasted with coal, her face black (they had been sheltering in the coal hole). I went looking for Patricia as soon as it was light enough and was told the sad truth. The next day the hospital was evacuated. Not me, though. We had a ward open within a week.

Patricia's funeral was a sad affair. Just her mother, brother, House Sister and me. No clergy to bury her, but the hospital padre came along with a friend pushing a handcart filled with sacks. You don't need me to tell you what the sacks contained. They were thrown into a large hole in the cemetery. The padre read the funeral service for Patricia. My mother belonged to Ynnsdu Primitive Methodist Church and they held a service for her at my request. War was very sad.

That Christmas was quiet and I was to be sent home to Wales for a rest in the New Year. It was the day after that awful night when the City was bombed that I remember standing on the flat roof of the Nurses' Home and seeing St Paul's in the distance amongst the flames. The only way I could get to Paddington was via Liverpool Street. I knew my way around pretty well because I had worked in that area previously. I seemed to be walking down endless subways when an elderly man wearing a morning suit and black top hat asked if he could help me. He led me to the train I could catch. Some years after, I was visiting Madam Tussaud's and there he was, the man who helped me: King Haakon of Norway (his waxwork of course). I only stayed in Wales for two weeks although our doctor thought I should have stayed longer, but the worry of wondering what the others were doing was worse than being there. We did have *some* quiet nights, or perhaps we got used to it.

When the hospital was eventually evacuated the nurses were only allowed to take a small amount of essentials. One of the young Welsh nurses had a book of poems by Byron which she valued and didn't want to throw away, so I told her I would look after it until we met again. We didn't. I still have the book and cherish it. The funny thing is I found inside it a card which said in lovely coloured print 'The safest place in the world is the place of DUTY'. Somebody had sent it to her, but it gave me, who was to stay behind, great comfort.

One of the maids, living with her elderly parents, climbed over the rubble and never missed a working day. Once, leaving her parents in a Blitz-damaged house, she came to work without the charwoman who usually came with her. She hoped to find that her friend had come to work earlier but had no luck. Her friend was later found dead on the top of a church where she had been blown by the blast.

It wasn't all gloom and doom. There was much laughter and when the bombing ceased we were able to live our lives.

I was married in 1943. My husband had come home in 1942 from the *Mauretania* to find not a lot of ships available. He went on the pool and in October 1942 set sail in the SS *Dahomian* – what he called a 'coffin ship' – to take supplies to North Africa for the Americans. His ship was in trouble and had to be left behind by the convoy. Still, they arrived safely and he eventually went on to Naples. It was rather funny that when he came home, he brought me make-up, but they were all dusky beauties in Oran and the lipsticks were not quite my colour!

He came back just before Christmas 1942, went on the pool again and eventually got a carpenter's mate job on the SS *Ranchi* which was laid up in Southampton until September 1943. We were married on 11 September 1943. He came home on the Friday, we were married on the Saturday and he left again on Sunday. For eighteen months that's how it was: home on Friday, off again on Sunday.

I remember seeing one of the first doodlebugs flying along in the distance. I said to my mother-in-law, 'That's a funny looking plane.' When I went to Bow the next day I was told a German plane had come down in Grove Road but there was no sign of the pilot. I have to admit the air raid sirens terrified me and I was glad when they stopped using them for doodlebugs. You could always hear them and knew that when they stopped you had a fifty-fifty chance.

When the rocket V2s started, although they were devastating, I found them more acceptable because if your name was on it there was no panic beforehand. I remember making semolina by the stove one evening and one dropped a few streets away. The walls seemed to be squeezed together, the fire in the sitting room came out as far as the hall door and the front door lock blew off and imbedded itself in the window frame. I realized afterwards that if I had not been bending over the semolina it would have passed through my head. Still I had my guardian angel looking after me.

Margaret Le Page

I reached seven years of age in June 1939. In September when war broke out, it did not at that time affect my happy Channel Island home. I was the youngest of four, two elder sisters, my brother the eldest child.

I remember going to the Red Cross hall where we knitted long strips, for blankets. Also having to try on gas masks, and having a 'case' made to carry it in. My cousin, aged eleven, arrived from Southampton to be in a 'safe' place; I did not understand only *her* home was not safe. I remember hearing my sisters singing 'There'll always be an England' for the school concert. Life went on quite happily for me till two weeks after my eighth birthday, 20 June 1940. There was a 'family conference'. Should we evacuate the children? I did not know what 'evacuate' meant. Next morning at 5 a.m. my mother woke me up, dressed me, gave me a paper carrier bag with two passports, a packet of dried fruit, and my gasmask. She buttoned up my winter coat and took me across the road to the school where she put me on a bus. I was too frightened to cry. I did not see my parents, brother or many relatives again for five years. My sisters were evacuated with their school.

After a three-hour wait on the beach, hundreds of us children were put on the boat. I was seasick and cried all day. That evening we were given a drink and crammed on to a train. We travelled all night and next day till it was evening, and dark. (We had had one third of a cup of water, and a sliver of ice cream during our journey.) We were told we were in Glasgow, and thirty-six of us went to a church hall. Scotch people are very kind, but we hated sitting on our camp beds while people came and looked at us.

My aunt fetched me, and my cousin fetched her daughter and my sisters from a school in Rochdale, and took us to

Southampton. They all said 'The war will be over by Christmas.' But we were caught in the Southampton Blitz; day and night we had the bombs.

Just before Christmas, the next sister to me and I were sent to an aunt and uncle in Devonshire, as the raids had made my sister ill.

I remember 'collecting salvage' (paper of all sorts) from the village houses. We did this in school time. We also picked blackberries, and rose hips, for the Red Cross. All boys of eight years and upward were expected to help on the school allotment. Summer holidays were two weeks and three weeks, at different times, to coincide with the potato and corn harvests, so the boys could help the farmers.

When I went to Grammar School it was harder. We only had Red Cross Messages, twenty-five words as 'letters' from home, all through the war.

I remember the headmistress coming into our classroom and saying 'The war is over. Unconditional surrender signed at 3 p.m. on 8 May 1945.' I did not rejoice with the rest; I could not believe I would go home – but I did, in August that year.

We still have Liberation Day here on 9 May, but I'll *never* forget the first Anniversary of Liberation Day.

My father died eighteen months after we came home. He never got over the occupation. People nearly starved, and there were no medicines.

I hope this account helps the children. Please learn to live together without war. It brings *so* much misery.

LIEUTENANT-COLONEL

ERIC WILSON

VC

It is not too difficult to think back and find some memories of the day war was declared. What happened to me as a consequence is not so easy to determine. Over the fifty years so many things have happened and it is not always possible to pick out those upon which my experiences during the war can be held to have had a bearing.

In August 1939 I was in England, on leave from Somaliland where I was serving on secondment to the Somaliland Camel Corps. About the last day of the month I received a telegram ordering me to report to Victoria Station. Here I found a number of friends from the King's African Rifles. By train, channel steamer and then train across France we reached Toulon where we were packed into the cruiser *Devonshire* which took us across the Mediterranean. At Port Said four of us – a fellow officer of the Camel Corps and two Indian Army officers – were transferred to a small steamer which lay at anchor.

Next morning we were on deck, leaning on the rail and looking at the shore. Immediately opposite our ship the German flag flew over the office of the German Consulate. Then we saw the flag lowered and removed; that was how we learnt that war had been declared. I do not remember that we discussed the implications of this for us and there was no element of surprise.

As to what happened to me as a consequence of the war I can only pick on one or two of what appear to be the more important things.

In 1940 I learnt that I had been awarded the Victoria Cross. This was to recognize the valour with which the

Machine Gun Company of the Somaliland Camel Corps fought at the battle of Tug Argan in Somaliland. It had been my task to train the company; early in 1940 I was issued with a dozen Vickers machine-guns, thirty-five Somali recruits and thirty-five reservists recalled to the colours, and told to train the lot as machine-gunners. Later our establishment was increased by the posting from Rhodesia of a subaltern and two sergeants. By August of the same year we were in action at Tug Argan.

Prior to taking over the Machine Gun Company I had had little close contact with Somalis as, although in the Camel Corps, I had commanded the company of *askaris* from Nyasaland which was part of the Corps. My brief but hectic association with Somalis left me with a lasting admiration and affection for them.

After the war I did not keep in touch with any members of the Company. Nearly thirty years after the end of the war I received at my home in Somerset, out of the blue, a telephone call from London. The caller was Hussein Omer Kujoog. His father, Sergeant Omer Kujoog, had been killed instantly in action by a shell which also wounded me and deposited three fragments which are still in my body. Hussein came to stay with us; it was exciting to meet this Somali with whose family I feel I have such an unusual relationship. I am still very much in touch with Somalis as I am Honorary Secretary of the Anglo-Somali Society and editor of the Society's newsletter. All this has certainly happened as a consequence of the war and to me it is important.

On a more mundane note, my considerable and increasing degree of deafness is a constant reminder of Tug Argan!

WILFRED THESIGER

I was on the liner *Montcalm* in the Clyde just about to sail for Egypt, having been called back to the Sudan where I was an Assistant District Commissioner in the Sudan Political Service, when Chamberlain announced at about eleven in the morning that we were at war with Germany. Unlike Churchill later there was no fire in his voice, and the announcement sounded dreary and depressing. We sailed in convoy one hour later.

My feelings were hopeful that Italy would also come into the war, and that I should be employed fighting against the Italians in Abyssinia. This indeed happened months later. At the time I hated the Italians bitterly for their invasion of Abyssinia and the atrocities they had committed there. I had been born in Abyssinia and was emotionally drained by what they had done to that country.

COUNT

J.A. KIELMANSEGG

I was a young Captain, thirty-two years old and a professional soldier in the 1st Armoured Division since 1926. This fact alone suggests a quite distinct range of ideas, as it did and still does with British and French officers. It happened that we soldiers, with a few exceptions at the top, were not tainted by National Socialism – even though in many books today it is told otherwise. We did not like it and we certainly did not like the SA and the SS. As for Hitler himself, that was something different; he had captivated us with his success in getting reparations for the Treaty of Versailles of 1919 which had so mutilated Germany. All the horror that we know of today we did not know of then.

So that you do not get a false impression of my attitude to Nazism I must tell you that I belonged to the Resistance, was thrown into prison, should have been sentenced to death, and only by chance, by pure luck, was not hanged.

I should also like to add that the war with Poland did not appear unjust to us soldiers. After the First World War Poland had annexed not only land that was originally Polish but also German land, and had not engaged in negotiations, had rejected the last German offer, but in return in the weeks before the war had dispossessed, ill-treated and murdered a large number of Germans still living in Poland – the worst case being the 'Bromberger Blutnacht' ('Bromberg's Bloody Night'). We were all aware of this. Nowadays it is largely forgotten and goes unmentioned. We saw it as only a border war, no one thought then that Great Britain would intervene, but rather that they, together with France, would let things go ahead as in the case of the Sudetenland and Czechoslovakia in 1938/9. I think that Hitler himself had assumed this, but I don't know for sure. Three days later things looked very different, but on the day before the outbreak of war we had no idea of this, at least not in the army.

The 1st Armoured Division had been stationed in Thuringen (now in East Germany) and some time around 20 August received orders to march to Oberschlesien (now in Poland) in the district around Oppeln – I don't know what the Polish name is today. There we waited for whatever was to happen. I quote now from my notes on 1 September 1939:

'In the morning, shortly after 4.00 a.m., at the Divisional Headquarters, close to the border. The pale morning light reveals a grey sky, it is bitterly cold. Silence reigns everywhere and only by watching very closely can one notice careful movements here and there. The General walks up and down a woodland path talking quietly with the Chief of Staff. The lull before the storm, a phrase often used without thinking, but here with uncanny reality. I'm sitting in a dark tent and my thoughts swing to and fro from the past to the future.' The order to attack was there and was to be carried out at 4.45 a.m.

How would it all turn out? What was war really like? On the march to Oberschlesien the people had greeted us everywhere with flowers and flags – not with enthusiasm but with a solid determination. It was quite different to 1914, but then this war would also be different to the Great War. However in spite of all the accounts of veteran soldiers, in spite of all the books, in spite of the fact that I myself had done practically nothing else for the last thirteen years except learn the military profession and study the phases of war like every other professional soldier, I still found it very difficult to imagine what it would actually be like. How would one stand the test as a person and as a soldier?

'The telephone rings, a final message is passed down. My interrupted thoughts take another direction, towards my home, my wife and children who are sleeping peacefully and have no idea that when they wake up they'll be at war. Deep in thought I hear someone say "So near and yet so far". I look at the time. It's 4.43 a.m. I light a cigarette. When it goes out we will be at war. Another two minutes and war will begin. It's a strange, indescribable and moving feeling to experience so consciously, so directly a historic moment the significance of which can in no way be foreseen.

4.45 a.m. Two reconnaissance planes fly over the border. The brigade announces "Action stations". War has begun.'

HUBERT PFOCH

At the time of the outbreak of war I was just nineteen and I had been working for 3½ years as an apprentice cabinet maker. During morning break my workmates and I discussed

Hitler's speech which we had heard on the radio earlier that day. The key sentences of the broadcast went something like: 'Polish hordes have crossed the frontier, penetrated German territory and occupied the German radio station at Gleiwitz. There are dead and wounded. Germany cannot stand for this and since 4.35 we have returned fire.'

I took the view that Hitler's speech could not be believed. I was certain that there had been no assault by 'Polish hordes' on the Gleiwitz radio station, rather than Hitler was looking for ways to justify occupying Poland. This was done to risk the war for which he had been systematically preparing. That they had returned fire since 4.35 a.m. was also a lie to make the German population believe in the threat from Poland.

I spoke to friends of the consequences which were to be feared. My doubts at the time concerning the reports of the invasion of Germany and the defence which became necessary were many years later confirmed through research sources (amongst other things also through documentation which was published under the title *Tannenberg Undertakings – the cause of the Second World War*, written by Alfred Spiess and Lichtenberg, published by *Limes*, Wiesbaden, Munich, 1979).

The consequences of this occurrence were forseeable and the allegiance of England to Poland I found understandable and necessary.

It is notable that all the terrible things I, an Austrian, feared at that time in 1939 through the reality of atrocities went far beyond the normal and unfortunate experiences and horrors of war. Millions of young people lost their lives on the battlefield and millions more died in the hail of bombs which laid waste whole towns, and with the murder of millions of defenceless men, women and children of Jewish extraction in the Holocaust, a new and appalling low was reached.

Lord Allen of Abbeydale

We had been expecting war for some time. That summer my wife and I had had a holiday in the South of France which we could ill-afford in the belief that there would be no further opportunity of getting abroad for a long time to come. We were under no illusion that, if war came, it would be short.

But in the end we did not hear the Prime Minister's announcement on the day. We drove up to Westminster to church that morning – and there was then no radio in the car – and the sirens went as we were parking in Smith Square. An air raid warden, suddenly conscious of his grave new responsibilities, at once ushered us into a nearby office block (why it was open on a Sunday we never discovered), and made sure that we were clutching our newly-issued gas-masks. From an upstairs window we watched a barrage balloon going up beyond the roof of Westminster Abbey. I write 'going up'; but it kept going down as well as up, rather like a slow-moving and inverted yo-yo. We might have been tempted to feel that our lives depended on its ascent, as some of the forecasts had been that the outbreak of war would be marked by an immediate raid by the Luftwaffe on the very area where we were now situated. But, oddly enough, the main feeling was of relief rather than apprehension – the feeling that the long preliminaries, in which the role of this country had not been a matter for great pride, were now over and that we were involved in a clear-cut contest which in the end, however distant that might be, would surely result in the destruction of the evil regime which held the world in jeopardy. I had known some Jewish people in Germany, and had been there, and knew a little of what had been happening, although I was not aware of anything like the full horror; and we were only too conscious of what had happened to Czechoslovakia and, within the previous few days, to Poland.

I was in the Home Office at the time and had been concerned with the police and their preparations for war. On that Sunday morning, after the All Clear, my wife went back home with some friends and I went on to the Home Office. I can still vividly remember, after all these years, that some of us went out to lunch, rather extravagantly by our standards, to the Lyons Corner House at Charing Cross. We had, as it now seems, a somewhat hilarious meal. If we had known the long and dreary days ahead, with so much to do and so little good news to cheer us up for such a long time, we should no doubt have been much more subdued. But, again, it was the feeling of relief that something had been decided that was uppermost.

We knew that life could never be quite the same again, and I think even then realized that the place of this country in the world would be bound to decline; and we had all of us been led to believe that the slaughter of the civilian population would be on a horrific scale and might well start forthwith. Although that forecast turned out to be wrong, like most forecasts, we were indeed embarked on years of death and destruction all around us, of separation, and of extreme shortages – but also of new friendships and the bonds of shared experiences. At any rate, we considered that we knew what we were fighting for, and there was now one main objective in all our work. Perhaps we were naive, but, in a sense, everything had become much simpler.

CARDINAL LUSTIGER

ARCHBISHOP OF PARIS

Extract from Le Choix de Dieu, *Editions de Fallois, 1987*

Before the war broke out, in 1939, Paris experienced a moment of sheer panic. All children had been brought up in the memory of the Great War. A new war was starting with

Germany! My father is called up. Paris is drained of her children. What to do? Where to go? Where to take shelter? For this first exodus, just before the declaration of war, I said to my parents: 'We are going to Orléans.' Because of my science teacher.

Why not Orléans rather than elsewhere? It was south of Paris. My father was called up. I still see him in his uniform, he was on leave. With our cases quickly packed, we set off. And there were crowds of refugees in Orléans.

Having arrived in Orléans, in no way can we find this science teacher! My parents get organized, we sleep in a hotel. And my parents decide to leave us children in Orléans whilst my mother returns to Paris to keep the shop. It was the only sensible solution. The children must be put into safety, they said. In Orléans Town Hall, there was a reception bureau for the children of refugees. These are the scenes customary to the beginning of war. My parents entrusted us to people who came forward. And I joined the 4th form in the *lycée* Pothier in Orléans.

I am not really certain of the chronology. I have asked a very close witness to confirm my memories. He told me that he is now too old and that his memory fails him. Neither have I kept a record of what happened. I would like to be able to check what are but fleeting impressions or uncertainties, memories with gaps of what I may have done or thought at such-and-such a time. What eludes me is the sequence of events but I have a precise and certain memory of inner experiences.

Facts first: my parents took us back to Paris during the 'phoney war'. The threat seemed to have lessened before the summer exodus took place. This return to Paris was short lived. I was back in the 4th form of the *lycée* Montaigne with my best friend.

I remember vividly the rupture the arrival of the Germans represented. For me, the collapse of France was beyond belief. A breach, a wound, a humiliation, all appalling. And when I saw the Germans arrive I knew that the Jews were going to be killed. I was better aware of it than my parents. I was clear what was going to happen. I see again the uniforms of the German army . . . I understood what they were saying since I spoke good German. I can still see the first soldier in a side-car stopping in the Rue St Marc, at the cross-roads where I lived. I was confronted with the unthinkable. I still remember the Senegalese infantryman who was shot on the little road bridge leading to the Faubourg de Bourgogne; he was the last to defend the bridge. His corpse lay beside Peguy's bronze bust. He had been billeted in the house where I lived, he hardly spoke any French, laughed like a big kid and caught mice with his hands! He defended the honour of France to the end. Yes indeed, I experienced this defeat like an unthinkable humiliation.

I still see the Place du Marrois in ruins, after the bombardments of 1940; and I see the German tanks streaming across the square. My memory replayed this scene to me, unchanged, when, as Bishop of Orléans, I presided at the festival of St Joan of Arc in 1980. I had expressed the wish to attend the military parade and saw the French tanks there. I struggled to hold back my tears as all of a sudden the two images merged in my mind. It was the second time in my life that I saw tanks streaming past on the Place du Marrois; but this time the tanks were French. And I understood that, hitherto, the humiliation of German tanks crossing a devastated Place du Marrois had remained intact. It may sound strange to say this today but that's how it is.

The way I perceived the political problem is not the way in which, even today, people continue to analyse it. Like all kids I heard people talking of the Spanish Civil War; of the unrest of the extreme right, of the demonstrations and of political violence in France; I mean, of all the things adults talked about and which filled the papers. But beyond this it seems to me that I was aware of some of the fundamental issues at stake: the right to justice, the fate of mankind, and ineluctably, given all I heard, the problem of the Jews. This problem was at the heart of the political conundrum, for there was in Germany Nazism and anti-Semitism; in France, there was anti-Semitism with Leon Blum as its target. Therefore, the Jewish factor was tied up with the political factor and, for me, the Jewish factor was concerned first of all with the relationship to faith, to God and to the question of salvation.

GINA GERSON

After the Anschluss in Austria in the spring of 1938 I was living in Vienna and was forced immediately to enter a Jewish school. During Kristallnacht of 9 and 10 November that same year, when the Nazis moved against all things Jewish, we were all as a family locked out of our flat – for our own protection – and had to find shelter with friends. At that time the Nazis still respected foreign nationals and they all wore their flags. I had a half-sister and she was Latvian by marriage, although by this time the marriage was over. She managed to get out of Austria on a domestic permit and once she had arrived in London she arranged for me to come as a 'trainee'.

In January 1939, just after my fourteenth birthday, I travelled to England alone, without the help or protection of an organization. The journey was very frightening and when we were about to cross the border at Aachen I was ordered, with all the other Jewish passengers, to dismount. I was taken to a little wooden building where a large woman stripped and searched me. Two men were reading my diary in which I described how my uncle committed suicide when the Nazis came, by throwing himself from the window of his flat. They squashed my chocolates, slashed the lining of my new winter gloves and cut up my manicure set – a parting birthday present. I was very fair and looked Aryan. Perhaps they thought that, as a child, I was being used to smuggle something. Of course with the delay I missed all my connections.

Leaving by sea I recall it was very rough and this was my first time on a boat. I was very sick. In England, when I got on the train, I saw that my compartment was upholstered and I was used to wooden seats in Third Class. I was frightened they would throw me off the train. At Victoria station, twelve hours late arriving, I must have sat down on my suitcase and gone to sleep, because my sister passed me several times without recognizing me. She was frantic. Finally when we went back to her room by Underground I was terrified again because I thought the railwaymen in their black uniforms were from the SS.

Through the rest of 1939 my parents remained in Vienna, but when the Germans marched into Poland that's when my sister and I became really desperate. My sister phoned my parents and said for them, for heaven's sake, to get to the frontier, to try and get out because war was imminent. My father was over sixty; he was not very strong and, I suppose, it was just more than they could face to go into the mountains and go illegally into Switzerland. It was not something that was in their nature, to do something illegal. They were law-abiding citizens and they had a permit to go out of Vienna, out of Austria. They had a ticket. They had their suitcases packed. It was only another few days, and they probably said to my sister: 'Wait. We'll hang on. It's Saturday now and we've only to wait until next Wednesday. Surely we'll make it?' On 31 August my sister sent me a telegram from London saying: 'Parents arriving Wednesday.' That would have been 6 September . . . But they never came. This is what I put in my diary:

31st. August.

Shall we be lucky? I can hardly believe it any more.

1st. September.

The Germans have marched into Poland. Does this mean war? Is it all too late? Dear God – only a few more days. Help just this once. Only five days.

2nd. September.

The English ultimatum. I have no hope left.

3rd. September.

England declares war against Germany. Now it is all finished. Too late. Three days too late. Where is there a God who can allow such a thing to happen? Poor, dear parents. Shall we see each other again? I could kick myself when I remember how cheeky and disobedient I often was. I didn't understand of course what the love of parents meant, and now perhaps it is too late. What do I care if the whole world falls to pieces.

That is how I welcomed the war.

BARONESS RYDER OF WARSAW CMG, OBE

Extract from Child of my Love, *Collins Harvill, 1986*

The congregation at Great Thurlow was in church as usual at eleven o'clock on Sunday, 3 September 1939, and there on a portable radio we heard Neville Chamberlain's announcement from 10 Downing Street that Britain was at war with Germany. The war had started two days earlier with Hitler's invasion of Poland, a crime the direct and particular effects of which were destined to have a special and lasting influence on my whole life.

We felt a sense of very deep shame when the Prime

Minister in his broadcast mentioned the failure of the ultimatum his Government had sent Berlin after the expected invasion and bombing and killing in Poland had begun, an ultimatum vainly demanding a German withdrawal. In March 1939, and indeed at Munich the previous year, the Czechs had been sold down the river, and now, owing to unbelievable political blindness, it was too late to be of any assistance to the Poles whose territorial integrity against Germany we had guaranteed and with whom we had signed a mutual defence treaty. When I see the pre-war British Embassy in Warsaw and remember the crowds who assembled there calling for the Ambassador and cheering him because they vainly believed that we would send arms, I marvel at the Poles' lack of bitterness today.

Immediately after the broadcast, sirens sounded but people reacted calmly. It was in fact a false alarm. There followed a series of false alarms which typified the start of the eight-month period of the phoney war.

The nearest bomb to us was subsequently dropped near the sheep pen on the Home Farm. My brother Stephen's friend, John McAnally, aged twenty-one, watched with us from the door of the cellar, and we talked about the courage of the Poles and their resistance and how remarkable the cavalry were to fight back against German tanks. We expressed indignation at our inability to help them and the knowledge that we and the French had let down their country and our common cause.

The National Service Act had been rushed through Parliament at the outset of war. It was to be supplemented later by a law making everybody, men and women alike, aged eighteen to sixty, liable for some type of war work. I decided to join the FANY as a volunteer. The First Aid Nursing Yeomanry was the full title of the corps. All recruits (who were volunteers and not conscripted) passed through the corps training school and, if selected for work with the Special Operations Executive (SOE), went to further training schools where they received instructions in the use of small arms and signals.

On the training course, each morning began with drill, at the time taken by a sergeant from the Devonshire Regiment, whose accent made his commands quite difficult to follow. Ethel Boileau, the well known author, who was Commanding Officer, inspected us, paying particular attention to our appearance: hair had to be well above the collar, and our shoes polished vigorously every day – the insteps were expected to be as shiny as the uppers. The Sam Browne belts, too, had to be polished to resemble a mirror. The course included route marches, training in army procedure, military groups, fire drill, security, respiration and stretcher drill, night vision, mechanics, advanced first aid nursing, convoy driving, night map reading, and driving different types of vehicles ranging from cars to five-ton lorries. We later received 11*s*. 2*d*. per week. We were addressed by our surnames only.

In addition to all the practical work we had to pass written and oral examinations in all these subjects. We attended lectures in corps history, and were reminded that during the freezing winters of the First World War the FANYs slept in tents and the girls had to wind up the vehicles every twenty minutes throughout each night to prevent the engines freezing. Several of us were overawed by what those FANYs had endured and the high standards expected of us; we were more than a little apprehensive as to whether we would come up to the mark.

The course lasted about three weeks, and then lists were put up with our names indicating to which sections we had been posted. I was to report to SOE headquarters in Baker Street, London, a rabbit-warren of offices and a prosaic threshold to a new world. When we signed the Official Secrets Act we were, without realizing it, signing our names to a new way of life. The head of SOE believed in our capacity to do difficult and secret work and that security would be impeccable. He gave encouragement to all, but especially to those of us still in our teens. The familiar, ordinary world was left behind, and I never returned to it.

I was posted, very briefly, to the Czech section, but otherwise served with the Poles. No reasons were ever given regarding postings and no questions ever entertained. As part of my training I was taught the rudiments of the Czech and Polish languages, but never succeeded in speaking them well, though I can follow conversations.

It would be very difficult indeed to describe in detail the size and complexity of the Polish section of SOE and to explain the activities of the underground in Poland. Their work covered acts of sabotage against enemy installations, collecting vital information for the Allies, organizing and training new groups and distributing BBC news. (It was forbidden by the Germans for any Pole to possess a wireless set – all were confiscated and anybody found with one was promptly imprisoned or executed.) To live and share, however briefly, in the lives of great, yet unknown, people made a great impression on me and I felt it was a privilege never to be forgotten.

BRONIA NIEDZWIECKA

I was eighteen years old, living with my parents, when the war came to Poland. My father was a small farmer with cows, pigs, chickens and two horses which the family used for transport from the small town of Lawaryszki where we lived.

At first we did not see much of the war, but eventually rationing was introduced and we began to see long queues of people waiting for bread, milk and meat (we were only allowed 3 oz each per week). There were no air raid shelters and only occasional buses.

When I was nineteen I married a Post Office worker and our son was born a year later. My future husband invited

German soldiers to our wedding and they were good company and very kind. Two years later when the Russians overran Poland my husband joined the Army; he had no option as the Russians found and killed all men of military age unless they fought. Many were sent to Siberia, including my husband's brother who was only nineteen years old.

At this time there was very much bombing around Warsaw. The bombers passed over Lawaryszki, sometimes dropping their bombs on us, and two of my friends were injured as a result. Lawaryszki, though, with about 300 inhabitants, missed most of the fighting, but a hundred miles away in Warsaw it was very bad and we could see the reflections of the fires in the sky at night.

My brother-in-law returned from Siberia after about two years but his health had been wrecked as a result of working in the mines.

F.G. GILLARD

CBE

I was a schoolmaster and freelance BBC broadcaster in September 1939, living and working in the West Country. On the Sunday morning when war was declared, I was at Church, praying that it would not happen. No doubt millions of Germans were doing the same thing.

I had been appointed a billeting officer, responsible for finding local temporary homes for hundreds of children who had been evacuated from London just forty-eight hours earlier and sent to this safer area. Much of the first day of war was therefore spent in going around to all the houses where evacuees had been placed, to see how they were getting on. In most cases they had been well received and made to feel at home, and seemed to be settling in reasonably well. But some of the children were bewildered and desolate at the separation from their parents, and were quite inconsolable. They were deeply unhappy, and there was little that I could do to comfort them. In just a few cases, children from the East End of London were making life miserable for the local people who had taken them in, because of their bad and unruly behaviour. They clearly came from undisciplined homes, and they were dirty, noisy, destructive and totally disobedient. I arranged for them to be moved into institutional care; it was impossible to cope with them in decent homes.

The rest of the day I spent in making blackout screens to fit the windows of my house so that no interior light could be seen from outside at night. This was quite a job. Air Raid Wardens pounced on any householder who allowed even the smallest chink of light to be visible from the street. I also fitted specially designed, and rather expensive, blackout masks to all the lights of my car. These prevented any light from shining upward, even to the smallest degree. It was important that no enemy aircraft should be able to spot cars moving about at night. All the cars' lights were greatly dimmed, and deflected down on to the road. It was necessary to drive very slowly indeed after dark, because the lights illuminated only a distance of about twenty feet, and quite faintly at that.

That night I stood on watch for four hours, midnight to 4 a.m., at a hilltop post, as a member of the Royal Observer Corps. At that post we kept twenty-four-hour observation of the skies, on guard against the approach of enemy aircraft. This duty was maintained from the first day of the war to the last. While I was committed to this work, I put in about twenty-four hours a week at the post, mainly at night, in addition to my normal occupations. Quite early on in the war I was able to direct RAF fighters on to an invading German bomber, in the early hours of one morning, and they were able to shoot it down. But I remained a member of the ROC for only a few months. Under the Direction of

Labour regulations, I was drafted into the BBC because of my broadcasting experience, and following a period of probationary training I spent the bulk of the war years as a war correspondent with the British, American and Canadian armies overseas.

MAJOR
EDWINA COVEN
CBE, JP, DL

War was imminent so my mother sent me away from our home in London to live with one of my married sisters and her husband in Sussex.

On Sunday 3 September 1939 I was entered in a tennis tournament in East Grinstead, Sussex. We were due to start play at 2 p.m. Just before 11 a.m. we switched on the radio in time to hear Neville Chamberlain make his announcement that because we had not heard from Germany by 11 a.m. we were at war. Immediately my sister phoned the tennis club and cancelled my entry – she felt that as she had responsibility for me and we expected to be bombed by German planes at once, she owed it to my mother to keep me at home! Of course, no bombing took place for over a year and the phoney war, as it was called, set in.

Subsequently I joined the Red Cross, after a month or two working on my brother-in-law's farm learning how to milk cows! Then as the phoney war continued I was allowed back to London where I took a secretarial course which led to my working with the Home Guard on Waterloo Station.

Then, in 1942, I joined the Auxilliary Territorial Service. This proved to be the most important influence in my life, both then and up to the present time. I joined as a Private and was then commissioned. The ATS became the Women's Royal Army Corps in which I remained until 1956. I served in many places in the UK, in Germany and Holland. The Army developed my character, and the training enabled me to turn my hand to most things. So when I eventually left the WRAC, a happily married woman, I had achieved a confidence in myself I had never thought possible. I wrote a children's book and worked in television and sound radio. Today I am a Councillor, a Magistrate and have served as Chief Commoner of the City of London. I was the first woman to become one of Her Majesty's Lieutenants of the City of London and I am now a Deputy Lord-Lieutenant of Greater London; I am also a director of TV-am.

So, terrible though the war was in every way, with the experience of being a teenager at the outbreak of war and my subsequent service with Her Majesty's Forces, it is directly through the outbreak of war in 1939 that I have had the immensely varied and happy life to this day. However, I may well have grown up in a different and equally interesting way had the Second World War never started. This, I shall never know.

TRUDE DUB

Article from The Listener, *14 May 1964*

The last train from Prague

Twenty five years ago, on 15 March 1939, I woke up from an uneasy sleep and switched on my bedside radio. The time was 5.30 in the morning, the place was Prague.

The voice of the announcer said:

'PLEASE KEEP LAW AND ORDER – the German army is invading Czechoslovakia from all four sides . . . PLEASE KEEP LAW AND ORDER – the German army is invading Czechoslovakia from all four sides . . . PLEASE KEEP LAW AND ORDER . . .'

I woke my husband and together we listened to the voice that proclaimed not only the death of one of the finest democracies in Europe, but also the end of an epoch in our lives – an epoch that meant roots, security, and human dignity. Even as that voice droned on, we were being turned into fugitives, our crime being that we were Jews.

The first German tank

By about midday, the first convoy of German tanks entered Wenceslas Square. I had often stood there, watching processions in the colourful Czech and Slovak national costumes and cheering with the onlookers. But the crowd that lined both sides of the square when the first German tank rolled down this beautiful thoroughfare was as still and silent as the statue of St Wenceslas – the patron saint of Bohemia – towering above the square. The Germans did not waste much time. A curfew was called immediately and their lorries rumbled long into the night collecting the first blacklisted victims.

In the days that followed, my husband and I ran from embassy to embassy, trying to find a way of escape. By one of those strange coincidences that shape human destinies, we met an old friend, who told us that until the end of March, Czech nationals did not require a visa for England. We made up our minds on the spot, although it seemed impossible to get all the necessary documents in the remaining eight days. We did not even have a passport. Still, it was worth trying. Never shall I forget this breathless paper-chase, the hours in endless queues, with hope mounting and hope disappearing while time was running out.

The National Bank was closed and you could get no money out of the country; you could not even get a railway ticket abroad. Again by chance, I heard that foreigners could obtain tickets. If you were lucky enough to find one, he might be persuaded to part with his return ticket and buy a new one. The price of such a transaction was fantastic, but life was more precious still.

My God, where can I find a foreigner? But it seemed easier than I thought. The clerk at a little travel agency did know of a Dutchman. 'Please, oh please, money no object . . . Yes, of course I pay in advance'. In a back alley that was our rendezvous, I was waiting for two hours in the pouring rain for the clerk and his Dutchman. They did not come.

But when I returned home, another good friend telephoned that some tickets were being sold at the main railway station – something that the efficient German administration had overlooked. I rushed there immediately but the news had got round and I found a queue a mile long. After three hours, when I was about the fifth from the grille, the window shut down: the tickets were sold out. Nobody knew whether there would be any more. So I crawled home to a weary husband who had spent his day chasing the passports.

God knows how we managed at all. Looking back on it, I can see a divine scheme in which each step was counted and each minute measured. For if we had not met just one of the many people who helped us at a particular moment, or if a train or a taxi had not come just when it did, we would not be here today. Eventually, we held in our hands the precious passports, the tickets, the inland revenue permit, and all the other documents – everything except the Gestapo permit to leave. That was the hardest thing of all.

There was the possibility of my husband being arrested, so I decided to go to the Gestapo myself. When I came out of that building, I knew that I should never be afraid as long as I lived – I spent the fear of my lifetime in there.

The passports had to be left behind and were to be collected with the permits – if any – three days later, on the day when the last train was leaving Prague to reach England without a visa.

‘Shall we never reach the door?’

Early that morning my husband Izio and I set out for the Gestapo. We closed the door of our home on all the precious things we had collected in our young married life, as well as on our hopes and dreams for the future. We joined the long, long queue. Friends brought us food, while the family waited at the flat for our telephone call to bring our luggage to the station. The hours passed and we made only little progress. My God, shall we never reach the door? Round about midday we were getting within sight but then the officials called a break and the queue became once more motionless.

Two o’clock came and the door opened again. We were not far away by this time but to our dismay the jackbooted Nazi in charge started to pull out his friends from the back of the queue. At three o’clock I plucked up all my courage and pointed out – humbly and politely – that our train would be leaving just after four o’clock. The man yelled: ‘Keep your mouth shut, Jewish swine, or you’ll go to the back of the queue’.

More waiting . . . At 4 p.m. we were at last moving through the door. A woman in front of us undertook to ring my parents and ask them to bring our hurriedly packed personal belongings to the station.

We arrived at the station within minutes of the train’s departure – perhaps it was better so – there was no time for prolonged goodbyes . . . The train moved slowly out of the station and I saw the dear faces of my parents disappearing in the distance. I never saw them again. None of the 300 fugitives on that train knew that the husbands who were going out to prepare the ground for their wives and children would never be joined by them, nor were the separated sweethearts to meet again.

And now we were on our way into the unknown. We

reached the border of the Czech protectorate, where all the permits were taken away from us. This was a bad omen. The permits entitled us to return within four weeks and now the way back was irrevocably closed. What would happen if England refused us entry? Our speculations were cut short by an order to change trains. This was to be a direct train from Prague to the Dutch port of Vlissingen, but Jews were not supposed to ask questions. We had to change twice more and so precious hours were lost. It now became obvious that we should not reach England before midnight on 31 March. Panic seized those who came on the train straight from prisons and there was a good number of them. They said that they were going to kill themselves rather than go through it again.

Full of foreboding, the transport reached Bentheim, on the German-Dutch border. There we were told that England would not let us in. It was too late. The treaty would expire before we could reach the English shores. Now the Dutch also refused us entry, fearing that we would be left on their hands. Besides, their reception centres for refugees in transit were already overcrowded. Negotiations with the Dutch authorities were set afoot, while our luggage, papers, and persons were examined by the German customs and police officials. Carriage after carriage was emptied and filled again, as people went to be investigated and returned.

'Oh, we shot him!'

By and by everybody was back except for three men – one of them my husband. For six hours they kept him standing near a wall – not leaning on it, mind you – while Nazi officials checked with Prague his identity and awaited clearance. I was nearly out of my mind with worry and I was not comforted when I asked an official with a swastika armlet whether he knew where my husband was. Hearing the name, he said brightly: 'Oh, we shot him!' Just one of the delicate Nazi jokes, but how was I to tell at the time?

Meanwhile, the first half of our transport was allowed to move on to Oldenzaal, on the Dutch side of the border, and await their fate in Holland, while the rest of us had to remain in Germany. We spent another night on the train, which was shunted on to a side track. Months later I was to wake up in the middle of the night and imagine myself to be still on that stationary train. In the morning, the local inhabitants came to stare at us as if we were some strange animals; and we felt indeed like rats in a trap. We could neither go forward nor back, and now the German railways were asking for the carriages. Rumours reached us that we might be transferred to a concentration camp.

But now the world was told of our plight by desperate telephone and telegraph messages. Finally a British immigration officer arrived in Oldenzaal, and it was rumoured that if you found an English guarantor, you were given a visa. Izio and I had had a chance meeting with an Englishman on the day Hitler marched into Prague. We wired him in desperation to send a guarantee for us to Oldenzaal. One clutched at every straw.

Another night came and still our fate was undecided. The train had to be sent back now and we were told to deposit our luggage in a room at the station and form two orderly lines, men separate and women separate. We thought that this could only mean a concentration camp but to our great surprise we found ourselves at a youth hostel, where we were given black coffee and bread with margarine, thanks to the mayor of Bentheim. Then the men were accommodated on straw – sixty of them in a room – and women were given a bunk between two of them.

In the morning, the good news was brought to us that all women, and the married ones together with their husbands, were permitted to present themselves to the British immigration officer in Oldenzaal. It was only one railway station away, but what a different world awaited us on the other side of the border. The Dutch went all out to welcome us, and I shall never forget the warmth of their hospitality. There was food ready for us in a school and we certainly needed it. And here we had another pleasant surprise: the guarantee from our chance English acquaintance arrived and so we faced the immigration officer with easier hearts.

Yes, we got the visa and were taken to Hengelo, one more railway stop down the line, to spend the night. As in Oldenzaal, the whole town turned out to greet us. People threw their homes open to us and Scouts took care of our luggage and shepherded us to our lodgings. Izio and I followed our Boy Scout as in a dream through the darkening streets of Hengelo. The crisis was over – this was the beginning of a new life.

That night, after what seemed like a lifetime, we rested again on clean and comfortable beds. Next morning our group left Hengelo to the chorus of 'Long live Holland' and 'Long live Czechoslovakia'. The Boy Scouts formed a guard of honour at the station. I often thought of this scene, when, a few months later, Holland herself became the victim of the same cruel oppressor.

The journey on the boat was uneventful. We felt that whatever lay before us could never be as bad as our first glimpse of Hitler's rule. True, we did not know a word of English; we had exactly sixpence left after sending postcards from the boat and treating ourselves to one cup of coffee between the two of us; we did not know a soul in England, apart from that chance acquaintance of ours, but we were young and not afraid of hard work.

And so, during the week of Passover, when Jewish people all over the world celebrate their deliverance from slavery to freedom – we landed on these blessed shores.

CAPTAIN

GUY GRIFFITHS

When war broke out in 1939 I was serving as a Royal Marine fighter pilot in 803 Squadron on board HMS *Ark Royal*, our latest and largest carrier which carried seventy-two craft.

Our squadron was equipped with the Navy's latest aircraft the 'Skua', the fleet's first monoplane, a two-seater fighter/ dive bomber. It had four front guns and the air gunner in the rear had one machine-gun. As a dive bomber it carried a single 500 lb bomb on a sling, so when diving near vertically it swung the bomb clear of the prop. It also had racks to carry anti-personnel bombs on each wing. Its top speed was only 230 mph, sufficient to catch slower modern bombers, but not Germany's latest types. However as a dive bomber it was a very accurate and deadly machine, and a few months later in Norway our squadron was to sink the cruiser *Nuremburg*, the first major warship sunk by bombs.

All summer of 1939 *Ark Royal* aircraft had practised attacks on German warships in exercises, and by August *Ark Royal* was at her war patrol area to cover the vast area from Northern Norway to Iceland to track German shipping trying to return to Germany before war started and warships trying to get out ready to raid our commerce once war started. *Bremen*, the huge German liner, was one of the prizes we were searching for, and trying to get out unseen were the battlecruisers *Scharnhorst, Gneisenau* and *Hipper*, and the pocket battleship *Graf Spee*. We were to learn later they had set out unseen weeks earlier! However by the day war was announced we had been at war stations and war routine for weeks, expecting German bomber raids the moment war was declared. We had left one fighter squadron of Skuas (800 Squadron) at Scapa Flow to defend the base until the RAF could take over, so the *Ark* was one fighter squadron short for fleet fighter protection. When we were called to the wardroom to hear the Prime Minister on the ship's loud speakers, when he did announce that we were at war, it was a quiet and sober anti-climax, for we had been ready for action for weeks. However when he announced that Winston Churchill had been made First Lord of the Admiralty there was a roar of delight and cheering broke out all over the ship. At last we had the man the Navy had wanted to lead them.

Then we returned to our stations, I to my hangar post to check that all aircraft were armed up and ready to be fitted with the correct bombs that any target required. The duty pilot slept in the hangar, and I found a spot under my aircraft, ready for the tannoy to blast out.

We continued patrolling the northern approaches to the North Sea until the liner *Athenia* was sunk by a U-30. We were then switched to the North Atlantic, with our destroyer screen, at full speed, to take part in the hunt for U-boats. (Nowadays we think we were mad to risk the vital carrier looking for subs.) We were, in fact, attacked by a U-boat, but it just missed us and was later blown up.

On 14 September, eleven days after the outbreak of war, we picked up an SOS from the *Fanard Head*, being attacked by a U-boat. My flight of Skuas, led by our commanding officer Lieutenant-Commander Campbell (now Vice Admiral), was sent off ahead of the main Swordfish attack squadron, to find and attack the sub. However, we were only carrying one 112 lb anti-sub bomb and four 20 lb Cooper anti-personnel bombs, so only a very lucky direct hit on the conning tower would be effective.

We found the sub, the U-30, after we had separated into individual search patrols, and attacked it at different times. My flight commander spotted it just disappearing and, at low level, dropped his bombs but was hit by shrapnel from the exploding bomb and crashed on fire, losing his air gunner.

Later on I also found the sub, but he too was crash diving. I attacked low down as his periscope was going under and I too was hit by shrapnel and crashed. Some way ahead was a deserted ship, so I swam to it and found it taken over by two crew from the submarine, which then surfaced. On board was the pilot of the other Skua, very badly burnt. The ship turned out to be the *Fanard Head*, whose SOS we had picked up. The captain ordered us to swim to the submarine and then he put a torpedo into the ship.

As we clambered aboard and below, we were attacked by the Swordfish sent out after we left the *Ark*. The sub was attacked with depth charges and damaged but we managed to limp back to Germany in fourteen days. We were to spend the next years to May 1945 in various POW camps, the last four years in the famous Stalag Luft III of the Great Escape fame.

A few weeks after I had crashed a Lieutenant of my flight shot down a Dornier 18 shadowing the fleet, giving the Fleet Air Arm the honour of shooting down the first German aircraft of World War II. The fighter? A Skua!

EINAR IVERSEN

I stretched gently, rubbed my eyes and peered out through the bedroom window; another lovely, sunny morning. I looked at the clock – it showed a quarter to six this nice spring morning. I thought to myself: 'You better hurry if you are going to get those fish-nets in before you go off to college.' Fishing was my hobby; it also gave us some good meals, and I was trying to save up for a new bike. I switched the radio on, and while that was warming up, went to the pantry for a glass of milk and some bread. I always switched the radio on early in the morning, for our local radio announcer, Mr Stinesen, invariably found some lively music

– marches or pop-records – to set you going in the morning. I always looked forward to getting downstairs to listen, and usually woke up the rest of the household that way. But I was disappointed this morning – no music at all, just somebody reading a story of some sort. Something about the war and Germans, so I didn't listen at all.

I couldn't stand war, I couldn't understand that people could be so stupid as to kill one another, or hurt each other, destroy other people's homes just for the sake of a political principle. I had grown up in a country that hadn't had war since the Napoleonic age, and our whole society was centred around peaceful coexistence with our neighbours. Life itself was the most sacrosanct thing in my young life, and the commandment 'Thou shalt not kill' meant something to me and all my friends. I was very glad that when war had broken out between Germany and Britain/France seven months ago, the Norwegian government refused to take sides and declared a strict neutrality. Anyway, we had practically no army, no air force (seven old German training aircraft) and just a 'homemade' navy with the largest ship like a corvette. 'If you don't provoke anyone, they will leave you in peace', was the slogan.

Suddenly I pricked up my ears: this was no ordinary story coming from the radio. I could hardly believe what I was hearing; there had been nothing on the late evening news before I went to bed. By this time I had been joined by my eldest brother and mother, and like me, they were completely dumbfounded. 'German planes have bombed and strafed the Royal family, but they are safe and hiding in a wood near Eidsvoll,' the radio went on, 'but reports of German patrols on motorcycles trying to catch them are coming in.' The members of the government had managed to escape from Oslo and had held an emergency meeting during the night, deciding to fight, and ordering all able men to report to regional defence depots, taking their hunting-rifles with them; all transport and buses were requisitioned.

All ships were told to report to 'allied' ports – and an enterprising soul had managed to find trucks during the night and got all of forty tons of gold out of the vaults of the Bank of Norway. (This eventually found its way to Aalesund and thence to England.)

I realized that although I was 'under age', I was now at war. The idea was abhorrent, and I had no idea how to go about it. I had forgotten my fishing nets, they didn't seem to matter any more. I decided to take my bike and go the nine miles to college to find out if they had any more news there. Wherever I went, people were stood in small groups, talking agitatedly. Rumours were rife everywhere, seagulls and crows had become German paratroops, fishing boats became German motor torpedo boats, and coastal steamers troopships. A friend of mine said he had heard the English were coming to help, and the Royal Navy would soon send the Germans back to where they came from. I wanted so much to believe him, for I had great respect for the Royal Navy and thought them invincible. (In fact, three English destroyers came to Aalesund a few days later, and provided us for a time with our only anti-aircraft defence – we had nothing but rifles.) At college our headmaster came and gave us a summary of what had happened up to that moment, but the only new thing he could tell us was that a man called Vidkun Quisling, whom I had never heard of – nor had he – had formed a new government in Oslo, and told us to greet our German liberators with friendship. Liberators? From what? Liberators from freedom? I had always thought of myself as free as the seagulls that would come and eat the offal out of my hands while I was fishing.

As I cycled home again, many strange thoughts went through my mind, strange for a young boy who had been brought up in such a sheltered environment. Stories came to mind, stories and names I had read about: Guernica and Zaragossa, Shanghai and Nanking, Verdun and Somme, of 'the unknown soldier', of horror and slaughter on the battlefield. Was my name and those of my friends and dear ones to be added to those? I still didn't know what lay ahead, and I didn't even know what to do. But after I got home, it didn't take me long to make up my mind. It came with the first proclamation over the radio from our 'new masters': 'Shot will be the one who —' and there followed a long list of things which were punishable by death, things that I had been doing all my life, and that I had taken for granted. It was called freedom. And this was what I would be shot for. No, not me, not after 9 April 1940. I would rather fight, and I did.

E.D. SPARKES

In 1939 I was living just north of Copenhagen where I was completing my studies in horticulture at The State Glasshouse Experimental Station. There seemed little chance that war could be avoided and Denmark was aware that they could be overrun in a few hours if Germany so decided.

Denmark was a peaceful little country, well aware of its vulnerability but proud of its culture and close ties in the Scandinavian brotherhood, and deeply feeling the invasion of Finland by the Russians. A young man walking along with a suitcase would be slapped on the back and wished good luck, so many of them went to help the Finns. The papers were full of stories of the gallant defence.

The first problem was the language, with the extraordinary glottal stops, pronunciation of the swallowed 'r's and a couple of extra letters in the alphabet. There was no way out: it had to be learned. Without it further study was impossible.

Being a student, money for entertainment was limited. I was naturally envious of my friends who had been conscripted into the army in which all Danes had to serve. They travelled at half-fare on the railways and the still-famous pleasure gardens of Tivoli and its many entertainments were half-price or free. I can't remember how it started, but somehow a bet was placed between two groups, one claiming that I would be able to pass a whole day in Tivoli in Danish soldier's uniform without detection and the others denying it. I had been in the country six months when on 13 May 1939 my silhouette was cut out, as it can still be done in Tivoli today, and the event was witnessed in writing on the back by companions who came along to confirm the conditions of the bet were met.

The temptation was too great and I continued to borrow the uniform and enjoy the lower rates. It was great fun but a dangerous game. One night I had left it too late and the last train was in the station, but guarding the gates were two large Military Policemen. I retired to the shadows wondering what to do. There seemed no way out. What I would have paid to be in civilian clothes. All seemed lost when I heard a low whistle. It was the guard of the train. A quick jerk of his thumb and I followed him into and through some offices, along a deserted platform, across two trains and platforms and I was past the police and on my train. He gave me a quick pat on the back and wished me luck. He would have served his time in the army and had probably been in a scrape or two, but I wondered what he would have done if he had known that I was not a Danish soldier. That was the last time and I had been lucky to get away with it.

The day war was declared I was at lunch with the family of my, then, girlfriend. Her family was large and extremely hospitable. At the special weekly meal many students were invited including myself and, on that occasion, a German student. As we sat around that huge table and finished our meal the radio was turned on and we listened to the words that started World War II.

Utter silence, oppressive, followed: it seemed that nothing would end it and then rose a tiny childish voice.

From the youngest daughter, 'What does it mean, Father?' 'It means many people are going to be killed.' The oppressive silence returned. It seemed an age, then that tiny voice again: 'Father, can I leave the table?' 'Sit still!' The silence was returning. Then, on the verge of tears, 'But Father I MUST go.' The spell was broken by a small girl's problem and everyone laughed and started to talk at once. My girlfriend asked me what I was going to do. I shrugged. The German said, 'I can get back. What are you going to do? Swim?' He laughed. He laughed alone and was suddenly embarrassed.

I had kept my eyes open to gain any information that may be useful if some means could be found to return to England. At least once a week I would walk along the shore noting where the boats were pulled up and where the oars were stored against the chance that the Germans made a sudden invasion. The lights of Sweden winked invitingly across the Øresund, the narrow strip of water between Denmark and Sweden. I would not go as far north as Elsinor, that would be too obvious. A slack tide and a dark night to avoid any pre-emptive German patrols, and a hope to slip over to the north or south of the island of Ven just inside Swedish waters. Every time I left my room for more than a few hours I wore heavy clothes and boots, prepared to sleep rough and not return. I did not trust the police and had no way of finding otherwise. It is no use going into the station and saying 'I am vulnerable, can I trust you?' I need not have bothered. When I returned after the war my old boss told me that immediately the Germans invaded, the police (who did not know that I had left a few days before) phoned him to say that they were coming to take me into custody. Since they were coming from Copenhagen the warning would give me ample time to escape. Better safe than sorry.

I was cut off from England but not from information. There was plenty of propaganda. From both sides. One of the most glorious, or infamous, depending on one's country of origin, was the 'Altmark Incident'. A German prison ship, the *Altmark*, with British soldiers imprisoned on board, had to put into a Norwegian fjord. A British destroyer made a surprise raid, overran the crew killing some of them, and the shout went up 'The Navy's here!' The soldiers were rescued and returned safely. The Danes were delighted, as, one suspects, were the Norwegians although they protested vigorously that their neutrality had been violated. Danish movie theatres were able to show both the British and the German newsreels of the funerals, with full military honours, of the sailors who had been killed. The same incident was portrayed with full national bias. The German pictures of the attending officers had all been taken from a low camera angle outlining against the sky clean-shaven, granite-jawed, tall and immaculately uniformed Nordic heroic sons of the Fatherland. The British newsreels had been taken from a high angle, dwarfing the Germans. They looked awkward and shambling and there was more than a hint of five o'clock shadow. I still wonder at the brilliance of the technicians who must have added that shadow on every frame of the film. The radio was equally interesting. The same incidents from opposing viewpoints were hardly recognizable. One became inured to this and tended to aim at a point between the two – but slightly biased towards the British!

Air tickets were almost impossible to come by and I was surprised one February day in 1940 to hear from the Danish airline that they had an air ticket for me in six weeks' time, but only as far as the Netherlands. So on that day I went to Kastrup airport and perhaps I was not surprised to see the German, also going home. He gave me a wry smile and said, 'Did you learn everything you wanted to know?' I did not know on that early April day that there would be an invasion within a few days. He thought I was a spy and that I knew what was to follow. I am sure that he knew and that his interest in the Danish military airport north of Copenhagen was not innocent. My plane, a Fokker-Wulf Kondor, never returned. It was taken over by the RAF and spent the rest of its time with Coastal Command. Aircraft recognition charts for pilots' information noted that the type was much in use by German patrols over the Atlantic, but to be sure of the markings because there was one in use by the RAF.

Fortunately I had worked in the Netherlands for a few months so accommodation was no problem. The Dutch were preparing to defend themselves by flooding the land that they had so dearly won from the sea. They had no illusions as to their fate under Hitler. I was able to get a plane within the week which flew with blacked-out windows to prevent passengers seeing anything of military interest. We landed at Shoreham, Sussex, the only civilian airport open at that time. As I was in agriculture I was in a reserved occupation and not eligible to join the forces. I went to work in the family business, now turned over to food production in glasshouses on the south coast.

It could have stayed so but one morning an aircraft, flying low, dropped two bombs about fifty yards away. Perhaps he mistook the glasshouses for a factory. A few minutes later he dropped another string of bombs. I hopped on my motor-bike and went to see if there was anything I could do.

He had made a direct hit on another glasshouse complex near the sea. About two acres of glass were shattered. Near a bomb crater was the body of a man, almost cut in half. A little line of ducklings with no mother to lead them was running in a crazy circle, each time round dabbling through the entrails. A grey-faced man was lying on his back; thinking that I could do nothing for him I went off to help those who could be helped. Returning some time later I saw people holding up his head, still grey, and urging some water through his lips. His eyes fluttered and opened and he said, 'I wish I'd had me bloody rifle'.

That was the end of any feeling but fury: we were now short of pilots so I applied, and in due course was released by the Ministry of Agriculture. By the time I was flying Spitfires air fighting was changing and eventually there was a posting to India. While waiting for my operational posting there was a time of test-flying and flying the aircraft to various stations across the subcontinent. Then the chance of the formation of a new squadron, No. 10 in the Royal Indian Air Force.

It meant goodbye to my beloved Spitfires and on to the Hurricane IIb. I had test flown them but had not yet come to love them. They were a phenomenally firm gun platform for the four 20 mm Hispano Suiza cannon, with a withering cone of fire that must have been terrifying to face. Many of them had seen operational service in England and North Africa before we had them. After that the tropical weather was the last straw. Often an aircraft would return with only a few whiskers of fabric left. A hole left by enemy action or perished fabric and the air would rush in, stripping the rest off like an old glove. It looked pretty bizarre to see just the skeleton of the longerons holding the tail to the rest of the aircraft, but it wasn't too dangerous, the flying surfaces being metal-skinned. We were a small squadron of thirty-two pilots at full strength, based mainly as flying artillery for ground attack. We could also carry two 500 lb bombs to the Spitfire's two 250 lbs, and two 20 mm cannons.

Our field of operations was the Arakan coast of Burma. Stories of Japanese atrocities coloured our thoughts. One such sticks in my guts now. We were told that, if we could evade capture, we should make for one of the Muhammadan villages near the coast as they hated the Japanese. One of our pilots managed to, but was betrayed. The Japs pegged him to the ground with tent pegs and executed him by pouring boiling water over him.

We were told to escape in the first two days if we were shot down or we should be too weak. Some of us even carved our names on one bullet in our revolvers. That was supposed to be the last one. Romantic? Perhaps, but we were out there at the sharp end and we were young too.

A frequent question often asked is: What is it like to fly into anti-aircraft fire? It is a little like driving fast into large snowflakes. They seem to float towards one and increase speed until they flash past. Then remind yourself that most of the cannon fire is not tracer.

I was very proud of my squadron with its various religions. We felt ourselves to be the élite but then so, probably, did other squadrons.

I was invalided back to England with amoebic dysentery and felt morally and physically shattered. It is unpleasant to remember that towards the end of the war I had a lust to kill, and that that was entirely directed towards the Japanese.

Most of the darker side has dimmed in memory, so the enduring memories are of the happy times and there were many of them to savour. They come so easily to mind: the joy and excitement of a perfect day flying over the knife-edged mountain ridges of the Burmese Arakan, looking to left and right to see the sun shining on the full squadron strength of twelve aircraft. Perhaps a flash of colour of a scarf at the neck of the goggled, helmeted, masked figure in the next aircraft. Instant recognition of the vital, living young man. He too would be sitting in his little cockpit with his left hand on the throttle control and his right hand on the control column, the thumb never more than an inch or so from the firing button. Eyes constantly scanning the other aircraft, sky and jungle below and with ever-vigilant glances to the instruments, running over in his mind the action to come.

Sir Hugh Dundas

On 3 September 1939 I was on Doncaster airfield with No. 616 (South Yorkshire) Squadron, Auxiliary Air Force. I was just nineteen years old. I had eighty-four flying hours in my pilot's log book, twenty-three of them dual, sixty-one solo. My main concern was that I might not have added to them sufficiently, or that the Squadron might not have been re-equipped with Spitfires or Hurricanes in place of its delightful but antiquated Gloster Gauntlet bi-planes, in time to play a full part in any fighting which was to come.

Often enough, over the next 5½ years, I was to look back and reflect ruefully on that boyish personal reaction to the outbreak of a war which brutally affected hundreds of millions of people all over the world and certainly became the most dominant single factor, by far, in my own life.

It was the day which so many of us had been waiting for – not just for the week or so since it had become obvious that Hitler's Germany had finally decided to take military action in the east, or for the forty-eight hours since the actual invasion of Poland had begun, but over a period of two or three years. Yet on the actual day itself there was little enough in the way of action or heroics on Doncaster airfield. Indeed, so far as I was concerned, as an Acting Pilot Officer and one of several pupil pilots in the Training Flight, there was really no business to go about on that momentous day.

I remember that, after breakfast, we were all hanging about in the Officers' Mess, or just outside it, listening to BBC radio. There was no flying training that day. The Squadron Adjutant and Assistant Adjutant, regular RAF officers who were responsible, among other things, for teaching us to fly and training us up to full Wings and operational standard, were busy doing all the things which had to be done following the Squadron's embodiment in the Royal Air Force (Auxiliary Squadrons were the RAF equivalent of Army Territorial units) and its premature recall from Summer Camp, at Manston in Kent, two days earlier. I remember that I, with two or three fellow pilots, occupied myself by polishing up the bodywork and chrome of a ten-year-old Rolls Royce tourer which the Assistant Adjutant had bought a few days earlier. It was with that trivial pursuit that we were engaged when the Prime Minister spoke on the radio and told us what we really already knew, that we were at war with Germany. And we were still at it when the air raid sirens wailed out for the very first time.

It was a long, hard road from Doncaster, 3 September 1939, to Treviso, in north-east Italy, where I found myself on 8 May 1945, the day the war in Europe ended. At Doncaster I had been a boy, just one year out of school, with no knowledge or experience of anything at all except boyish things. At Treviso, as a Group Captain, with five fighter/bomber squadrons under my command and five years of almost continuous campaigning behind me, I had – though still more than two months short of my twenty-fifth birthday – plenty of experience and knowledge. But it was experience and knowledge exclusively of war, experience and knowledge gleaned in the hostile skies over Dunkirk in the spring of 1940 and over south-east England a couple of months later; over north-east France in the summers of 1941 and 1942; over Tunisia, Sicily and southern Italy in 1943; and in support of the allied armies in their hard slog up through central and northern Italy in 1944 and the spring of 1945. I had left very many friends and some of my family along that road and I knew that I was extraordinarily lucky to have reached the end of it myself.

There is no doubt at all that my journey down that road shaped my life and my character to an extent immeasurably more powerful than anything else which has happened to me along the way.

CAPTAIN

HUGO BRACKEN

CBE, RN

In September 1939 I was in command of the ship's flight consisting of two Walrus amphibians of HMS *Suffolk* which was refitting at Portsmouth. We were disembarked at the Royal Naval Air Station at Lee-on-Solent.

Both prior to and in the first part of the war it was considered that the Germans would use poison gas as they had in World War I. On the morning of 3 September the order was given that those who wore beards must shave them off: if you had a beard – as I had – then your gas mask did not fit sufficiently tightly at the sides to give full protection. I went to my cabin in the Officers' Mess and started to shave mine off. The rule was then – as it is now – that officers and men in the Royal Navy could either be clean-shaven or wear a full set of moustache and beard; in the Army and Air Force they could either be clean-shaven or wear a moustache without a beard. By way of amusement I first of all shaved off my beard but left the moustache. Looking in the mirror I saw that this changed my appearance considerably and I decided to play a prank on my fellow officers.

I changed into plain clothes, left the Officers' Mess by a side door and went round to the main entrance where I announced myself to the Hall Porter as Major Hawkins, Royal Artillery, in command of the local AA Battery, and said that I had come to call on the Officers' Mess. The senior officer present was summoned and I was invited in and entertained most generously with drinks as is the custom in the Navy. Nobody penetrated my disguise.

After about an hour the Commander of the Air Station

came into the Mess and approached me from behind. He put his hand on my shoulder and started to say 'By the way, Bracken . . . ' I turned towards him and he started to apologize, but suddenly I saw a look of recognition in his eye. I turned and fled. After removing the hirsute adornment from my upper lip, I returned to the Mess having changed into uniform. I was greeted with a cheer and much laughter. To my relief I saw a broad grin on the face of the Commander.

I served in HMS *Suffolk* until April 1940 when she was badly damaged by German Stukas off the coast of Norway. I was then appointed to command a squadron of Walruses and operated from shore bases in Norway and then in Iceland. In July 1941 I was sent to navigate a force of torpedo bombers which was to attack German shipping in north Norway (where I had been in 1940) from a carrier task force. Unfortunately our arrival in the target area coincided with the return of a German fighter sweep over the Russian lines near Murmansk and we lost sixteen aircraft out of twenty-one – heavier losses than we sustained in the whole of the Falklands campaign. We were shot down by a Messerschmit 110 and crashed in the sea. We were very fortunate to be picked up by a German minesweeper. I spent the next 3¾ years in various POW camps in Germany and Poland, but mainly in Stalag Luft III – best known for the Wooden Horse and the Great Escape. I was finally liberated by the Red Army from a camp south of Berlin and reached home on 5 May 1945.

RUTH WELLS

When I was a schoolgirl news flashes came in newsheet form with the cries of 'Extra! Extra!' from the paper boy. That's how we heard that war had been declared.

The third of September is easy to remember because the siren sounded that first night and my parents, brother and I all went into the dusty coal cellar. (We already had gas masks and ID cards.) I was terrified and sat on a makeshift loo for the duration of the alert – how long for I don't know but it seemed an eternity. We'd forgotten our drill. As the All Clear sounded we put on our gas masks, but then we heard the Air Raid Wardens calling 'All clear!'

Our wartime memories are an odd mixture of the happy and the harrowing, but they give an idea of the odd times in which we were all living. Blackout is something unforgettable especially when mixed with fog or smog: alighting from public transport required both nerve and skill! Some nights I spent on First Aid duty in the basement of the largest department store in Leeds – I still don't know why as there were no staff in the store! One night in 1943 or 1944 we thought we were having an air raid in Leeds without any sirens. It turned out to be a small earthquake!

My husband and I joined up in early stages of the war when under age; I was sixteen and my husband William was seventeen (this was old compared to my father-in-law who joined up at fourteen in World War I). William joined the RNVR as a telegraphist in August 1940. He trained at a Skegness holiday camp (HMS *Royal Arthur*) and he remembers ruefully the freezing conditions of those unheated chalets where they slept. German planes often came over at weekends machine-gunning and bombing. One weekend they machine-gunned the complete row of chalets but William was fortunate to be home on leave. He and his companions were each given a bike, a broomstick and a section of beach to patrol. Goodness knows what the enemy would have thought if they had landed there!

Another vivid memory is a trip to Iceland by converted trawler during which the men were all unwell and lived on condensed milk. On their return to port it was found that the water tanks on board had not been cleaned out since the beginning of the war and were full of huge white worms.

One Christmas Day William and the other Sub-Lieutenant decided to have a church parade on deck in bitter conditions. The crew were not happy as this meant best uniforms. When all were assembled the other No. 1 arrived, straight faced with collar reversed, vicar-like. He named the song, one of the most bawdy of naval songs, which was then sung with great gusto. This was then appropriately rounded off by Christmas dinner served by the officers.

On another occasion William and another Sub-Lieutenant brought two landing craft from Ayr to Appledore and they stopped at Plymouth for orders. The officers decided that all the men not on duty watch could have shore leave. An hour later William and the other No. 1 saw twenty crew members drinking mournfully in the bar. They called the bosun to form the crew in three outside the pub and marched them down the street. The crew obeyed but their glum faces lit up with laughter when they were escorted to the corner fish and chip shop and ordered to consume fish and chips at the expense of William and the other No. 1.

In April 1942 I arrived in Henley-in-Arden for my duty in the Women's Land Army. On arrival at the hostel we girls were supplied with bikes. I kept quiet about not being able to ride one even though I could have been given a lift to work by van. Next morning I gritted my teeth and learned – the hard way – on my way to work. There was plenty of hair standing on end that day including mine!

We WLA girls often worked on or near airfields and saw empty lots where there had been a plane the day before, and the flag was forever flying at half mast. One night, just after lights out, there was a terrible explosion. Next day we heard that two of the planes had crashed – one returning and one going out fully-laden with young lads we'd talked to and danced with only a week before.

One hostel was a beautiful old house set in lovely grounds. Perhaps for this reason Mrs Roosevelt was to visit and meet some of the Land Girls there – but not the ones who were staying in the house. Where the welcoming group came from is anyone's guess, but they all had new uniforms! We, from the house, were sent to work in an open lorry on that cold Saturday morning. When we arrived some distance away we were deposited and the lorry left. There was no sign of the farmer and no work. We felt we had been swept under the carpet and so we wasted no time. Despite our large number we got lifts back as we weren't fussy how we travelled – we all had our boots and dirty working clothes on. All ended well as we arrived in time to push to the front and give Mrs Roosevelt a real down-to-earth welcome. We were told off later by the authorities, but it was too late!

There's much said about those killed in action, but I remember the deaths of many Land Army girls killed by falling into farm machinery or off horses.

When all's said and done I think most people prefer to remember the better incidents of the war or the funny moments and especially the camaraderie that was so much in evidence in those times.

GEORGES SIMENON

At this time, I was expecting at any moment to be called up into military service in Belgium. I had just become a father for the first time, and I was living with my wife and tiny son at Nieul sur Mer, in Charentes Maritimes, in a property surrounded by a large garden. I remember well that the day war was declared, I pulled up all the flowers in my garden in order to plant cabbages and potatoes so that I would be able to feed my little family when provisions became scarce.

THE RT. HON.

TONY BENN

MP

I was 14½ years old when the war broke out, on holiday with my brothers in Essex, and my father, who was the Labour MP for Gorton, was in London with my mother because Parliament was meeting.

We heard that the Prime Minister Neville Chamberlain was to broadcast that morning so my brothers and I sat round and listened to it, and were acutely aware of what it all meant.

Living in a political family we had followed the advance of fascism during the thirties and knew exactly what was at stake, but even so the declaration of war itself was very moving to hear and we knew its significance, and we talked long and seriously about it.

A few days later the RAF made its first bombing raid on Germany.

MOLLIE CRISFORD

On 3 September 1939, I was eighteen years old, and living with my mother and brother in West London.

It was a beautiful cloudless autumn day, and the blue sky was full of sparkling silver barrage balloons, which looked like a lot of flying baby elephants! For weeks we had been preparing for war, but always with the hope that it wouldn't happen. We had painted the window-panes with a rubber solution, and stuck adhesive paper from corner to corner, to prevent shattering from a bomb blast. We had strengthened the ceiling of the dining-room with wooden beams, in case the house collapsed. We had stocked up a store cupboard with enough tinned food to last for several days, and tried to make the room gas-proof. We also had a commode in readiness!

We listened with a sense of horror and apprehension to Mr Chamberlain's speech. My mother, remembering the last war, shed a few tears. My brother, twenty-four years old, knew that he would have to go and fight for his country. I wondered what it would be like, and found it hard to believe it was really happening. I had been a very delicate, asthmatic child, with a great imagination, and often day-dreamed, picturing myself doing brave and daring deeds. Pictures now flashed into my mind of rescuing people from blazing houses while bombs rained down from the sky! I wished I was physically strong, and could really do the things I dreamt about.

My brother joined the army, and went off to Burma to fight the Japanese. Thankfully he survived the war. My mother and I went to live in Sussex, which although much safer than London was in the direct line of the doodlebugs when they came in 1944.

When I was twenty I joined the Women's Royal Naval Service, and served for three years as a coder. Working deep in an underground tunnel brought back my bronchitis and asthma, and I was eventually invalided out in 1945, and was in poor health for several years. It was not only the wounded who were 'war casualties'.

MUNDEK MARGULIES

I was living in Lvov. In June 1941 the city was occupied by the Germans and within just a few days we all knew, in the Jewish community, that it signalled the end for us. Immediately the Nazis ordered the execution of the most distinguished members of our community and from the minority Ukrainian section of the local population a militia was formed whose job was to terrorize Jews.

Later we were forced to give up our houses and our jobs and before the year had ended we all had to move into a ghetto. This was north of the city centre in the poorest part of Lvov and had to house about 100,000 people. Gradually food began to run out and there was starvation, and diseases like typhus and cholera became common.

Early in 1942 the Yanovska Concentration Camp was built on the ruins of a Jewish cemetery and people were taken from the ghetto to work there as forced labourers. Soon, though, people began to be taken away to death camps in very large numbers – from March to November 65,000 were taken. By May 1943 there were only 7000 left in the ghetto.

At eleven o'clock at night on 21 July 1943 the Gestapo and Ukrainian militia burst into the ghetto and spread everywhere. There was a dreadful panic, people running in every direction, shouting and screaming. The Germans were shooting left and right with flame throwers; they didn't even bother to look. Fearing that something like this would happen, a group of us had already dug a tunnel down into the sewer and when the final liquidation came we escaped.

In the cellar where the tunnel began there was panic too as some people did not want to go down. Christina, the daughter of Mr Chiger who had organized the tunnel, was crying that she didn't want to go, but someone took her and pushed her down to a person waiting in the water below.

In the sewers it was pitch black, with a roaring noise of water. To move we had to stay close to the wall which was running with water. Many other people tried to escape down into the sewers and there were lots of people moving in the pitch darkness, pushing and shoving. We didn't even know who they were – they were going crazy shouting, screaming, crying. One man I knew had a handkerchief full of diamonds and cried 'Margulies! Save me! Save me!' Somebody pushed past him and he fell, with the diamonds, into the water. It didn't matter if you tried to talk to people, they didn't even listen. They just made a long queue against the wall while other people tried to get past. This went on for three or four hours, many people fell into the water and were drowned. We only had two ropes and when we tried to throw the ropes in to help people the water was so fast that we couldn't hold them and people were just swept away. It was really like a torrent and no one could swim against it or even hold themselves against the sides. It was so deep too – about two metres – that if you fell in you just didn't have a chance.

We just couldn't rescue everybody. We didn't have enough food or water to give them. Some committed suicide by taking cyanide. With some a doctor gave them an injection. About twenty-six people we kept, and told them to wait for us, but they committed suicide. When we came back we had to throw them in the water because the rats were eating them. It was hell.

In all the chaos our group got separated and only when things began to quieten down were we able to find one another with the help of Leopold Socha, the Polish sewer inspector who had helped us right from the beginning. With him to guide us we got back together in a spot where we could rest. My wife (then my fiancée) and I were sitting quietly on the damp floor when the Chigers arrived to join us and we ended up staying there for six weeks, in a hole with water running down the walls from the toilets above. We only had cold water to drink – half a glass for each person each day. There were twenty of us: Mr and Mrs Chiger and their two children, Mr Weisz, me, my fiancée Clara and thirteen others.

While we were there the Gestapo searched the sewers for Jews but Socha, who acted as their guide, kept them away from us. We were imprisoned in those pitch black, stinking tunnels, the rats always bothering us. In the end Mr Weisz and two others left to try and find somewhere safe to hide outside. For weeks we had no food at all and so I decided to go out to see what I could find. There were no other Jews about, they were either in the Yanovska Camp or had been taken away to Auschwitz or Belsen. Soon I found the bodies of Weisz and the other two. They had been shot. In the burnt-out buildings of the empty ghetto I found a frying pan, a primus stove and some blankets, and I also came across bodies in cellars or cupboards, bodies of people who had killed themselves. After all, on the day when the ghetto was liquidated there had been 7000 people there and many had been shot or had taken their own lives.

Back in the tunnels we sat in pools of raw sewage and it wasn't long before we were all ill with dysentery. The two children were very bad and they had to go to the toilet there where we were living. Fresh water was very important and very difficult to get. Each day someone had to crawl on their stomach through very small tunnels with a special bucket over their head. It was a round journey of about a mile, grovelling along on your knees and elbows to fetch the water which trickled down from a fountain in the main square of the city. Eventually too Socha managed to get us a regular supply of food, mainly bread and soup to start with. He used to give part of his own lunch to the children. He really was our lifeline. We gave him money to buy food like bread and potatoes.

In August we decided we had to try and find a better place to live in. Socha led the way and we all crawled off through the tunnels until he brought us to a sort of L-shaped area. It was dry and much better than the place we had left. Here we managed to settle ourselves and establish some sort of simple routine. We were now able to wash once a week in clean water and even to take some simple exercise. We took it in turns to fetch drinking water, cook food and fend off the rats. We always marked the Sabbath with candles.

Now too we began to think about friends and relatives. Some should have come into the sewers with us but in the actual moment were too afraid to go down – people like my wife's sister and Mr Weisz's wife. What had become of them? Were they dead or were they in the Yanovska camp? I decided to try and find out and even perhaps rescue them. Late one night I came up from the sewer beside the Opera House and made my way towards the rail yards where the factory workers from the camp used to gather. There I mingled with these workers and at the end of a shift I changed places with one of the brigade members and returned with them into the Yanovska camp wearing an internee's arm band. I did this four or five times.

Inside the camp the women and children were separated but I finally made contact with my wife's sister and brother, but I just couldn't find a way to smuggle them out. I also found Mrs Weisz, whose husband had come with us initially into the sewers. She screamed at me, asking 'What's happened to my husband? What's happened?' I told her he was dead. She wouldn't believe it and started tearing her hair out, and she shouted 'You're not telling the truth.' My fiancée's sister, called Manya, gave me a letter for Clara and I started crying and kissing her because I couldn't help them any more. I had to say goodbye to them and to her little brother Milek, who was only twelve. I ran away from Mrs Weisz because I couldn't stand it. She was screaming and I was afraid she would give it out that I was illegal in the camp. I was afraid and I didn't want her to see me any more. Two brothers whom I met there, called Zucker, were very strong and I said we could do with them down below in the sewers, but they said no, they had to die anyway and they didn't want to drown in the water, it was better to die in the camp. I didn't ever see them again.

Back in the sewers winter came, and apart from the terrible cold there was always the danger we would be flooded. After long periods of rain the tunnels filled with water. Once the water came so high that the children had to be held above it or they would have drowned. Sometimes it was so cold we had to sleep piled on top of one another to keep warm.

Through all this Socha kept us supplied with food even when our money ran out. He told Mrs Chiger, 'I'll go on until the job is finished. I won't back out. I've decided to save you and that's that!' He brought us news too of how the war was going, how the Russians had crossed into Poland in January 1944. It was not until July though that the Russians began to shell Lvov. We could hear it. As they retreated the Germans began mining the streets and I thought that now we would be finished. We thought maybe they would come down to us, so Socha told them that if they dug any more they would hit gas and water. Luckily they stopped then and retreated.

On 29 July, two days after the Russians had occupied Lvov, Socha came to get us out. He knocked on the street grating and called to us and out we came – the children first. We had been there for fourteen months. Twenty of us went in and ten survived.

MAJOR-GENERAL G. ARMITAGE

It is not easy to remember precisely what happened the day war was declared fifty years ago, although some points are clear enough. My regiment was stationed at Colchester, and we all knew that we would be off to the continent at short notice, when the war started. My first personal concern was my two dogs and their future: my beloved spaniel went to my home in Ireland, where I saw her again on my first leave four months later. The little Shetland sheepdog was taken over by friends in Suffolk.

PROFESSOR

Nicholas Kemmer

On 3 September 1939 I was in a boarding house within sight of the Albert Memorial in London to hear Mr Chamberlain on the wireless and the first (bogus) air raid siren. However, my feelings at that instant may have been different from those of the others around the wireless.

I was just too young to share with my parents the corresponding experience of the start of World War I, which would have been within sight of the River Neva in St Petersburg, capital of Imperial Russia. However my memories do start to include the rejoicing over the Armistice outside our flat in Hyde Park Gate in London (not quite within sight of the Albert Memorial!).

A Plenipotentiary of the Imperial Russian Government, which my father was, who had lost not only his job but his home, possessions and citizenship, can't easily manage to stay within sight of the Albert Memorial even if his son has started his school life at Mr Orlando Magner's school at 90, Queens Gate (within sight of etc. . . .) so that by 1921 I found myself a pupil of the Bismarckschule in Hanover, Germany, being taught in my *third* language and taught modern history and attitudes of mind *very* different from those that, mercifully, still prevailed in my home. No wonder I veered towards 'objective' studies like maths and physics, which I was taught well. The aim became to graduate at the great University of Gottingen some seventy miles away, with strong recommendation to seek to be accepted in Professor Max Born's school. The political atmosphere changed, however, and was periodically eased for me by return to my parents' home which by then had been moved to Zurich in Switzerland. While visiting them I heard that Max Born and most of his colleagues were sacked from their posts. I returned briefly to Gottingen to pack my belongings and dodge forcible enrolment into the Stormtroopers (SA) by getting a hernia seen to. Zurich had a physics school equal to Gottingen so I had my solution for getting qualifications – but not employment since my passport had, of necessity, by then become German.

Imperial College (within sight of the . . . etc.) advertised a Beit Scientific Research Fellowship for graduates under 25. At the age of 24¾ I applied and got it.

This nearly closes the circle except for the 'enemy alien' status that I acquired as Mr Chamberlain spoke. Internment at once? Well, scientific qualifications were otherwise immediately in demand – from British colleagues. Perhaps because of my Russian past I never got to the Isle of Man. Instead, it was realized by the powers-that-be that there *was* a branch of physics that *might eventually* become important, but at very long range. That was where all the awkward aliens belonged – working on The Bomb – and when it came to moving them to the US or Canada (that was me) they needed to be naturalized British. Many of my friends subsequently became American. I chose to think that I could not change nationality yet again. Only for the last thirty-five years I have been growing more and more Scottish. Here I am, retired from the chair passed on to me from Max Born.

What did I feel then in 1939? A year earlier, in 1938, was perhaps a better and more memorable moment – Chamberlain coming back from Munich announcing the quite incredible: yet another surrender to those thugs and criminals! Why doesn't anyone listen to Churchill? And yet we are going to go on living with our gas masks and sandbags for some time longer. *Of course* I felt the same relief as everybody, but that war was about to come anyway. So, a year later, there it was. What will internment be like for me? How much worse for my friends? Then the 'phoney war'. What followed, all the ghastly realities, did not really affect me. I was an extraordinary exception. I did not see the Russian revolution. I was shielded from the 'German spirit' prevailing in Germany in the '20s and '30s. I never saw real war service or heavy air raids.

If I ever publish a biography, I'll call it '*Alibi – I wasn't there!*'

PROFESSOR HELMUT G. KOENIGSBERGER

We listened to Chamberlain's announcement on the old wireless in the landlady's sitting-room, my mother and I. It was not a surprise. We knew too much about the Germans to imagine that they would tamely give in to the British ultimatum and withdraw from Poland. But the landlady had still hoped for peace. 'They are wicked', she repeated over and over again, meaning Hitler and co. Mother was intrigued. Wicked was a word from a religious vocabulary. She didn't disapprove but she herself usually used words from the more general range of moral epithets: evil, for instance.

Of this evil Käthe Koenigsberger had had plenty of experience in Germany since the Nazis came to power in 1933. Early on, she had correctly seen that there was no future for her children in Germany. Neither being christened nor my father's war service in World War I made any difference to our classification as Jews, sub-humans who had to be got rid of in one way or another. She sent all five of us out of the country, to England, America and India. Käthe had been widowed in 1932. She stayed on alone in the big house by the lake, near Berlin, trying to keep a home for us when we came back on holiday or on the off-chance that things should ever get better. They didn't. In the spring of 1939 she had to leave Germany with a couple of suitcases. The house and garden had been stolen from her by the

Nazis. Later, they were to murder several of her cousins and old aunts.

I was the youngest of the five and had been to school in Newport, Shropshire, since 1934. Since 1937 I had been reading History at Caius College, Cambridge, on college and West Riding of Yorkshire scholarships. During the summer vacation of 1939 I had stayed up. Mother had joined me. There was nowhere else to go. Our digs, in a dingy Cambridge side street, were typically cramped but clean.

After Chamberlain's announcement we naturally talked only about the war. Both of us were reasonably optimistic about the final outcome. There was, after all, the precedent of Germany's defeat in 1918. 'The Germans can always be relied on to commit the ultimate and decisive stupidity,' my mother's physicist brother, Max Born, had assured her. We did not realize how unprepared this country was and I, at least, did not realize how effectively Germany had rearmed. Mother, having lived there until a few months previously, knew better and was afraid. 'Oh well,' I said, 'I don't imagine I will survive this war.' I remember this now quite distinctly; but I am no longer sure what I meant. Will no one survive? Will young men not survive? Or just I, personally? I don't think it was this last meaning; and the others sound, now in 1989 at any rate, rather theatrical. But while there was satisfaction, even joy, that Britain had finally said 'no' to Hitler, we were under no illusion about the horrors of war, and we expected them to start almost immediately.

That night the air raid siren woke us – a shocking sound, not yet become familiar by nightly repetition. We all scrambled down and huddled under the stairs, my mother and I, the landlady and her little girl, perhaps ten years old. I don't think there was a father, or perhaps he was away. Like many other people, the landlady had not yet learned to black out the windows properly and we were afraid to attract German bombs. Later, one was to be more afraid of attracting an air raid warden. It seemed hours before the All Clear sounded, although it may not have been more than twenty minutes.

The next day we learned, on the grapevine, that there had been no raid on Cambridge. We told the landlady we would organize the blackout. From then on we had light in the house and we also decided it was better to risk the bombs in one's bed than shivering under the stairs. The essential survival mechanisms of war, the comforting grapevine and a certain degree of personal fatalism, had slipped into place within the first twenty-four hours.

My mother stayed in England until January 1940 and then sailed to America, in a neutral Dutch ship, to live with my eldest sister for the rest of the war. I volunteered for HM Forces but was turned down as an 'enemy alien'. In May 1940, two weeks before I was due to take my Part II exams, I was interned and shipped off to Canada. When I was released and brought back, in January 1941, there was still only the option of the Pioneer Corps. No one I consulted thought it would be a good idea for me to spend the rest of the war digging latrines. I was of more use as a teacher, first at Brentwood, then at Bedford School. In 1944 the Royal Navy changed its policy and I was accepted for active service in destroyers. There were some twenty-five or thirty of us, ex-Germans and ex-Austrians, in the ships of 21st Destroyer Flotilla and, unofficially, we called ourselves 'His Majesty's most loyal enemy aliens'. They demobilized us in October 1945 and I returned to Cambridge as a postgraduate student.

SHLOMO LIVNEY

As a German Jew brought up in Berlin and having immigrated to Palestine in the year 1934 at the age of twenty, I found myself at the outbreak of World War II working away in a Kibbutz. At that time pioneering and the redemption of Israel's ancient land were in high fashion and one found profound and genuine satisfaction in a life of toil and sweat.

It is sometimes forgotten that the small Jewish population of those days in Palestine sent forth not less than 36,000 volunteers who joined Britain's fighting forces in various theatres of war. Like many of our boys I was allowed to volunteer for the RAF in April 1940, choosing the medical services. Though I could read English, the RAF provided my first encounter – no brief one – with a section of British society whose language and mentality were, naturally, very different from mine. Having undergone training as a male nurse and dispenser in RAF general hospitals in Egypt – Helwan, Kabuit (canal area), Western Desert and Cairo – I spent the long years of that war on firm daily routine, never wasting a day's duties. Of course, one made friends with many a British lad and one discovered new land: I was still young enough to absorb and appreciate English thoughts and habits; truly new horizons in my case. During the war Cairo was a unique centre of Commonwealth activities in many respects. One could meet everybody in various clubs, libraries, theatres, debating and other societies – there did exist a Forces Parliament – in short that period in Cairo left an important influence with me until the present day.

Having demobilized in April 1946 I returned to work the plough and the land. In fact, for the last forty-three years I have again been a member of this Kibbutz, but memories of World War II are lingering on.

J. DONAGHY

To recall the day war broke out is to try to compress one's mind into the limited experience and knowledge of a fourteen-year-old girl of that time. Awareness of life outside the village was restricted to the daily paper and the scanty news bulletins on radio.

I cannot remember any school lessons touching on politics or European affairs, but these may have been taught to older girls. A fourteen-year-old was still fairly sheltered and cosseted. Home and parents represented the ultimate security, and my own parents seldom discussed anything in front of the children which might be deemed to be 'upsetting'.

However, it was from them that most of my perceptions of war came, Father having been gassed in the trenches of the Great War, while Mother had memories of sheltering in the cellar during Zeppelin raids, and the difficulties of food shortages.

It was not until I grew up that I learned how that war came about, but insulated as we were in 1939, children were still aware of the menace of the Third Reich and Hitler's mounting demands. Ever since the Munich Agreement the previous autumn, we had received Government instructions and advice on how to be prepared for war – and so it was that Sunday 3 September found us already issued with our gas masks; with blackout curtains ready for the windows; with our 'gasproof' room equipped with survival kit; and with Father appointed as an ARP Warden. Our household had already been turned upside-down by the arrival of two evacuees, for we lived in a reception area and from 1 September onwards, schoolchildren and expectant mothers had been arriving for billeting on local householders. Those poor expectant mothers – no one wanted to have them, and their first night was spent bedded down on straw palliasses in the nearest cinema!

And so to The Day – and the dread proclamation by the Prime Minister. I feel sure that matins must have been brought forward to allow people to get home in time, as we certainly went to Church that morning and it was packed to the doors. I next remember us all standing round the radio and listening to Neville Chamberlain, the words 'consequently this country is at war with Germany' producing a frisson of grave horror all round. Then I remember Father pouring sherry and the menfolk (my uncles had joined us) discussing the implications with hearty patriotism and a short-lived optimism that all would be over by Christmas.

Apart from my one question – 'Will we still have school?' – which was greeted with high amusement, I cannot recall anything else about that day, even though it is well documented that the air raid sirens did sound that morning. I think we children felt we must be suitably serious to fit the occasion, but there was a secret enjoyment of the novelty and drama of it all, and an utter conviction that if we all worked hard and did our duty, everyone would live happily ever after. Well, of course, a few did – but for most people that day changed the course of their lives as inexorably as it changed the course of history.

For me and most of my contemporaries, it was a matter of *hoping* that the war would go on long enough for us to 'do our bit', doing one's bit being the natural and laudable aim of most citizens. Until then, outside of school and then work, it was knitting gloves and balaclavas, washing up in a canteen, joining the Girls Training Corps to learn drill and marching, jelling and jamming with Mother to preserve every last fruit, and filling in those great geographical gaps in one's knowledge of the world as the war spread.

And then, at eighteen, it was into the WRNS and I grew up. Schooldays having been curtailed by wartime travelling difficulties, it was not until I joined up that I realized the full impact of the war, and not until then that the world of books and music, conversation and debate, experience and companionship of new nationalities and differing viewpoints, all conspired to mature one overnight.

The overriding recollection of the day war broke out and the years that followed is the complete belief in the righteousness of the Allied cause and a unique pride in serving one's country, something which has never diminished and binds most ex-servicemen and women into an indissoluble comradeship.

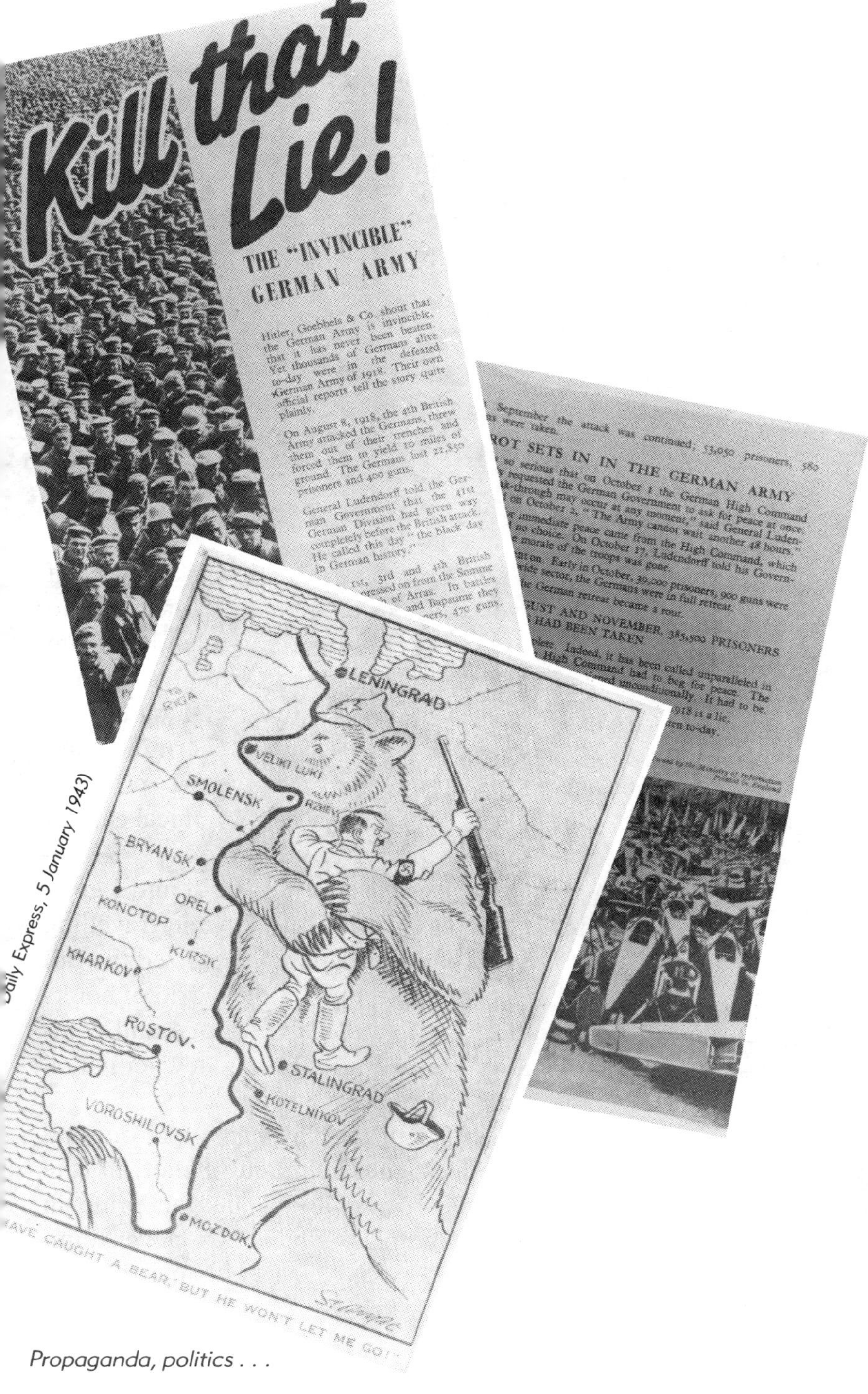

Kill that Lie!

THE "INVINCIBLE" GERMAN ARMY

Hitler, Goebbels & Co. shout that the German Army is invincible, that it has never been beaten. Yet thousands of Germans alive to-day were in the defeated German Army of 1918. Their own official reports tell the story quite plainly.

On August 8, 1918, the 4th British Army attacked the Germans, threw them out of their trenches and forced them to yield to miles of ground. The Germans lost 21,850 prisoners and 400 guns.

General Ludendorff told the German Government that the 41st German Division had given way completely before the British attack. He called this day "the black day in German history."

... 1st, 3rd and 4th British ... pressed on from the Somme ... of Arras. In battles ... and Bapaume they ... ners, 470 guns.

... September the attack was continued; 53,050 prisoners, 580 ... ns were taken.

...ROT SETS IN IN THE GERMAN ARMY

... so serious that on October 1 the German High Command ... y requested the German Government to ask for peace at once. ... ak-through may occur at any moment," said General Laden- ... d on October 2, "The Army cannot wait another 48 hours." ... r immediate peace came from the High Command, which ... d no choice. On October 17, Ludendorff told his Govern- ... e morale of the troops was gone.

... ent on. Early in October, 30,000 prisoners, 900 guns were ... wide sector, the Germans were in full retreat. ... he German retreat became a rout.

...UST AND NOVEMBER, 385,500 PRISONERS ... HAD BEEN TAKEN

... plete. Indeed, it has been called unparalleled in ... High Command had to beg for peace. The ... ed unconditionally. It had to be. ... 1918 is a lie. ... ten to-day.

aily Express, 5 January 1943)

Propaganda, politics . . .

. . . and the Front Line

Nancy Smith

I was on holiday in the Wirral with my family on the day war broke out, staying at our grandparents' house. I was sixteen and still at school.

My younger brother and I were on the front and heard people talking. We were at war! We rushed back to tell our father. He didn't believe us until he heard it soon after on the radio. Mother and I rushed out to the nearest haberdashers to buy blackout material. Someone had had great forethought and there was a good supply in the shops. We quickly covered the grandparents' windows and bought enough to do our own at home.

Grandmother's 'wash lady' bustled in to say her husband was off to join up, to see if he could get his old rank back. He had been a sergeant-major. Everything was suddenly different; new words, new ideas and an excitement in the air everywhere.

My father, a teacher, had to return home to cope with evacuations, but he was not needed and so returned to pick us up. He had had an invitation to visit an RAF station on the way home. We called in and were shocked to find we couldn't visit – there was a war on!

Returning home we found that some of our friends who had spare rooms had evacuees from Liverpool billeted on them. These did not stay long. They were back home within a week. They didn't like the food and there was no local fish and chip shop.

Back at school for a new term the number of children had increased. Boys from a Birmingham school were integrated with us – great news! New teachers were interesting and new, inhibited boys were there to make friends with. We all felt cheerful, excited and invincible. We were all at war.

For the next few years, until I joined the WRNS, it was a

case of fighting on the home front. Fire-watching at school, Dad in the Home Guard, digging for victory. Going easy on the bread and eating spuds instead. Keeping poultry, making do, making camouflage nets, helping in Service canteens. Occasionally feeling hungry, lusting after chocolates, altering clothes, unpicking woollies to make new garments, knitting seaboot stockings and balaclava helmets.

I don't remember being miserable, depressed or even bored.

ELLA JERRAM

I was born in Estonia in 1925 and from the age of nine my time was split between school and work. In the winter months I attended school and in the summer I was hired out to different farms where I was employed mainly on tending cattle and sheep. A herder was necessary as Estonia had no fences or hedges between the various holdings. I transgressed at times in that I fell asleep and, on waking up, was faced with the task of finding and rounding-up my charges. My wages were paid part in kind (farm produce) and part in cash, all of which went to my father.

This went on until 1939 when the Russians invaded Estonia. This was a result of a pact between Germany and Russia in which it was agreed that Poland should be split between these two powers and that Russia should occupy the Baltic states of Estonia, Latvia and Lithuania. So at the age of fourteen I found my country occupied. My first knowledge of this was when I saw what seemed to be unending columns of marching Russians. Up to this time we had been a country with plenty in the shops (for those who had money to buy). My family were poor but that year I had prevailed on my father to let me have part of my hard-earned income to get myself some clothes.

I eagerly made my way to Tartu, the capital, to buy a winter coat and a pair of shoes. The Russians and their wives had beaten me to it though and the shops had been practically denuded of goods. My first big spend was not to be.

The next year, 1940, was a period of anxiety as the Russians were in the process of purging the country of anti-communists. We lived in fear of a midnight knock on the door and several of our neighbours went missing. Sometimes, I regret to say, that was as a result of denunciations made by Estonians with a grudge against other Estonians.

The Russian-German pact made provision for the evacuation of German citizens from Estonia to Germany. My father and his brothers were of German stock and they decided to try and get out. Their wives who were all Estonians by birth were not in favour of leaving. As Russia and Germany were still, at least on paper, friendly, the Germans were allowed to send a Commission to Estonia for the repatriation of German nationals. We were lucky to qualify.

When we finally left in about March 1941 we could only take with us what we could carry, but this was no great worry as we owned few possessions. Our journey to Germany was by train and took a long time. I remember that our meals *en route* consisted mainly of Edam cheese; as a result I was put off cheese for a long time to come.

We were well received in Germany, even being greeted with a brass band. However one of my uncles was not impressed and opted to return to Estonia. The Russians sent him to Siberia for his troubles.

At the time I was not aware of, and was unaffected by, the fact that Germany was at war with Britain. We lived in the Swabian area which at that time, apart from a certain amount of rationing, was not very involved with the war. This happy state continued until the outbreak of hostilities between Germany and Russia and I must admit that my sympathies lay with the Germans as my family could see the possibilities of a return home if Russia was defeated.

Whilst in Germany we were accommodated in a camp (an old lunatic asylum) and we were employed in farming. Later we moved to an old school building where I worked in the kitchen and also in domestic service. I did not relish the latter as my employers were very mean and sparing with the food provided: breakfast consisted of one slice of dry brown bread and skimmed milk. By 1944 things had really deteriorated what with severe rationing and incessant air raids, and then all-out shelling. My brother and I attempted to flee but we only managed a few miles before being forced to turn back.

By spring 1945 Germany was in a state of collapse and the members of our camp were dispersing (I know not where). I finally realized that the war was over, as far as I was concerned, when I saw a soldier, an American whom I mistook for a German, tear down a swastika flag and wipe his feet on it. I was surprised to find the American troops were quite normal, as German propaganda had portrayed them as being outright ogres.

Later on the area was taken under French jurisdiction and they moved what was left of our camp (about forty of us) to some old barracks where were confined hundreds of young Russians who had been employed in forced labour in Germany. Many of them were running loose. They were looting and I caught one of them making off with my few possessions. I asked him why he didn't rob the Germans instead of me, a foreigner like himself. He must have understood as he abandoned my bag and ran away. He, like all the others, was destined to be returned to Russia, and the French obviously had the same plans as far as we were concerned. Fortunately one of our group could speak French and was able to explain that we weren't Russian. We were lucky that the French, in collusion with the Americans, arranged for us to be returned to our former camp. We then scattered and took to squatting in bombed-out properties and were lucky to find employment in a spinning factory.

By this time the Americans were sorting out all the many nationalities and accommodating us in German houses. This lasted for about a year until the Germans were allowed to re-possess their properties provided they agreed to accommodate us.

Being in the American zone we were given the opportunity to go to the United States as trainee hospital workers, but I feared that if I went and didn't like it, it was too far away to get back. I therefore went north into the British zone and applied for a year's work in a textile factory in England. I intended to return after one year. This was 1947.

My first impression of England via Tilbury Docks and London was 'What a horrible place!' We were sent to Bradford to work in a weaving mill. This I thought was lovely, although we had some awful 'digs' at times. I was introduced to kippers and fish and chips which later I loved, and I think I had them daily for several years. I decided that this was the life for me and I loved England so much that I abandoned my plans to return to Germany or Estonia (which is, of course, still occupied).

I received my naturalization papers in 1951.

JOHANNES JOACHIM DEGENHARDT

ARCHBISHOP OF PADERBORN

At the beginning of the Second World War I was thirteen years old. I can remember on 1 September 1939 that over the radio we were told that German troops had marched into Poland. Of 3 September when Great Britain and France declared war I know nothing more. I can recall only that my father, a participant in the First World War, told us children very earnestly when he came home from work that evening that a very difficult time was beginning and we would have to adjust ourselves to a long war. As far as I can remember there was no enthusiasm amongst my generation for the war.

AIR VICE-MARSHALL
I.R. CAMPBELL

Aged nineteen, I was already a first year cadet at the Royal Air Force College, Cranwell, and we had been recalled from leave at the end of August to continue flying training. I suppose we were relieved that the die was now cast and were filled with feelings of excitement and anticipation. Many memoirs of young men in 1914 recount how they worried that the war would be over by Christmas and they might miss the action. I do not think that we were as naive as that, but the feeling was tense.

I did not consider that I was taking part in a crusade; indeed, although I had spent some time in Germany as a student, I knew little or nothing of Nazi atrocities. For a young man in 1939 it was, I think, natural to want to 'fight for King and Country' and to some degree we thought that it would be an adventure. There had been an uneasy period of what proved to be borrowed time since the Munich crisis of 1938. I had then, in my last term at school, felt annoyed and guilty that we had not – goodness knows how – gone to the help of Czechoslovakia. I did not know then, just as I did not know a year later, how unprepared for war we were.

So I, like hundreds of other young men, went to war undertrained and using inadequate and obsolescent equipment. I completed 1½ tours of operations and was shot down in the Mediterranean in January 1942 to spend 3¼ years as a prisoner of war.

Initially I felt guilty at, and later resentful of, missing the later years of the war when we were better armed and had air superiority. I was probably jealous of those of my contemporaries who survived with fine war records and I consistently forgot those who were killed.

My time as a POW did not affect me psychologically as it scarred many prisoners of the Japanese, but in later years I regretted losing some of the best years of my life, years which as a professional airman I could never make up as far as my career was concerned.

FIELD MARSHAL
SIR ROLAND GIBBS

At school I had elected to join the Army as a career and in early 1939 I took the Army Examination for what was then the Royal Military College at Sandhurst, with a view to starting my eighteen-months' training to become an officer. This was not through some prescience that war was inevitable, but because such a career seemed to me at the time to be a way of earning my living with an active outdoor life. And so in August 1939, and just eighteen years old, I arrived at Sandhurst to find quite a shock in store for a boy who had enjoyed the comfort, comparative independence and slow pace of life of his last year at school. From reveille until late into the night it was a constant race to get on parade at the right time, do the homework required and get the uniform polished for the next day. A small thing like war being declared might have passed by unnoticed in the circumstances, particularly as you were isolated from all other life beyond the walls of the College. Newspapers and the radio were available, but there was scarcely time to benefit from either. And so Chamberlain made his fateful broadcast on 3 September. We did not hear it. We may even have been on our bicycles, riding to attention in file, *en route* from one exercise to another. I cannot remember. But the news soon got around.

I do not believe there was any feeling other than relief. After Munich and the failure of our policy of appeasement, war may have seemed subconsciously to be inevitable. We had been brought up in the shadow of the Great War, our fathers' war. This would be our war. And such is the optimism of the young, we had no thought of failure or worry of the price that might have to be paid – only a supreme confidence in our country, in our leaders, political and military, and in ourselves. And in our own little lives it could mean the shortening of our uncomfortably hectic time at Sandhurst!

Indeed this was so: for on 1 January 1940, after less than six months training, we were all duly commissioned. A few unfortunates were to join their regiments and be killed or made POWs in the fighting in Europe in 1940 which led to the evacuation from Dunkirk; others were to suffer the same fate on later battlefields; the luckier ones like me were to fight and survive.

ROBERT BAYNE-POWELL

In 1939 I was a barrister, but, after Hitler took over Czechoslovakia, I was certain that war was inevitable. I thought that London, where I lived, would be bombed immediately the war began, so I took a course in first aid and enrolled as a stretcher-bearer at Swan Street, near the Minories in east London. We worked twenty-four hours on duty and twenty-four hours off, and 3 September was my day off. I was then living with my wife at a flat in Balcombe Street, Marylebone. I give my diary entry for the day:

Heard on the wireless at 10 that war would be declared at 11. At 11 Chamberlain spoke shortly and well. So it has come as I feared it would. God grant us victory and, after it, the wisdom to make a treaty which will not seem to the vanquished so necessary to be revised as the 'Versailles Diktat'. Germany, in the event of our victory, should be helped economically, but crushed politically, perhaps by dismemberment into the pre-1870 states.

At 11.30 air raid warnings sounded and Nancy and I retired to the bathroom in gas masks and admit felt for a few minutes very queasy. It was only, I think, a practice and the All Clear soon sounded. The sirens seem much louder than in trials earlier in the year.

Lunched at the Sussex and afterwards we walked in Kensington Gardens and sat on a seat opposite a lovely clump of pink and white hibiscuses. It was very pleasant with the sun and the green trees and the bright hibiscus flowers. The only reminder of war was the balloon barrage shining silver in the afternoon sunlight. To Paddington to see if there were crowds leaving London, but only saw a slightly larger crowd, mostly of women with children. Walked back as no 27s seemed to be running.

George Korwin-Rodziszewski

It is hard to believe that a whole half-century has passed since the first shots were fired at the outset of a long and bloody struggle which was to last almost six years. For, even after this long lapse of time, it is all still as vivid in my mind as if it had taken place a year or two ago. And I have no records or notes to help me, as I had in later years in Siberia and in the army, when I kept a diary. Relying entirely on my visual memory I see those remote events of September 1939 in pictures undimmed by the passage of years.

I was not in the Forces then and was neither fighting nor otherwise engaged in defence of my country, so I can boast of no heroics. As a civilian I observed the happenings of those days as they were taking place, and can remember my reactions and those of the other inhabitants of the city of Lvov on the south-eastern fringe of Poland (now in the Soviet Union) with its multinational population and its turbulent history.

I heard the early morning news on the radio announcing that the enemy had attacked our country. The announcer mentioned a few localities somewhere in the west, where fighting was taking place. The communiqué ended with a rousing martial song.

I was not greatly surprised. We had been expecting the war for some time now: it was the logical outcome of earlier events, notably the rejection by our Foreign Minister, Joseph Beck, of Hitler's demands on Gdansk, for territorial concessions in the so-called Polish corridor and that Poland should join his crusade against the Soviet Union.

At first the hostilities did not affect us. Cities like Vilnius and Lvov, both on the eastern borderland, did not at first feel the impact of the onslaught. But within a day or so we heard alarming news of the German advance and of the air raids on Warsaw and other cities. The fine weather favoured the enemy. His armour advanced over dry fields and roads and his air force had no difficulty in locating its targets.

I went to work in my office, which was housed in the enormous residence of the former Governor, dating from the days of Austro-Hungarian rule. Everything there looked much the same as usual. The head of our section, a spry, rotund little man, was running silently, at a gentle trot on his thick rubber soles, along the corridor to report to the head of the department, just as he did every morning. Then, as usual, on his return he climbed on his stool, lit his pipe and enveloped in a cloud of smoke, wrote diligently for an hour or two. At the next table Janina R., a lively and humorous girl, was clattering away on her calculating machine. I, too, was busy writing official letters to various landowners. We were still carrying on with the job of allocating land to the peasants, as if nothing had happened.

Sitting at my desk, by a window on the second floor, I glanced from time to time at the sky, expecting to see an aircraft. But there was no object in the blue expanse, not even a cloud.

In the second week of September the German army reached the outskirts of Lvov from the west and south. We heard about the skirmishes of our units in defence of the city, in which cadet officers of the local military school took part. Alas, most of them were killed attacking enemy positions.

The Germans began to shell the city. Our Citadel on the hill in the city centre was returning the fire, thus starting a duel which was to last a week. And watching men and women in this precarious existence, I never heard a single complaint or whimper. The inhabitants suffered their plight with determination and fortitude.

The air raids started even before the shelling. From time to time we could hear the intermittent staccato bursts of fire from the anti-aircraft machine-gun placed on the roof of our building. Apparently it was not well camouflaged, because the enemy Stuka soon spotted it and began to dive with a terrifying siren whine. We were ordered to go down into the cellars. As we ran downstairs, there were two explosions which shook the foundations, but fortunately the bombs fell in the nearby garden without causing any damage.

That particular air raid put a stop to our work. We were told that the office was closing until further notice, and we were sent home.

The next day I was standing in front of the city's Garrison Command in a crowd of several hundred young men who were asking to be employed in any defence capacity. Here, too, we were told that the military authorities had no plans for the employment of the civilians.

While I was sitting at home, not knowing what to do next, my friend from university days, Henry K., came to see me. Trying to catch his breath after running and climbing the stairs, he told me through the ear-splitting roar of our guns that all men of military age were to leave the city and go eastward to avoid being captured and drafted into the German army. He was leaving with a party, now assembled in a nearby square, and urged me to join them.

I had not heard anything of such an order and it sounded to me rather panicky and premature, but Henry assured me that it was true (as it later proved to be). I pondered for a while. Whether true or not, what was keeping me? I had nothing to do and was of no use to anybody. Why should I not take this step into the unknown. The fine weather and a youthful sense of adventure decided me. It took me ten minutes to pack my rucksack. There was no time to notify friends of my decision, as we left in a hurry.

The group of about forty men was waiting for us, impatient and anxious to leave at once. It was an odd assortment: students, bank clerks, artisans, small Jewish traders, factory workers, gypsies, dubious characters from the suburbs, representatives of the city's small Armenian colony, but not a single Ukrainian.

Where were we all going?

Heading east. Presumably as far as it will take us – to the Soviet border. And what then? Nobody gave it a thought. We'll see when we get there.

Passing the Lyczakov toll-gate, we climbed the wooded hill with the anti-aircraft gun emplacements. Here we stopped for a while and turned round to get what we thought was the last sight of the city. The view was breathtaking – white buildings, church towers, tree-lined avenues, the lush greenery of parks – all in the glow of the afternoon sun.

Then, exchanging friendly hand-waves with the gunners, we descended the hill on to the road.

There was not much traffic, mostly villagers returning home in their horse-drawn carts, pedestrians, singly or in groups, all moving at a leisurely pace. They seemed unmindful of what was going on, of the enemy's proximity. Their peasant imperturbability suggested that come what may, it was not going to interfere with their daily routine.

We must have covered about fifteen kilometres when darkness fell. We decided to stop for the night. Standing on the road by a long fence, we saw a big yard beyond it with a house in the background. Seeing light in the window, one of us went to ask if we might stop there until morning. It turned out to be a village school. The teacher came out to meet us. Surveying us, she asked a few questions. I sensed a feeling of animosity in her voice. She obviously thought that we ought to have stayed back, fighting the enemy, though she did not express her opinion. She could not let us into the classroom, as the children were coming to school in the morning, but allowed us to settle for the night on the huge pile of firewood in the middle of the yard.

We were hungry by now. The few provisions that we had with us, we had eaten on the way. One of our men, who went into the village foraging for food, soon came back accompanied by an old peasant woman, who brought three loaves of bread and a pail of milk. Not much for a bunch of forty young men!

Lying down among logs and still hearing the distant rumble of guns in the stillness of the countryside, we soon fell asleep. The nights were still warm, but the chill of early morning woke us up.

Resuming our journey, we met an infantry unit heading in the opposite direction. A few kilometres further we saw a convoy of military lorries with an escort of motor-cyclists. It stopped by the side of the road. Some lorries had machine-guns mounted on them; all were full of soldiers. Our attempts to strike up a conversation were soon interrupted. The officer in command came and told us that they were going to Lvov, and that was all. Otherwise his men had orders not to speak to civilians.

Passing through one village, we managed to get some food, then we drank water and washed at the pump. Soon after midday we reached a small town. We must have covered about forty-five kilometres. We entered an inn for some refreshment. As we sat talking about the next leg of our march, the landlord butted in: 'My advice to you is to turn back! We've just heard the announcement that this morning the Soviet army has crossed the whole length of the border and is marching westwards. There's no point in your going any further!' The few customers present confirmed that they, too, had heard the communiqué.

The date was 17 September.

Indeed, two days later the Red Army approached Lvov from the east, thus completing the encirclement of the city.

There was nothing left for us but to follow the landlord's advice and retrace our steps. Exhausted by the long march, we were approaching Lvov. The familiar rumble of guns grew louder with every kilometre. On entering the city, I made my way to my home on the top floor of a new block of flats. It was a mere few hundred yards from the Citadel and the ear-splitting boom of our guns was just as unbearable as before.

Walking along, I suddenly saw a plume of smoke over my head. A quick jump to the wall probably saved my life, for a split second later a hail of shrapnel splinters fell on the road with a swish.

In all this confusion it was admirable to see postmen who, risking their lives, still carried the mail. I found two messages in my letter-box. One was from our accounts department asking me to collect my back pay. The other – delivered by hand – was from an office colleague who lived nearby and with whom I occasionally exchanged small services. Its content was a cry for help. Alas, the date showed that it was already two days old. She asked me to come at once, 'because something dreadful has happened'.

As it turned out, in her absence a burglar forced the door to her flat and got inside. Fortunately nothing was missing. Presumably, disturbed by someone on the staircase, the intruder fled. When I came, somebody had already found a carpenter for her, who had repaired the door and fitted iron bars on the inside. But she was still suffering from shock, so that a neighbour had to stay with her. Soon, however, they were all sitting in the cellar. The shelling was more intense now and the proximity of a military objective meant that there was more destruction and there were more casualties in our district. I accepted their invitation to join them, feeling safer there than in my own flat on the upper floor.

On the second night a policeman came to our shelter. He was calling all able-bodied males to help in the defence of the city. We came out and began to pull up flagstones and paving from the road and pile them up across the approach road. Very soon we built an imposing anti-tank barrier about two metres high, with narrow passages for the pedestrians.

As the dawn was breaking, I dragged myself home. Dead tired and indifferent to anything round me, I flung myself on the bed.

It was early afternoon when I woke up. The first thing that struck me was the dead silence. The shelling and firing had stopped. I went out to see what was happening.

The streets were full of people, shopping for food or just strolling. They were glad to be out again. There was a feeling of general animation; one could even hear jokes and laughter in this city, still in the tight ring of the blockade.

Noticing a crowd in front of the Garrison Command, I approached it and was told that Soviet representatives had arrived to negotiate a surrender. And there in the centre of the crowd stood an armoured car with three Red Army soldiers, three village lads, sitting on the running-board and looking surprised at everything around them. For this was probably their first glimpse of the outside world. As a Russian speaker, I was curious to engage them in conversation, to ask about life in that huge country, so near and yet so little known to us. Alas, my attempts to have a friendly chat soon petered out. All my questions met with the same non-committal, stereotyped reply from the lad: '*Znachit tak nado*'. And every time he glanced at his companions, as if seeking their reassurance. Finally, feeling that I was getting nowhere with him, I told him that if we had to choose between the two armies (as we then thought), I would prefer the Russians. Hearing of German atrocities, when for instance their airmen were machine-gunning refugees on the roads as they were fleeing from the bombed cities, I though 'surely the Russians cannot be as bad as that'. He did not reply. Instead he looked at me intently. I felt that he was trying to convey to me something which he was wary of putting into words. Unfortunately, I could not read his meaning then and it was not until much later that I understood what he meant. But that is another story.

Soon afterwards we heard that the city had surrendered to the Red Army.

A few hours later I was standing in the street watching as the tanks rolled into the city. Polish administration came to an end. It was taken over by the Soviet authorities. The date was 22 September.

HANS LANDAUER

My personal memories of the day England and France declared war on Nazi Germany are closely linked to the pre-war policies of both countries. Until then, they had in no way tried to halt Hitler's and Mussolini's aggression. Rather the opposite. Against any international law, Spain was deprived of the means which would have enabled it to fight the rebels and their foreign accomplices. London and Paris shut their eyes to the open interference of the totalitarian powers.

Just over eighteen, after two years of combat as the youngest Austrian volunteer of the '12 February 1934' battalion of the 11th International Brigade, I found myself in an internment camp in Gurs, France.

Every warning we had made had come true. Chamberlain and Daladier had not brought peace in our time nor saved us. Their policy had incensed the aggressors' greed even more. With their deplorable behaviour they had infringed their own national interest.

We showed Guernica to the world. In vain, for London and Paris thought it impossible that the same could ever happen to Coventry. We showed the Spanish republicans who had been slaughtered in the arena of Badajoz to the world. London and Paris did not yet believe Oradour-sur-Glan, Marzabotto or the gas chambers of Auschwitz.

On 5 September 1939, despite bitter experiences, 2,220 of 4,509 interned former members of the International Brigade – Germans, Austrians, Poles, Czechs, Italians – entered their names on a list stating their willingness to join the French army (but not the Foreign Legion) in the fight against Hitler. Another 1,890 enlisted for the work brigades.

But fate held other things in store for us Austrians. After France had been defeated we were trapped. For most of us Dachau was the end of the road. Seventy died in various concentration camps.

PIERRE GODET

I was born on 10 August 1922 in Montmedy in the Meuse, a few kilometres away from the Belgian border, and I lived in the Ardennes in Neuvizy with my parents and my sister about 30 km away from the Meuse river. Both counties were under German occupation during World War I. As I grew up I kept on hearing of the war which had been, of its atrocities (massacres of civilians and so forth) and of the war to come. The £50,000 question was always the same: 'Will they get this far? Will we be forced to evacuate?' But I was far from imagining that the approaching war would be so disastrous for France.

May 1940: the exodus.

My village was not far from the Belgian border so, from the declaration of war onwards, many regiments were quartered there.

On 10 May 1940, the sun shone gloriously. We are woken up in the small hours by plane formations which scour the sky at very high altitude. On the radio, we are informed of the invasion of Holland, Belgium and Luxembourg. In the course of the morning on the Orleans – Givet road, which lies 1 km north of the village, the first cars of refugees drive past, mostly Belgian. For one month now the CA of the first battalion of 329th Regiment of Infantry of Caen had been billeted on my parents' farm. No anti-aircraft missiles in the vicinity, in the distance a dull rumble.

In the afternoon, first bombardments of the main crossroads and machine-gun attacks on the trains using the railway line lying 2 km west of the village.

The two following days the bombardments increase. The Belgian cars are now joined by French ones: the people from the Meuse valley and of the Sedan area. There are teams of horses harnessed to carts and some people are on foot pushing a push chair, a wheelbarrow, in front of them. They have been promised a train at Amagne, at Rethel, nothing more precise.

On Whit Sunday we attend, unbeknownst to us, our last high mass in the village. When the planes fly overhead, we feel none too safe. Air bombings intensify. Strangers to the village join us in our cellar which is sizeable; despite the thickness of the walls everything shakes, we feel rather fragile. Power cuts are more and more frequent.

On Whit Monday, 13 May, the stream of refugees has become a flood in which soldiers from other regiments are carried. The cannon rumbles endlessly in the direction of Sedan, of Charleville. We still hope to stay put. Captain de Neuville who is billeted at my father's tells him that, at nightfall because of the planes, his men will go up into the front line. At 10 p.m. the battalion leaves the village. We go to bed as usual.

Towards midnight, my father hears soldiers entering the farmyard and finds, to his amazement, the troop who had left a few hours before barricading themselves in the yard. German tank units have been sighted. My father goes to tell the village mayor who in turn informs the populace. We decide to leave. My father directs me to retrieve a mule from the meadow. Having found it – after some tribulations in the night – I harness it to a light cart and take it to the priests so that they too can leave. Having thus discharged his duty as sexton, my father jams his entire family – his wife, my sister aged fourteen, three grandparents, me and himself – in a Renault Prima 4 designed to carry five people with very, very little luggage. In the night everything looks sinister. We have let the dogs loose and they howl.

For fear of the bombardments, we avoid all the main roads. We discern here and there some flares. At daybreak, we reach Soissons. We head for Normandy where we stay for a week. As the situation plainly does not improve, we flee to Vendee; we will stay in les Sables d'Olonne until July 1941. The war over, we find out that the tanks which had been reported that night were Guderian's, held up at la Horgne by the third brigade, Spahis and at Bouvelmont by the 15th Dragoons. These villages are 10 km away from Neuvizy.

June 1943. The STO.

Our region had been declared a 'forbidden zone' and it was difficult to re-enter it. After the departure of some of the occupying forces for Russia, my parents were able to find a free house in the village. Returning to our own farm was out of the question as it was occupied by a German 'Agriculture Chief' who managed the land of one or two villages, working French POWs and Polish or Italian deportees plus some local people. The winter of 1941/2 seemed very long and very hard. There was very little food; all that was produced was for German use and sent to Germany. Things improved with garden production.

In the spring of 1943, alert! In order to meet the German demands for the French work force, Laval (premier in the Vichy government) set up the Service du Travail Obligatoire for the young men who should have been called up in 1942, the *classe 42* to which I belonged.

A distant cousin, who had not returned to his land in the Ardennes, since it was also under German control, had re-settled in the Berry, not far from Issoudun. Early in 1943, he wrote to my parents, offering to take me on if I was worried. I had no wish to go to Germany but needed to make sure that my father would not be picked up in my place. With this in mind, I went with a local priest to discuss matters with a county civil servant. His advice: to procure a false ID card, and on the day of departure, to turn up at the German work agency, check in at the station and then, disappear. If my father was questioned – as indeed happened – he could say that I had been killed in a train bombardment, since I had checked in at Charleville station. First operation: to obtain a false ID card. I approached the village mayor who after much palaver obliged. I had become two years younger. My joy was short lived: Laval having delivered another speech to the effect that those who helped defaulters were even more guilty than them, the mayor came to recover the aforementioned card. Fortunately, thanks to another connection, I obtained a card from a neighbouring council.

About 20 June I received my summons for the big journey which was to take place at the end of the month. I first went to Charleville to find out how the departures were organized, how closely watched they were. The young men for the STO, after showing up at the work agency, would catch the 15.00 hours train for Paris and travel in a wagon which was reserved for them. I then went to Rheims to observe the passage of the train in question and to make a note of the carriages which stopped by the underground passages, as I was anxious to go unnoticed by friends who might stand at the doors and windows. At the same time, I visited a friend and asked for his hospitality the night I would break away. He accepted and lent me, in great foresight, a bicycle which I left ready in a café.

The evening I was to leave, 29 June, only my mother was informed of my intentions. I caught the stopping train to Charleville where I arrived at 7.30 p.m. As I got off the train I made contact with a young man whom I had noticed in my previous forays. When I saw his bike, I guessed his intentions for he too was STO-bound. He would just check in at the work agency then ride to Rethel, 50 km south-west, where he would catch the Paris train. He introduced himself: 'Jean-Noizet from Creve-Coeur' in the Ardennes. 'Do you known Monsieur Faillon?' I asked. 'That's where I am going,' he said. 'So am I. If you arrive first, you can say I am on my way!' Thanks to him I gained a few more useful leads for my journey to Issoudun.

I then set of to the German work agency. A medical check-up was carried out by a French doctor: fit for duty! I was given 1000 francs and a pouch of tobacco. A friend went and bought my Charleville-Paris ticket, which was obviously not covered by my German travel entitlement. I concealed my false ID card and my ticket in my sock.

There remained one problem: some friends had arrived on the scene who expressed their delight at the idea of travelling with me. I didn't want to inform them of my project – how could I shake them off? I opportunely remembered that the French are often late. We had to be at the work agency at 14.00 hours; at 13.00, there I was in company with a few others whom I did not know. At their insistence, on the grounds that they wanted a seat, some employees took us to the station. We were let in via the exit – second check, non-existant surveillance – and taken through the underground passage to the train. They walked very fast, I very slowly, but I spotted the wagon into which they went before dashing into the one I had earmarked for a speedy getaway in Rheims. The wait for departure seemed long; it was a relief when the whistle blew. I made a speedy exit in Rheims station without untoward encounters, entrusted my luggage to the left-luggage, retrieved the bike at the café and set off for Cernay where I spent a pleasant evening.

The following day at 6.30 a.m. I was back in the train for Paris. No problems. But what was I going to do for a whole day in a town that I did not know, where I did not know anybody, and where, so they said, there were raids?

The train from Issoudun did not leave until 20.00 hours. Austerlitz station which serves the south-west is very close to Paris cathedral. So I went hither and did not regret my idea for there was a pilgrimage of the Versailles diocese and I went unnoticed.

At 7.00 p.m. I returned to the station and, by sheer strength on this first day of the holiday, I succeeded in forcing my way into a wagon corridor. The train was choc-a-bloc so there was no risk of controls. I alighted at Issoudun towards 1.00 a.m. As I knew no one in the town I decided to stay in the station and to feign sleep. After a while, a police round . . . but they walked by. Half-an-hour later, they are back, with a plain clothes inspector: 'What are you doing here? *Vos papiers*.' They sift through my false ID. I tell them I am waiting for a train. They move on. Phew! I think to myself that it is not healthy to hang around so, at daybreak, I set off but at 5.00 in the morning the streets are deserted. With relief I notice someone entering a church. I follow him, hide my case under the pulpit and attend two or three masses.

At 7.30, I asked a curate how to find the school run by the fathers of the Holy Heart of Jesus where the Faillon children were boarding. The city streets were now busy and I walked there undisturbed. At the boarding school, I asked to see the father superior and told him that I was an STO defaulter. 'You are neither the first nor the last; how can I help you?' 'Could you let Monsieur Faillon know that I have arrived? And may I wait for him here?' 'Certainly, but don't mention what you have been up to,' I was enjoined, 'not to a soul.'

At that moment I felt real relief and went to sleep in a chair. I woke up at midday and was fetched by Monsieur Faillon in the afternoon.

I needed more convincing papers than those I had travelled with, which would not have withstood many controls. The *secrétaire de mairie* in the village where Monsieur Faillon lived was a football nut. No sooner had he figured that I played goalie (which he happened to need) than he found it within his powers to oblige. My new ID card had me a member of the first intake of *classe 39* which had been called up. I had been a prisoner and I had escaped (in the free zone, escaped prisoners enjoyed some respect). Thus I went the width and breadth of Berry. After the Normandy landings, controls tightened up and we had a few close shaves which turned to our advantage.

Before I arrived in Berry, Monsieur Faillon had done a lot for the Free French by organizing on his farm many a Lysander night landing. But now, he and his farm were under close surveillance so he went and did it elsewhere. So he was often away and the arrival of a defaulter, a farmer to boot, did not come amiss.

In conclusion, my regret is not to have joined in 1941 the army which General Weygan was creating in North Africa, the one which was to win fame in Tunisia and Italy under General Juin, then in France and in Germany under General de Lattre de Tassigny.

The British and French governments acted with unforgivable levity in declaring war whilst so unprepared. An occupied country is sick at heart and ails for a long time. Political strife (a national sport) is soured by the settling of old accounts; something De Gaulle did not do much to alter or discourage. In his eyes, only those who had made it to London were resistants. Fortunately Colonel Remy, who was among the very first to reach London, has set the record straight in his book *In The Shadow of the Marechal*, in which he establishes that out of the twenty people who served in the Vichy cabinet, one was killed outright by the Gestapo, four were deported to Germany, and two arrested by the *Milice*.

Herbert Morgenstern

At the end of the First World War I often listened to the conversations of the adults living at my grandparents' house. Without understanding them I heard words like 'revolution' and 'civil war'. I cannot recall when I started to ask questions about my father, but the desire to gather information about him has never left me, more so because he had been known as a good natured man and a skilled craftsman. A strong feeling of likeness made me miss him very much, and I wanted to know who was to blame for his death. An old teacher explained to us war orphans that our fathers had been shot by the bad Russians or French, but the 'why?' was not easily satisfied. Other adults told me it was the mistake of the rich or influential people because they wanted to make money and gain more power by leading a war. This made more sense to me. So I blamed those who turned people's blood into money.

In our small kitchen were two ornamental pictures; one showed the leaders of the Social Democrats – Wilhelm Liebknecht, August Bebel and Paul Singer – with the quotation: 'We want peace, freedom, equality, the right to work and the right for everyone to lead a humane life.' The other was a picture of August Bebel with the quotation: 'Working men, you have the power; nothing can be achieved without you.' Those two pictures taught me to read before I went to school. My inquisitive mind wanted to have the meaning of the quotations explained, and the answers were satisfactory. Thus, my longing for peace and my hatred for those who started wars was aroused.

As fascism grew stronger in Germany, the danger of another war grew with it. Since I saw the communists as being the strongest opposition to war, I joined the communist youth unit in 1929, which cost me my job in the German Post in 1933.

Ernst Thalmann taught us that war was inevitable if we could not prevent fascist rule. For me and my friends this was a challenge we had to take on. Consequently I joined the illegal anti-fascist resistance, which fought for peace and against the increasingly threatening danger of war. In December 1934 I and many of my fellow fighters were arrested and charged with high treason.

While Hitler was constantly talking about peace until 1938, Germany armed herself heavily. I could only follow the events from the prison in which I had been confined for 3½ years. Filled with helpless rage I had to watch Hitler's associates cashing in on the preparations for an impending war. Unceasingly the people were bombarded by mendacious smear campaigns. 'The threat from the East' became a nightmare for most Germans. But why? The majority could not see the imminent catastrophe, or was it that they did not want to see it?

In the summer of 1938 my sentence should have ended. But the barbarous Nazis feared every voice that could be raised in defence of peace and cruelly terrorized everyone who dared to oppose them. So I was transferred to Buchenwald concentration camp as an incorrigible communist, and it was there that I subsequently heard of the outbreak of war. We were embittered, but not surprised, because listening in on broadcasts from Moscow, London, Beromunster and elsewhere kept us well informed, even though the death sentence had been introduced for listening to so-called enemy transmissions. But even in the subhuman conditions of Buchenwald the resistance work was carried on. Despite all the frustration we were convinced that the days of the Nazi regime were numbered.

Shortly after the first few foreign prisoners were brought to Buchenwald, an anti-fascist resistance group was formed, indifferent to ideology or religion. We dreaded every victory won by the Nazis and cheerfully welcomed all their threats.

On 11 April 1945, as the first American tanks approached, the prisoners of Buchenwald freed themselves with the help of an illegal international military organization. Thus the triumph of the Allied forces became our triumph as well. After our release, the 21,000 ex-prisoners took the world-famous oath of Buchenwald and swore to root out fascism in order to secure peace on earth. Today those roots spread from the people who kindle the arms race and thereby make money. What distinguished the anti-fascist resistance fighters of all countries applies today to the world peace movement; the unifying power of all peace-loving people of all ideologies and religions will bring peace to the world.

LORE KRUGER

On 1 September 1939, my husband and I had just returned to our flat in Paris from our first vacation spent together. As refugees with very limited financial means, we had camped in a homemade tent on the coast of Brittany. We were just settling down, when we learned by radio that Hitler's troops had invaded Poland without even a declaration of war. This meant that Nazi Germany had started World War II, as we had been anticipating all along: German anti-fascists had foreseen Hitler's war of aggression for many years – the reason why they had become such militant opponents of his. We had passionately tried to warn the world it was coming.

We German refugees who had found shelter in France were ready to muster all our knowledge and all our strength for the defence of the country that had received us, and to fight its enemy who was our enemy – that of all mankind. Everybody was aware of the fact that Hitler had sent swarms of his agents into France: Hitler's Fifth Column. But against all common sense, not these agents were imprisoned the first day of war but we, the German anti-fascist refugees! Already during the night of 1 September, many well-known anti-Nazis were arrested in their flats and taken to prison, among them one of our closest friends who lived in the same house as us. He was a medical doctor who suffered from lung-TB and had been assistant director of the Sanitary Service of the International Brigades in Republican Spain. On 3 September, the French government published an order to all men born in Germany, regardless of what their nationality was and whether Hitler had declared them void of their German citizenship, to assemble the same day with plaids and fifteen kilograms of luggage in order to be interned for examination of their cases. We, the women, were prohibited to leave the place where we lived.

So I had to pack a knapsack with the most urgently needed things for my husband on this first day of World War II, and he was interned, even though a wound from a recent complicated stomach operation had not quite healed. We were not to meet again for many months, and never again in our flat.

For more than ten years, as a responsible leader of the German Workers' movement, he had stubbornly struggled against the more and more threatening Nazi upsurge and continued his fight after they came to power. The Gestapo had arrested him and imprisoned him in a concentration camp. Afterwards, they took him to court and sentenced him to 2½ years of imprisonment. When he got out, he did not wait till the Gestapo took him once more to a concentration camp, but crossed the mountainous Czechoslovak border by night and found shelter in Prague. From here, he helped to create many secret ties with Germany, in order to spread there the knowledge about Hitler's war plans and to mobilize the German people to resist them, as well as to help endangered anti-fascists to escape and let the people abroad know about the crimes committed in Germany.

When the Spanish civil war started and Hitler and Mussolini sent arms and soldiers to Franco, my husband became a volunteer in the International Brigades, like 5000 other Germans who wanted to fight Hitler with weapons in their hands and who hoped that this way he would be stopped from starting a world war. The flags of the International Brigades bore the inscription: 'For your and our Freedom'.

He fought there till the autumn of 1938, when he badly needed an operation for some ulcers which threatened to perforate his stomach. Since it could not be done in Spain, he was sent to France, where doctors sympathetic to the Spanish Republic operated upon him in 1939.

And now many, many months of internment in various French camps lay ahead of him, under the most primitive conditions, tortured by hunger and cold, but much more so still by the awareness that he had to watch helplessly as during the entire so-called 'comic war' nothing was done to defeat the Nazis; and when Hitler put an end to it, how the French armies withdrew even further, practically without a shot, and the situation of France, which was dear to our hearts as the country that had given us shelter, grew worse and worse. When the Nazi troops at last approached the internment camp near Bordeaux where he then was held, he managed to escape from the camp, together with some friends. Ahead of the German armies, mostly on foot, sometimes taken aboard some lorry or other for a stretch of the way by retreating French soldiers, they joined the streams of refugees that poured southward over the roads of France, and got to the foot of the Pyrenees and up to the camp of Gurs, where I had been interned in the meantime.

I came from a Jewish family and had left Germany already in 1933, because of the radical persecutions by the Nazis and because of their evident preparations for a hated new world war. I had first found asylum in England and lived 'au pair' with a young married couple. There I learned to speak English. After a year I had gone to France via Spain. In France, I got to know a group of German resistance fighters and helped them with their work. Here I met my husband.

Together with a small number of like-minded German refugee women, I had, like my husband, succeeded to escape from my internment camp at Gurs. We were just walking along the road near the camp when suddenly my husband and his buddy who had fled with him turned up. What happiness we felt! Together with our friends, we marched for three days, to Toulouse. A French family who lived in bitter poverty themselves (the four of them in one room) gave us shelter in a large empty wine barrel lying in their garden. It was our dwelling for many months. We got material help from the French underground which was then taking shape, and we participated in the organized work of the German anti-fascists who, in great numbers, had fled to Toulouse.

The Mexican government had declared their readiness to grant immigration visas for Mexico to all former members of the International Brigades in France and their families. The responsible leaders of our underground group decided that a number of well-known foes of the Nazis mentioned on Pétain's extradition lists to Hitler should try to get to Mexico, there to continue the struggle against Nazi Germany. With false identity papers furnished by our friends in the French underground, we got safely to Marseilles and the Mexican consulate, in order to arrange for the necessary formalities for our whole group that was to cross the ocean.

Taking leave from us, the German anti-fascists, the family who had hidden us for so long opened one of the two bottles of wine they had tucked away for a special occasion. The other bottle was to be kept for the return of their son, a prisoner of war in Germany.

After many difficulties, we and a number of our friends got berths in the hold of a merchant boat, coveted by thousands and thousands of applicants, that was bound for La Martinique. From there we hoped somehow to get to Mexico.

Just before our three weeks' voyage across the Atlantic came to an end, our Vichy-French merchant ship carrying about 1,200 refugees instead of freight was captured by a gunboat belonging to the Dutch government who continued the war against Nazi Germany from London. We were taken to Trinidad, then still a British colony. Right from the boat we were led into an internment camp for German refugees living on Trinidad. The British army examined all our cases, and after a few weeks we were permitted to continue on our way. But there was no way of getting from Trinidad to Mexico. Our group of friends wired the Assistance Committee of the Abraham Lincoln Brigade, the American veterans of the Spanish war, asking them to help us. They did, and sent us the necessary papers and money to travel via the United States. And so, early in June, we left our Trinidad camp and boarded a genuine passenger boat bound for New York. From there we wanted to go on to Mexico. But we had hardly landed when we learned that a new law concerning German nationals prohibited our leaving the United States, and so we never got to Mexico at all but stayed in the US till the end of the war.

There, we continued our struggle against the Nazis. By spoken and written word, we did our best to spread our knowledge about what was going on in Germany and occupied Europe. We especially addressed the German Americans of whom quite a number were under the influence of Nazi propaganda. After the US entered the war, we did what we could to mobilize the former to help the war effort of the Allies, denouncing the crimes the Nazis committed in the countries they had invaded, which now included also the Soviet Union, and making known their crimes against their own nation, thus giving voice to another Germany. We knew that the longer the Nazis were able to wage their war, the more not only the allied countries but also Germany would be destroyed and the more people must die.

We founded a bi-monthly paper written half in English, half in German. Many famous German anti-Nazi writers contributed to it. Later on during the war, when German prisoners of war were sent to American camps, we endeavoured to influence and enlighten their minds, sending them our paper and other printed matters. We were part of the movement 'Free Germany' that was active on many fronts.

Our daughter was born in New York. In the autumn of

1946, when I was expecting another baby, we finally were able to return to liberated Berlin. Shortly after we arrived, our son was born.

Since then I strive to pass on to younger people my experiences of that time, and do what I can to help develop friendship among nations. For dozens of years I have been translating British and American classical literature for one of our most prominent editing houses, since developing friendship among nations also means making their cultures known.

For almost forty years now, I have been participating in the work of the Committee of Anti-Fascist Resistance Fighters in the German Democratic Republic. Together with former resistance fighters and war veterans of many countries, we dedicate our activities to the defence of peace, for we who have gone through the suffering of war feel we owe it to our children and grandchildren, as to the children of the entire world, to protect them from the horror of a third world war – which would be the last, for it would surely mean the end of mankind.

Georgette Simone Cockburn

A blue sky, the beginning of spring! It is 10 May 1940, and I am fifteen years of age. I remember my sister calling me as the sky was full of planes, and we soon found out they were German planes, and they dived down and killed a few of the population then. That was my first taste of war, Germany was invading Belgium. This was followed by the marching of the troops, the 'cream' of their army down our main boulevards, pointing their rifles at the inhabitants. How many times, after that, did we hear them, walking on our cobbled streets with their heavy boots, singing their awful German songs which still ring in my ears! They used to round people up, make them get off buses, face the walls, hands in the air, searching them, and God help those without papers. We used to listen to Winston Churchill, with difficulty as the Germans used to jam all transmissions from London, and had great faith in him: he gave us strength. But we lived in fear of being caught.

The Gestapo twice came to my home, as my sister was in the *Résistance*. I was lucky: each time, I was out. My cousin spent five years in a German prison camp in Germany. My best friend's father was in the *Résistance*, and had to be smuggled to the Belgian Congo where he died from a tropical disease, his *résistance* being too low to survive the atrocities of the Germans!

We had coupons for food but could not always obtain the food with them. I remember a dark brown bread which we had to cut with two knives as it was so wet and sticky. And the air raids! My father had arranged the cellar as a shelter. We were bombed by the Germans, then by the English and the Americans.

I shall never forget the fear when the actual invasion took place. The sky full of German planes, and the eventual sight of the masses of troops, German tanks, and troop carriers! The Occupation was difficult to tolerate. I hid many times, when house-to-house searches were carried out, the general idea being to find suitable civilians to be herded away to work in the German factories.

At the Liberation, we heard 'put the Belgian Flag out, the English are there . . .' then shooting . . . and 'put the flags in again, a few Germans are still near here.' And we saw the last of the Germans walking down our *Chaussée*, rifles at the ready, going God knows where: they were not the 'Cream of the Army' any more. And I laughed.

A lady opposite us used to rent rooms. She had German soldiers on the first floor and English and Americans on the second floor, hiding them, and her brother guiding them through the *Résistance* lines. I think you need courage for that. Her brother was sent to Dachau concentration camp; I saw him when he came back and did not recognize him. My blood still runs cold when I hear Germans speaking. I cannot forget. The past has long shadows!

ANON

Prison Camp

Day follows day in dull monotony
The sun hangs heavy in the changeless sky
Dust devils eddy down the sandy road
The long drab rows of huts lie mute within
The shadow of the encircling wire
And this is life

The hours slip silent to eternity
The days stretch into weeks, the weeks to years
Time ages, yet its features do not change
Time sweeps along on feet that never move
Feet fettered by the wire's weightless bond
With night comes sleep

And sleep brings dreams to flout these timeless days
And life runs sweetly as before
Bright eyes, sweet lips, cool drinks, good food, soft beds,
The thousand fantasies of vanished peace
Till morning light returns with hopeless hope.

Jack Wright

Two extracts from a POW's notebook:

A LETTER TO MYSELF. 'LEST I FORGET.'
TO BE READ PERIODICALLY WHEN THE WAR IS OVER, PARTICULARLY WHEN GRUMBLING OR COMPLAINING IN POST-WAR LIFE.

Germany
4th November 1944

Dear Jack,

Time is about 3.45 p.m. on the above date. You are sitting in Room 15 Hut 32 and in the miserable gloom can just see what you are writing.

The view from the windows, never very inspiring, is at the moment what is termed as 'the absolute bottoms'. Hut lights have not been switched on and this miserable cold dull November day seems to take ages to tear itself away.

Red Cross Parcels have ceased over a week ago, our last eight weekly issues were on the scale of one parcel between two people and for the odd week even between three.

In your cupboard is a piece of bread (German bread) about the size of a 'Swan Vestas' match box. This is the remains of your *funf*, your daily ration. You must not eat it now, it must be kept for your breakfast and this, spread with that axle-grease-looking-and-tasting PRIMA margarine will, until the arrival of Red Cross Parcels, constitute your breakfast for the uncertain future. Some days you weaken and all your *funf* has gone, then breakfast consists mainly of tea the quality of such, that could the NAAFI tea but see, it would blush to be classed in the category of beverage.

Remember Jack that from a *funf* of bread you can obtain at the most four slices. This bread, sprinkled with sawdust from the local bakery, when topped with PRIMA provides you with one of your chief delights of the day.

Also in your cupboard is a Red Cross Box containing five empty tins with perhaps just the scrapings of German jam clinging to one.

Your sugar issue went two days ago. There is body in cocoa, yes but no sugar! You wrote a letter today and if you are lucky and it isn't censored you'll get a reply in about four months, if the reply isn't bombed.

You've got a pile of dirty socks to wash and after that they need darning if the holes aren't too big.

It's a fact that right now if they existed, 12 dry Canadian biscuits would fetch 150 marks which is £10 or one month's pay. You would be willing to give 'a fiver', but wouldn't stand a chance.

There go those – – bells! Will finish this afterwards. Blast all cold calls.

The fire is out and can't afford more coal. You are sitting on a hard stool and the table cloth is an old flea bitten Italian blanket covered in grease, food and holes which 'Reddy' uses on his bed. He has to.

Das Reich is our highest line in toilet paper and even that we want to keep for our map.

Churchill says the war won't end this year and another 'bag' Christmas draws near.

A large Private Parcel list has just gone up and you weren't on it. A letter from England gives no news but says there is lots of fruit in England and can you get any. No, they would rather the fruit rotted on the ground than give or sell it to you.

You shaved this morning but won't tomorrow. You were locked in at 5 p.m., no entertainments tomorrow. Church Services and a spot of shortbread you hope.

It's 9.30 p.m. and you have Sweet Fanny Adams to do, so you had better go to bed which is damned uncomfortable and cold, where you will dream of such simple foods as you now despise.

You haven't read an English newspaper for nearly two years. What you read in your 'locals' either makes you laugh or sick, while the truth about the war is left to your imagination.

In short you are a dumb, stagnant, unwanted, hungry, dirty, cold and bored idiot in the service of your country.

If this doesn't make you grateful for what little you now have in front of and around you, you are an even bigger idiot than that.

So with the prospects of two or three journeys down the long cold corridor during the night to ease away the cocoa you must get to bed.

Licht aus! Goodnight.

Yours ever,

Jack

The chief delights of the culinary art
lie not in the pudding and pie and tart,
nor in the complex gallicised runes
on a menu offering porridge and prunes.
These are but part of an ancient fraud
to entice you to an unwholesome board.

So remember the countless men who forsook
their wives because they could not cook
and think of the countless things you've eaten
that don't appear in Mrs Beeton.

O lend me a tin of margarine C
and a *funf* of bread will do for me!
Give me a fire where I can toast
and I will be mine own good host!

Doug Larnar
21st November, 1944

Sylvia Truss

When war broke out in September 1939, I was fourteen years old. I had been corresponding regularly with three girls my own age. They were from France, Germany and the USA. Unhappily, I did not hear again from Paris or Wilhelmshaven. My penfriend in Pennsylvania continued to write for many years. Her mother thoughtfully packed assorted items of food and clothing during our most severe shortages, and these gifts were most enthusiastically and gratefully received. My family and her family were finally able to meet in 1962.

Fred Prior

The year was 1943. The British Forces in North Africa were partly resting after the fall of Algeria and Tunisia to the Allies and partly rebuilding their strength prior to the invasion of Sicily. In an idel moment a young corporal, a Londoner, in the Headquarters of the 4th British Division, was reading a newspaper sent to a fellow comrade. It was the *Gloucester Journal* dated 24 April 1943. In that paper was a photograph of a group of ladies who were stallholders of a Church Bazaar being held in Northgate Chapel in the City of Gloucester. Among those ladies was a young girl who took the young soldier's eye. He thought he would write to her and wondered if she would reply. In the absence of a name and address he wrote to the Minister, asking him to forward to the young lady a letter, which he enclosed with the photograph indicating her.

Some time later, the soldier received a reply from the young lady which resulted in a pen friendship lasting until

Northgate Church Bazaar

SOME OF THE STALLHOLDERS AT THE ANNUAL TWO D
NORTHGATE METHODIST CHURCH.

Happy coincidence . . .

. . . and smiling faces

the end of the war, when the soldier returned to England in 1946, on leave.

The couple met for the first time in January of the same year and again in August 1946 when the soldier returned finally to England on release from the Forces.

They married in September 1947. What paths would their lives have followed had it not been for an idle moment in a remote part of war-torn North Africa?

CHARLIE CHESTER

Prior to war actually being declared, things such as race meetings were called off. Ascot was naturally abandoned. This gave Karl Hyson the famous producer an idea to call his new Cabaret show at the Grosvenor House in Park Lane 'Ascot'. It gave him an opportunity to show off his lovely ladies in fabulous gowns, and also included using the latest craze of 'Hobby Horses' from America: these were small wooden horses which by careful manoeuvring could be ridden forward, but, if not handled properly, could collapse. I was the Comedian Compere, and I had to invite the stars of stage and screen up on the raised stage to compete on these 'Horses' for the champagne stakes. It was hilarious as they fell about. It was during the run of this show that I was called up.

Conscripted into the Irish Fusiliers, I was later transferred and found myself doing field security and counter-espionage work. Later, I was sent for and helped to form a new regiment of professional entertainers in the Army. These men and women served a dual purpose: firstly they were soldiers, and because of their talent they were formed into small companies to be front line entertainers helping to keep up morale. The Regiment was initially known as 'The Central Pool of Artistes' but became known as 'Stars in

Battledress'. I wrote all the material for the initial shows, and went over a few days after the invasion, with my own company. We went right through Normandy, France, Belgium, Holland and then Germany. As Germany began to collapse, I was flown back to prepare many more shows as these would be needed for the armies of occupation.

GAY CLARK

I remember the day war was declared very clearly because my parents were on edge, but when you're young you don't thing about what your parents are thinking about. They'd been through the First World War and there was all this chat going on about Hitler, and we had a lot of officers from my father's regiment who were going out to Germany on holiday and coming back saying all this 'Heil Hitler' was going on and it was very tense.

My sister became a nurse, the boys went into the army and I joined the ATS. You could either go into a factory or join the forces and me and all my friends all wanted to join the Wrens because we liked their navy blue uniform with black stockings, not the khaki uniform of the army . . .!

I was called up with 2,700 girls and at that time I was living in Cornwall. My father's regimental depot was in Bodmin (he was in the Duke of Cornwall's Light Infantry) and the army promised to put everyone in the nearest base to their homes. For me this meant Honiton, but it was full, no room for even one more recruit, so when my papers came through I was posted to Wrexham in North Wales which couldn't have been further away!

In the ATS I was trained to do everything like gas drill and shooting, then we were selected for commissions if we wanted to be. I didn't want a commission as I'd made a lot of friends by then and we all kept together.

Before the war I'd been a semi-professional artist and I'd met a lot of stars. I also met people who entertained the troops because they came to the garrison where I lived. After I'd been called up I trained as a switchboard operator and was returned to Cornwall. Originally I was going to train to be a driver for my father, but I was too short in the leg to reach the car pedals so that didn't work out! I'd only been back in Cornwall about a month when my Commanding Officer wanted to see me about a message from Charlie Chester who wanted me to go to Plymouth and audition for a show for the troops. (Dame Vera Lynn was nothing to do with us, she was a civilian whereas we were all from the services.) The show was called 'Stars in Battledress' and I did my audition at the Palais, Plymouth and was chosen by a man called Donald Stewart. There were eighteen men, and me. So I had a 'minder' called Bill. Bill always stayed at my digs – I often had to sneak out at night! We played seven nights a week and sometimes did two shows a day. At this time the Americans and Canadians were arriving and we entertained them at all the different bases as well as the military hospitals.

Entertaining was now my job but I was still under the army for pay and discipline. Our digs were all checked out in advance, in case of spies. Some digs were nice, some were awful. I once slept in a cellar on a damp bed and caught pneumonia. All the men in our 'Stars in Battledress' show had disabilities which prevented them from doing active service. We called ourselves 'The Bombshells', and we did in fact get caught up in many horrific air raids, although often we did shows at odd times to avoid air raids. D-Day was dreadful: we worked until we couldn't stand to keep the troops entertained.

Looking back, though, we went through some ghastly things, like the smell of burning flesh in Plymouth after they dropped incendiaries on the Sailors' Rest Home which had 500 men in it at the time. All of them died. You'd go to bed at night and the next day the street would be gone. People you knew and loved were killed.

We did shows on aircraft carriers which was a real hassle, trying to get the piano on board! I used to hate going on to the ships as I was usually given the Purser's cabin which was alive with cockroaches! I'd come back with my costumes full of them. I was the first girl on Drake's Island: I was presented with a badge saying that I was the first woman there.

My husband Ron was also in the Bombshells and our best man was killed just before we were married. My husband was in another 'Stars in Battledress' show when I met him. We actually met in Aldershot in a 'potted pantomime' called 'Christmas Pie'. I was Cinderella and he was Buttons, and on Christmas Eve he chased me with a piece of mistletoe so that started us! We were married in May because we were warned that we would have to go to France. We only had a forty-eight-hour honeymoon as that was all that was allowed. However, when we went to Headquarters Charlie Chester, who was a sergeant, told us that we weren't going to France but to Irish Command, so we were posted to Belfast: we could have real milk and eggs!

Ted Tangye

I was fourteen when war was declared. Nothing changed in a material way in New Zealand, though the majority of families were emotionally involved – we all seemed to have relatives who had voluntarily joined our armed forces. My brother was sixteen years older than I and enlisted in our army, which sailed with a huge convoy to Egypt. He fought in Greece, Crete and Egypt, until being sent back to us in 1943. His wife was a WAAF. Those were anxious years: retreats and evacuations seemed the Allies' lot – Dunkirk,

Norway, Greece, Crete and most of North Africa lost to us. Then with the Japs capturing Singapore and our huge naval losses, we began to feel very vulnerable: no army at home and the Japanese heading island by island towards us. After Pearl Harbor and Guadalcanal, many thousand American troops used our country as a rest away from combat before returning to action. Our harbours had been ruined and many merchant ships sunk by German armed merchant cruisers, who could escape detection in the vast oceans that surround us. Some food rationing was imposed here: tea, meat, sugar, eggs and clothing were on coupons. Whisky and spirits were unattainable. I think we were rationed mainly to enable us to send more supplies to Britain.

Petrol was practically non-existant; cars were jacked up and left in garages for years. Some fitted gas producers to their cars, lit the coal fire and chugged around, but it was cumbersome and dirty. I remember a friend and I raking the bunker out on the roadside and setting fire to the grass! Tyres were unavailable as the Japs controlled the world's rubber supplies.

I worked as a grocer, till I was old enough to volunteer for the navy in 1943. After three months' training I joined an escort carrier, HMS *Patroller*. My draft was to South Africa, but I never got there. About twenty of us had joined the carrier which was ferrying aircraft from California to India. After loading Black Widow night fighters at Oakland, across the bay from San Francisco, a signal came for us to cross the USA by rail, then on to England and commission *Achilles* to bring her out East. *Achilles*, which won fame at the River Plate, was being repaired at Portsmouth.

Can you imagine the thrill and excitement we eighteen-year-olds had in places like 'Frisco, Salt Lake City, Chicago and New York. We had our own sleeper carriage restaurant car attached on our five day journay across the States. 'Frisco remains a favourite place in my memories of places I've been and cities I've seen. We were about ten days in

New York at HMS *Saker*, where we were for St Patrick's Day. I went to a world boxing match at Madison Square Gardens, was shown over New York, Empire State, Rockefeller Centre, Waldorf Astoria – then one of the world's great hotels – the Statue of Liberty and everywhere by a lovely American girl, whose company I enjoyed until we sailed in convoy aboard the *Duchess of Bedford* for the Clyde. Our naval party was now about 400. A special train took us from Greenock to Plymouth, then on leave to enable us to visit relatives and generally explore Britain. Those early days were hungry ones, until our stomachs contracted: we found it awkward getting used to the austere rationing. The opportunity arose to transfer from the NZ to the Royal Navy on loan and many of us did. Eleven of my seamanship class did and were drafted to HMS *Isis*, a fleet destroyer that had come from the Mediterranean to get ready for the invasion. We joined her at Portsmouth, a great day for the lone New Zealander aboard, a Petty Officer Merv Williams. He relished our news from home. Now twelve Kiwis were in *Isis* ship's company.

We escorted invasion craft out into the channel on 4 June, but the weather was bad so we returned to the Solent. On 5 June, we were duty destroyer at Portsmouth and so did not leave with the troops for D-Day, but early on 6 June we were detailed to escort a commando landing ship and cover them while they stormed ashore to knock out a gun battery at Merville that was firing on to the Sword beaches and landing area. We sped towards Le Havre more than a little apprehensive about our role and were relieved when a signal told us that airborne forces had silenced the guns. We then took up station off the river Orne, outer screen for the thousands of vessels disgorging men and supplies on to the various beaches. Aboard we carried an army bombardment liaison officer who was in radio contact with spotters ashore. He directed our 4.7 guns on to targets ashore – we would sometimes be only a few hundred metres from shore aiming at tanks hiding in clumps of trees. By day bombarding was usually our role, at night we would join other destroyers and patrol the channel, mainly off Le Havre, engaging E-Boats, and on Asdic patrol. Night actions were really exciting: we chased and blasted away at German vessels and their planes would bomb our wake – the phosphorescence made by it could be spotted from quite a height in the darkness. There was many a near-miss but we were never hit. On more fortunate nights we were anchored as sentries off the Orne. Vigilance was imperative as the enemy were floating down mines, using very small submarines, manned torpedoes and explosive motor boats to inflict losses on us. One night I expected to be blown to smithereens: a white wake was heading right at me – but it was a dolphin, not a torpedo.

Lack of sleep was my memory of those incident-filled days. June's thirty days seemed like thirty months. Our guns banged away incessantly, cordite filled the air, spent brass cartridges were stacked everywhere. Back to Portsmouth we would go, ammunition lighters would come alongside; restocked we'd sail straight back to France.

After three very welcome days' leave in London, crew replacements came aboard before we left for Normandy. One of them was another New Zealander: we now numbered thirteen.

We steamed to our position off the Orne, to find our old workmate HMS *Swift* poking her superstructure out of the water at low tide. She had been mined while we were away, myriads of craft still covered the sea in all directions, the Mulberry Harbour was a hive of activity. We had complete control of the skies. German aircraft were seldom seen.

On 20 July, we had chased a submarine most of the day and lost it; at 16.00 hours we were to be relieved, but our replacement never showed up. At 18.00 hours I lay on the lockers in the Messdeck drifting off to sleep. The wireless news droned out that a bomb attempt had been made on Hitler's life. Sleep came and with it a dream: I was sitting in the bucket of a well and was dropped into the dark shaft then yanked back to the surface like a yo-yo. Three times this happened, then I awoke. It was eerie: my life had changed. The ship was lying on its side, it was silent, no fans whirred, no radio noise – just an uncanny silence. I was alone amid a jungle of lashed hammocks. I clambered towards the hatch leading to the forecastle break: no way out there, the deck was all twisted, blocking the way out. I slipped on the oily steel, hit the coaming of the hatch to the stokers' Mess below and sloshed into the water, oil and muck by the ship's canteen.

The ship's side was now the deck head. A glimmer of light showed above me. Somehow I climbed up the washplace and found a hole had been blown in the side – it was large enough for me to squeeze through. I stood up on what had been the ship's side and saw the after part till upright: we had been twisted in half. I saw some faces at a porthole, one of them my classmate Dyer. I wondered what he had been doing down there, it wasn't his Mess. They were trapped. The picture of their plight has never faded from my memory. Our army officer was staggering around near B-gun. The ship was almost deserted and going down rapidly, so I swam off the lee side and, keeping my mouth clear of the oil that covered the sea all around, made for a small float, a metre square wooden raft which I was to share with our ship's writer. Many of our companions died as oil clogged lungs and breathing. We took turns at swimming or resting on the raft all through the long night.

Isis vanished when we were about sixty metres from her, the bow pulled the after part down quickly. As the oil dispersed large waves built up: one moment we were poised up high and could see for miles, then we slid into the trough. At dusk we could see our replacement patrolling the far horizon. From the moment I swam off *Isis* I realized we wouldn't be found until morning.

Our ship's butcher swam past our float, clutching a

butterbox, yelling out 'Taxi! Taxi!'. He never even saw us. Only about twenty-nine of our ship's company of 200 survived.

As dawn broke, a decidedly grey squally dawn, we drifted by some merchant ships that were standing two miles from shore, as it was too rough to unload their supplies. A coastguard cutter was signalled by one of them and it bore down on us with a scrambling net, and as we rose on a swell we clutched at the net and willing hands pulled us aboard. They wrapped me, filthy with oil and grime, in a white blanket, and put me in a wonderful warm bunk. Several hours later we were transferred to an American hospital ship which took us into Omaha beach where amphibious trucks swam out from the shore to fetch us.

We were well looked after, about ten of us in all, and once mobile, after four days, we made our way back to the beaches to await a ride back to England. We watched spellbound as a 1000-bomber raid flew over heading towards Caen. We hitched a ride to Southampton on an LCT, to be kitted up at Eastleigh and given three days' leave.

Our ship had been struck by an acoustic mine, a type drawn closer to the surface by the sound of ships moving overhead. When, on the trip across the Channel in the LCT, some steel crashed on to the deck while I was asleep, still semi-conscious I went to leap over the side. I was restrained by Stoker Dixon, or I'd not be alive today.

After VJ day New Zealand sailors, who were scattered all around Britain, gathered at Plymouth and ended their travels in Wellington, New Zealand on Christmas Eve, 1945. Our war was over, homecoming was exciting; but after four or five days of reunions with family and friends, a loneliness crept over me. For the first time in years I was an individual: I'd become so accustomed to being surrounded by shipmates, crowded Messdecks, incessant chatter, part of a team. A new world was dawning and it was taking quite a lot of getting used to.

SHIRLEY BECKE

I was twenty-two and had just completed a five year training in Gas Engineering and was living in a top floor bed-sitting room in a tall Georgian house in Chelsea. I listened to Chamberlain on the wireless. It is one thing to expect something, quite another to come to terms with it in the event. I felt shattered.

In those first months before the invasion of the Low Countries and our retreat from Dunkirk, Britain struggled hard to get totally geared for war. I had hoped that having obtained the full Institute of Gas Engineers qualifications the Gas Company (this was before nationalization) would give me a job which would allow me to use those qualifications. Alas, no, I was twenty years before my time.

So in 1941 I gave up the unequal struggle and joined the Metropolitan Police as a Constable. I spent the rest of the war years in police duty in the centre of London during the bombing, the flying bomb attacks, the influx of Canadian, American and other allied troops (a lot of work there!) and finally the celebration of VE and VJ days.

So did the war change my life? Yes, indeed it did. I figured that, if when there was a shortage of men the Gas Industry had no position to offer a woman engineer, it was unlikely to have one for me when the men returned. So I stayed in the police and had a most interesting career, finishing up as a Commander in the Metropolitan Police, the first woman in this country to hold chief officer rank.

DOCTOR

FRITZ BOCK

I spent the afternoon of the day war broke out in Baden (south of Vienna) and listened to the customary concert, which was interrupted by a radio announcement about the outbreak of war. I said to my wife, who was standing beside me, 'Thank God for that!'. Of course she objected, but I explained that now we could be sure of getting rid of National Socialism since the Germans could not be expected to win. My reasoning was that despite enormous armament Germany could never win a war on two fronts. European history is quite unambiguous about that. It was simple: Germany would win many battles, but would lose the last one. It is said that Stalingrad was the turning point of the war, but for me and many others the outcome was obvious from the first day. The speech by Winston Churchill, the greatest man of our century, which he made in the House of Commons in 1940 and in which he spoke of blood and tears, but promised victory, was verified by history.

As a former political prisoner (I was arrested and put into Dachau concentration camp on 1 April 1938) I enjoyed an odd status. Following my release from Dachau in 1939 I was declared unfit for military service like many others whose opposition to the Nazis was well known. Needless to say this pleased me. Nevertheless I was drafted into the army by mistake in 1941 and sent back home as soon as they realized their error. The battalion to which I had been attached for a few days was part of the German 6th Army which was later completely destroyed at Stalingrad. Fate works in mysterious ways.

Of course I was under police surveillance until the end of the Nazi regime. Consequently I had to report at the police headquarters regularly to show that I was obeying their orders and staying in Vienna. Fortunately I was able to get round this prohibition by using faked identity papers.

Early in 1945 I was informed of my impending arrest which caused me to go into hiding from which I emerged only during the last days of the decay of the Third Reich. Thus it was that I survived the time of National Socialism, which had been my greatest wish on that September day in 1939.

JACQUES-ÉMILE DUBOIS

In 1938, one year before the war, I had an exchange with a young German of my own age. He spent some time in my family and I in his in the Black Forest region, the town of Gaggenau. His father worked in the Daimler Benz factory there, making trucks for the German army, as we found out later. In 1939, Dieter's family asked me for a return visit. He was now with the Hitler Youth Movement and would not be at home, and I would, in a sense, replace him. The area was full of fortifications in the process of construction. When my family sent me a telegram requesting my urgent return because the situation was very serious, the family assured me there was no imminent danger and begged me to stay. I had to obey my family, of course. Crossing the Kehl bridge that forms the border between France and Germany, between Kehl and Strasbourg, I noticed bunkers being built in all haste along the Rhine. The very next day, war was declared. I had returned home none too soon.

At that time, conscription was at age twenty, and I was nineteen and due to start at the University of Lille in the Autumn, which I did. It was only the following year, in 1940, with the French defeat (*la débâcle*), when France was divided into an 'occupied' and an 'unoccupied' zone, that I left home with my younger sister to go south. Our idea was to find shelter with cousins in the Corrèze region. However, since I wanted to go on with my studies, I left for Lyon and then Grenoble where I registered at the university. Like many other refugees there, my registration was taken 'on honour', since my papers and diplomas had all remained in the north of France.

When I presented myself for conscription, I was refused, like all those of my year, since France was no longer officially in the war. Thanks to friends from my home region of Picardy, I entered the *Résistance* movement in which I participated very actively until the liberation. Indeed I was one of the nine members of the Comité de Libération de l'Isère just after the war.

Looking back, it seems to me that having to leave home alone and to manage my life by myself made me mature more quickly than might otherwise have been the case. Furthermore, Grenoble was then one of the centres for refugees of all kinds, and I met and made lifelong friends with Alsacians who had fled the German advance, Hungarians sent to study in France, Jews seeking refuge in the unoccupied zone and, in general, people of very varied origins and political tendencies. It was enriching, even if life was extremely hard and food hard to come by, Grenoble not being a fertile agricultural area.

ERICH SCHELLOW

I was a young actor then, a beginner, in the theatre of Hamburg. I returned to my hotel room very late that night and wanted to boil an egg on the electric stove, but I fell asleep and woke up only when the room was filled with smoke. The water had boiled away, the cooker had burned into the table and the fire brigade had to come. It was very early in the morning of 1 September 1939. From loudspeakers all around you could hear the news that our troops had invaded Poland.

I lived through the war in Hamburg and Berlin, with all the horrible days and nights of bombing. Because of my reserved occupation as an actor with the Prussian State Theatre until 1944, I did not have to join the army, but I was due to be drafted after that although in the event an injury made me unfit for service.

Early in 1945 I managed to escape from Berlin to a small village near Würzburg where I stayed until the end of the war. On 1 May 1945 we were liberated by the Americans: an extremely wonderful survival which makes me thankful every day and obliges me to prove myself worthy of my existence.

DAME

NINETTE DE VALOIS

My personal memory of the day that war was declared is concerned with a railway journey from Liverpool to Leeds with the then Sadler's Wells Ballet. Passing a small village station without stopping, we noted the following placard stuck up very prominently in the little station – it simply said 'War declared'. When we reached our destination, Leeds, we found that the theatre was closed. The Company embarked on a train for London.

Some time later the Company was reformed and danced its way through the war, both in London and the provinces. Over the war years we built up a very large public and they have supported us ever since. We were even taken, at the very end of the war, to Belgium and France under ENSA. Again we enlarged our own public and also got in touch with an American public, some years before we visited the States.

During the war people had money to spend on the theatre

world. They had no cars, no means of spending money on extra clothes, food or drink. Any form of expensive holiday, or for that matter any sort of holiday, was not to be contemplated.

Boys entered the Company from our school at the age of sixteen, dancing until their call-up date was due at eighteen. The girls were exempted, provided that they did not leave the Company. We had only two weeks' closure a year and the work was extremely hard. At times in London we gave an 'extra' performance for 'war workers'. This was inserted on Saturdays between the matinée and evening show!

AIR VICE-MARSHAL
'JOHNNIE' JOHNSON
CB, CBE, DSO, DFC, DL, C.ENG., MICE

At school I always wanted to become an RAF Fighter Pilot, and I was inspired by the legendary Aces of the First War – Ball, Boecke, Bishop, Von Richthofen, Mannock and McCuddon. When the Volunteer Reserve was expanded I joined this enthusiastic bunch of weekend pupils.

After initial training I was posted to 616 Squadron at Kenley. However almost immediately I found myself out of the front-line when the Squadron, which had been decimated by the loss of six pilots and five wounded, was moved to Coltishall. (Perhaps just as well, for I had only twelve hours on Spitfires.)

In February 1941 Billy Burton took the Squadron to Tangmere and the next few months were the most exciting of my fighting career. Then Douglas Bader arrived to lead the Tangmere Wing, and the great man elected to fly with 616 Squadron: 'Cocky' Dundas, Alan Smith and myself were selected to fly with Douglas in the leading section.

We flew and fought hard during that epic summer.

Douglas was a great and inspiring leader whose fruity language in the air was a joy to hear. He took time to teach us the intricate art of air fighting. His idea of an afternoon off was to take one or two of us over the Channel hoping to come across Adolf Galland and some of his chaps, then based at Abbeville in the *Pas de Calais*.

On 19 August 1941, we were badly 'bounced' by a bunch of higher Messerschmitts and Douglas did not return from this fight. After we had refuelled we searched for him for several hours over the Channel as we thought he might have baled out and clambered into his dinghy. Gradually it dawned upon us that he would not be returning, and this day marked the end of an era that was rapidly becoming a legend.

In the summer of 1942 I was promoted to command 610 (County of Chester) Squadron, and then in early 1943 I was promoted to Wing Commander to lead the Canadian Spitfire Wing at Kenley. My personal score at that time was eight victories. During the spring and summer of that year I led the aggressive Canadian fighter pilots on 140 missions over north-west Europe; my pilots shot down more than 100 enemy aircraft, and my personal score rose to twenty-five. The highlights of those days were escorting the Flying Fortresses of the Eighth Air Force.

After a short rest from operations, in March 1944, I was posted to lead another Canadian Spitfire Wing, and on D-Day, 6 June 1944, I led 144 Wing on four missions over the beaches. On 8 June, we made history when we were the first Spitfire Wing to land in France, and a few weeks later we began the exhilarating, buccaneering trek across France. In September 1944, I scored my thirty-eighth and last victory. Patrolling the Rhine, with 443 Squadron, we bounced nine Messerschmitts flying low in the opposite direction, and very quickly shot down five, but unfortunately on this occasion I lost a superb Canadian fighter pilot, Squadron Leader 'Wally' McLeod.

Early in 1945, I was promoted to Group Captain and commanded 125 Wing equipped with the latest Spitfire 14s. In the spring we crossed the Rhine and flew from Luftwaffe airfields. Soon it was all over and I had time to reflect that a boy's ambition of slightly more than a decade ago had, indeed, been realized.

William Roe

From Student *magazine, Aberdeen, 1947*

Per Ardua Ad Ersatz

'So you are going to Torquay on your next leave. Want to float around all day on one of these inflated rubber mattress things, getting nicely sunburnt, do you? Don't think much of the idea, personally. I never could stand the sight of these rubber contraptions after the night our crew spent in the emergency dinghy. Perhaps I told you about it. No? Well, it was like this – Another pint did you say? Well, yes, I don't mind if I do.

'As I was saying, it was way back in 1942, when the Squadron was equipped with Wellingtons. Things were pretty slack at the time. November, it was, and the weather had been bad over Germany. Most of the ops. were minelaying trips to the Baltic or the Friesians, and this night three crews of us had been briefed for a mining job in the Heligoland Bight. Easy these mining trips really, never much flak, and seldom any fighters. Just a long, monotonous stooge over water all the way, the sort of thing they give to "sprog" crews before sending them over a real target. I am not superstitious, but I did know that it was the Navigator and Wireless Operator's thirteenth trip.

'Everything was going fine, we found our pinpoint on the enemy coast dead on time, and set course for the dropping position thirty miles back to sea again. Ten minutes later we were in the "ditch", both engines having packed up.

'Well, there we were, still all in one piece, thanks to the skipper's crash-landing, miles from home, and precious little chance of getting there again this side of VE-day. Six bewildered airmen, squeezed into an absurd circle of inflated rubber, six feet across, slowly becoming aware that they were still alive, and had better start bailing some of the water out if they wanted to stay that way. Another Wellington passed low overhead, it must have been one of our own Squadron, but it was gone before we could send up a Verey signal, although they could not have helped us anyway.

'The navigator claimed the German coast was twenty odd miles due east, and if the wind and current stayed put, we might be ashore before dawn. He wasn't far out in his reckoning. We spent all that night in a howling gale, chewing Horlicks tablets from our escape kits, and trying to keep our cigarettes dry enough to smoke. Cold, did you say? Well, there are warmer places than a rubber dinghy in the North Sea in the middle of a November night – and the rum was in the ration pack which we lost in the scramble to get into the dinghy. There were some benzedrine tablets in the escape kits with instructions "to be taken only in an emergency", and if this was not an emergency – ! We had one each and they helped to boost the morale a bit, not that we wanted to sing sea-shanties, but we all felt better a few minutes afterwards.

'We spanked along at a fair dip all night, and just before dawn came slap bang up against the end of a sort of stone breakwater, about ten feet high, which for no apparent reason stretched out to sea from –; well that is what we were going to find out. We walked along the top of it for about half an hour, and, as it grew gradually lighter, we could make out the mainland ahead, a flat, monotonous country. It was funny to realize that this place, now seen in the daylight, was Germany. It could have been typical of a thousand and one spots on our own coast. Previously Germany had been a map on the wall with target areas, flak defences, searchlight belts, and night-fighter dromes, or else a flat two dimensional piece of blackness from whose surface long groping fingers of light sprang, or from which streamed up beautiful and deceitfully harmless-looking festoons of red and green tracer.

'Yes, it was strange to see this other Germany, and to find that all Germans were not flak gunners, searchlight operators, or fighter pilots. It was not long before we met the local inhabitants. At the end of the pier was a most formidable-looking pill-box, complete with machine-guns, with what looked like half of the German army to man them. The other half it seemed was waiting for us with fixed bayonets. We had walked into a part of the much vaunted Atlantic Wall. They were not such a bad bunch once they saw we were quite harmless, and, of course, Invasion was not started yet.

They fed us on Sauerkraut, bacon, sausage and ersatz coffee, gave us cigarettes – and an armed escort to the interrogation camp at Frankfurt. The farewell words of an English speaking NCO were: "For you the war is over." He was right.'

W.P.S.R.

From Nalgo *magazine, Tunbridge Wells, 1957*

Gardening

Before putting pen to paper, an author should, I feel, know sufficient about his subject to instruct, amuse or enlighten his readers. Let me state here and now that if anyone reading this wishes advice about his chrysanthemums or Brussels sprouts I cannot help him. Let him look to the shelves of our excellent Public Library or seek counsel elsewhere. There is, however, a type of 'gardening' of which I can write with first hand experience.

It is probably not generally known that this was the code name for the mine-laying operations round the coasts of Occupied Europe, carried out by aircraft of Bomber and Coastal Commands of the RAF, during World War II. The 'Vegetables', acoustic and magnetic mines weighing half a ton each, were sown in 'Allotments' at selected spots in the North Sea and the Baltic, where report has it they gave considerable trouble to our late enemies.

At the time of which I write, Bomber Command had been expanded until it could, with a little help from Training Command, send 1000 aircraft out on a single sortie, and with so much of our resources committed to this end it had to be used to the full. On nights when weather conditions did not favour the locating of land targets, as many as 300 Wellingtons, Hampdens and even lordly Lancasters and Halifaxes would be carrying out individual gardening operations.

These trips were looked on with mixed feelings by the squadrons. True, the opposition was usually less than what would be encountered over the Ruhr or other heavily defended land targets; and newly trained crews were often given a mining trip for their initiation, but they only counted as half an op. towards the thirty needed to complete a tour of operations.

Painstakingly accurate navigation was needed to get the mines to the correct place. The technique was to find a visual pin-point on the coastline not more than ten miles from the dropping point, descend to 1000 feet and set course on a dead reckoning run for the last few miles, keeping height, course and airspeed absolutely constant. Accuracy to about 100 yards could be obtained, provided the pin-point could be located, but to do this in overcast weather was often no mean feat of navigation; and without a definite pin-point the whole thing was scrubbed and the mines brought back home. At the end of the 'DR' run the mines, two from a 'Wimpey' and up to six from a 'Lanc', were released and floated gently down on their parachutes to land at precisely the preordained spot, you hoped.

After that you could think about getting home, that is, if you had not passed within a couple of miles of any flak, because flying at 1000 feet on a steady course a Wellington could probably be shot down by a determined small boy with a catapult. To make matters worse, particularly as you were flying over water nearly all the time, mines could not be fitted in the bomb bays unless the flotation gear was removed. This consisted of large airbags which inflated automatically with the impact of a crash landing and helped to keep the aircraft afloat, but as official figures gave the chances of survival in a 'ditching' as sixteen-to-one against, the benefit of the presence of flotation gear was probably more imagined than real.

Whatever the squadron reaction to 'Gardening', there is no doubt that the powers that be regarded it with favour, probably with good reason, as we were told that more shipping was sunk by this means than by all other methods put together. This rather surprising information was given to the assembled aircrews by a Captain, RN, sent from Combined Operations to sell 'Gardening' to the sceptics. His visit caused quite a stir since his driver was a Wren of such dazzling good looks as was rarely seen in a staff car of anything less than a full Admiral. A suggestion that the gallant Captain might care to accompany one of the crews on their next trip was regretfully but very firmly declined. Proposals of a more personal nature were pressed on the Wren, but these, too, were declined and one sensed that it was with some relief that the Navy took its leave of us.

EVELYN M. BUIST

I don't think our family will ever forget the day that the Japanese bombed Pearl Harbor and so the USA, China and Japan were at war.

We – my husband and two daughters, Kathleen and Beryl – were living in the city of Peking. We were Salvation Army Officers from England and thoroughly enjoying our missionary work.

My husband, as usual, switched on the radio and these were the words we heard: 'Britishers and Americans stay indoors. We are now at war.' We felt dreadful and wondered what would happen to us. We didn't have to wait long, because suddenly Japanese soldiers entered our home. You can imagine how we felt when we were told to stand up and these soldiers stood in front of us holding their guns with the bayonets pointing at us. They stamped round our bungalow looking at everything. When they saw our radio they barked at our cook to take it outside and put it in their van. He refused and looked at us, but when the soldiers stepped forward to beat him we quickly said, 'Please do as they tell you!'

We were all told to remain indoors for one week. Then all foreign nationals were given red arm bands with the words ENGLISH PIG painted on in Chinese characters. We had to wear them constantly and we were limited to a one mile radius when we left our home.

Life after this wasn't very pleasant. Our baby son was due to be born in four months' time and we had very little money to buy food. Our cook wouldn't leave us although we were unable to pay him any wages. The *Amah* was a young married woman with a family and she left us, partly through fear of the Japanese and also because she needed the money. Our cook said if only he could continue to live with us he would gladly work for no pay. He would eat what we ate. All the Salvation Army officers in Peking, British and Americans, had been given some money and told it was to last until the war ended. This made us feel we dare not spend too much on food so day by day we ate millet porridge and, surprise, surprise, when our baby was born he weighed ten pounds!

We had to wait a few months until the Japanese had a place ready for 1,700 internees to live in. Eventually the summons came that we all had to meet at the 'former American Embassy'. Adults were allowed one trunk each – but no allowances were made for children. This was quite a problem as we had three, including a baby. Then we were told to take all our beds and bedding. One of the beds had everything but the kitchen sink packed on it, so this relieved the trunks for clothing. Imagine sweeping brush, folding chairs, tin mugs and plates, cutlery, bedding, pillows, bucket, a few pictures and a little mat. How relieved we were when the Japanese took our goods without a murmur. Anything we could carry ourselves we were allowed to take.

I remember our dear old cook had baked us bread to take with us and he took my bread knife to some man who rounded off the top so that it couldn't hurt anyone.

When we met at the Embassy all our goods were tipped out on to the lawn for inspection and when the officer saw my bread knife he made quite a fuss. There we were arguing about a simple bread knife – he said it was dangerous and I disagreed. At last permission was given for me to take it with us.

The 1,700 men, women and children were put in line for a long march to the station. We had rolled up four blankets and Kathleen aged six and Beryl, three, had one fastened round their shoulders and my husband and I also had one. Little Gordon, about nine months old, was in a very cheap little Chinese pushchair. My lovely English pram had been exchanged for this poor one. The Japanese were sure that the Chinese would be happy to see all the 'Foreign Pigs' being sent away, but not so, for thousands lined the streets to see us marching away and many eyes were wet.

It was a deliberate act of humiliation by the Japanese. The internees were from all walks of life – lecturers and professors from the Peking Union Medical College and Yenching University; Missionaries of the London Missionary Society, and English Methodist Society for the Propagation of the Gospel; officers of the Salvation Army; business executives of the British and American Tobacco Company; priests and nuns from North China and Manchuria. Altogether there were 1,700 of us coming by cart and train converging on Weihsien, tired, apprehensive and ill-prepared for the manual labour and hardships which faced us.

There were three big kitchens, each feeding 500 (small children ate in the hospital): Kitchen 1 for the Tientsin Internees, Kitchen 2 for the Peking Internees, Kitchen 3 for the Tsinglao Internees.

Catholic priests from Belgium, Holland and America, mostly in their twenties, cleared the toilets and erected large ovens for the camp bakery. How fortunate we from Peking were, that by the time we arrived at Weihsien all was running fairly smoothly because 400 other internees had arrived earlier and had worked really hard.

The administrative machinery was most impressive. The Quarters Leader allocated two small rooms to us and they knocked a hole in the wall of one room to make it more convenient to get from one room to another. Then the Labour Leader gave us forms to fill in to indicate how much experience we had in teaching, engineering, cooking, baking, dressmaking and other spheres.

The 400 Catholic priests and nuns had made a great impact on the internee community. They had turned their hands to the most menial tasks cheerfully, organized baseball games and helped in the education programme for the year. But eventually all but thirty priests were transferred to an institution of their own in Peking.

We lived in this camp for nearly three years until one wonderful day, 17 August, a Friday, when in the middle of the morning we heard a plane. It got louder and louder and we saw it had the stars and stripes on it. Everyone stopped whatever they were doing and we all ran outside the camp. Without thinking of any regulations or of the Japanese, 1,500 people were running to see who the seven men were who were parachuting down to the ground. The Salvation Army had a small band which had practised for years the National Anthems of all the nationalities in the camp – playing without the lead so that the Japanese guard sitting in on the practice wouldn't recognize the tune. Now was their great moment. They all ran with their instruments and stood on top of the wall and played the National Anthem of each of the seven men as they were carried shoulder high into the camp.

We had lived for nearly three years in this internment camp. It had a high wall right around with electric barbed wire on top of the wall. On each corner the soldiers had machine-guns trained on the camp. I could tell lots more of our life in the camp, but no – we want to forget it, and I will just repeat my first sentence: we will never forget that day, but now we are free.

VICE ADMIRAL
SIR PATRICK BAYLY

On 3 September 1939 I was a Lieutenant RN in a China river gunboat, HMS *Cicala*, one of five which patrolled the West River (Si Kiang) between Hong Kong and Wuchow, a distance of some 150 miles. Our base was at Canton where we had moorings in the river off the British Concession and near the centre of the city.

The river was, and is, an important artery for trade in

South China and the gunboats' task was to discourage piracy. At that moment in time our patrols were particularly valuable because all China was in chaos, suffering from a Japanese invasion.

I had arrived at Canton to join the *Cicala* in mid-1938 with a Japanese bombing raid in progress. As we were not then at war with them the Japanese did not deliberately attack us but often flew over us at low altitude on their way to attack some target in the city. Soon afterwards they shot down a Chinese passenger airliner – my first close acquaintance with the casualties of war.

Towards the end of 1938 the Japs invaded South China, blockaded the river and became much more threatening, pointing loaded guns at us and so on. For the most part we ignored this but not without some flutterings in the stomach! The Chinese were not capable of serious resistance but started their 'scorched earth' policy and set fire to the city. We carried out foot patrols round the Concession, mainly to deter the floods of refugees who would otherwise have swamped us.

During one of my patrols an ammunition train, not far away, blew up and we took shelter from a rain of bits of freight wagons. One day I watched an old woman beat a dog to death and stuff it, hair and all, into a cooking pot. The Japanese soldiers bayoneted anyone who did not instantly obey and headless corpses floated past in the river.

I have recounted what I saw in 1938 and early 1939 to show that, when it came to 3 September, I and those around me were sufficiently familiar with sudden death, famine, disease and destruction to appreciate what Europe would suffer, only far, far worse.

The fatal signal arrived: Commence hostilities against Germany. The Captain read it out and added 'God save the King and keep safe all our families'. It was a highly emotional moment.

We had by that time abandoned the river, where trade no

longer moved, and were based in Hong Kong. War in Europe hardly affected us in the Far East until, two years later, the Japanese attacked us without warning. In the meantime, however, I had transferred to an old cruiser, HMS *Durban*, which patrolled the coasts of China, Malaya and Indonesia to prevent the movement of the many German merchant ships which had taken refuge in neutral ports.

In late 1941 I at last returned to England. Thus, after over three years 'east of Suez', avoiding, by a few weeks, the disastrous outbreak of the war with Japan.

My next posting was to Combined Operations in the Royal Naval Commandos where, as Principal Beach Master, I landed with the assault in the invasions of Sicily and Italy.

Later, back at sea again, I had a grandstand view of the most thrilling episode in my life, the landing of the Allied Forces in Normandy and D-Day, 6 June 1944.

It is extraordinary how young the thirty-year-olds look today!

DOCTOR
A.P. CURTIN

It was a challenge, a greatly varied and at times most stressful experience after qualification with both the Royal College of Surgeons and Royal College of Physicians in April 1939. After a short period of three months as Casualty House Surgeon at my teaching hospital – St Bartholomew's Hospital, London – I was called up for War Service by the Royal Navy early in September 1939 for an initial short period of service indoctrination at RN Hospital Haslar, Portsmouth.

Following this I was directed for Service at HMS *Drake*, Plymouth. I well remember this posting as it was my first experience of dealing with a wartime casualty situation when survivors of the Aircraft Carrier *Courageous*, sunk by a German U-Boat attack off the South Western Approaches, were brought ashore. This initial task having been completed, I was ordered to sea in a destroyer, HMS *Wessex*, for service in protection of westbound convoys in the North Atlantic.

Later, I was transferred to the Channel ports to participate in the evacuation of the Dunkirk beaches. We were kept very busy; the port of disembarkation this side was Dover. At this time there were no RAF planes over the Channel or beaches, and on a return outward journey we were attacked by Luftwaffe Junkers 88s and sunk in mid-Channel. I was blown clear into the water, and subsequently picked up, in oil-soaked clothes and much shaken, by a small French coaster bringing out British Dunkirk wounded, including two young RAF pilots who had been shot down over the Channel at this time. I may say, a dose of hot rum greatly helped to overcome my period of shock and assist my speedy recovery.

I well remember that one of the most disturbing aspects of our surgery was the discovery of ·303 bullets in some of our wounded, which led me to believe that either by accident or design British troops had fired on their own soldiers and airmen. I felt it could be possible that many of those left behind on the beaches were in such fear of death that they jealously and in a state of frenzy fired at those leaving. It was a most unpleasant fact to reflect upon at this time, but the thought kept recurring.

MARILYN PULLON

My war started on 8 December 1941, the 'day of infamy' as President Roosevelt described it. That was the day the Japanese bombed Pearl Harbor. I was nine years old and living with my parents and sister in Shanghai, China.

We were woken early that morning by the sound of planes flying low overhead. Fortunately for us, they were not on a bombing mission, but were dropping leaflets, one of which I still have. It declared that a state of war now existed between Japan, and the USA and the British Empire, and that the Japanese Army had taken over the International Settlement, where we lived.

At that time, life for my family was extremely comfortable. My father was the managing director of a large export and import company and a director of several other local companies. We had a large house and beautiful garden. We had servants to do everything for us. There was a great deal of lavish entertaining for the adults and parents vied with each other to give bigger and better children's parties. In fact, we were all pretty spoiled!

However, from that day in December 1941, things started to change. Though we continued to live in our house, and go to school, all the foreign businesses including my father's were taken over by the Japanese. Soon our car was impounded, and before long Japanese soldiers had come to the house and put stickers on every item of furniture, stating that these were now the property of the Japanese Emperor and must not be sold. All adults had to wear red armbands when they left the house, with the letter 'B' for British and a number on them. The idea was to humiliate the wearers, but needless to say they were worn with pride. We needed permits to go practically anywhere, and roads were barricaded by armed soldiers. Friends of my parents were arrested and taken for questioning by the *Kempetai*, or Japanese Secret Police, and we never knew who would be next.

Then internment for all allied nationals started to be talked of, and in April 1942 my family left our home to go to Lunghwa Civil Assembly Centre, as it was euphemistically called. We were allowed to take our beds, a folding table and chairs, and a trunk for our clothes.

Lunghwa had been a Chinese school but it had been bombed by the Japanese in 1937 and had been empty since. The remaining habitable buildings, and some wooden huts, became home for us for the next 2½ years. As a family, we were lucky to have a room to ourselves, measuring some thirteen feet by ten feet. There were twenty-six rooms along our corridor, plus a washroom with concrete troughs around the walls, and male and female lavatories. We soon learnt that running water was a luxury which only came on for a couple of brief periods each day, so keeping clean, and washing clothes, became a severe problem. In fact, when it rained we always rushed outside to get a free shower. Likewise with the lavatories: these were only to be flushed when really necessary.

The camp was set in about eighty acres of land, and was surrounded by barbed wire. Beyond the camp lay the paddy fields of the Chinese peasants, who continued their daily toil apparently oblivious of the 'foreign devils' who now lived on the other side of the barbed wire. In the distance, across the flat landscape, we could see the skyscraper buildings of Shanghai.

All our drinking water and food was brought in by trucks from Shanghai. The water then had to be boiled, and we queued for our daily ration. The food was extremely unappetizing and became less and less adequate as the months went by. It consisted mainly of *congee* – rice boiled to a sort of gruel; stews – sometimes fish, meat or just vegetables; a ration of bread, usually sour and mildewy; and green tea. Fortunately, most of us had been able to make arrangements with Chinese or neutrals to send in parcels, and these came once a month, unless we were being punished.

I can remember being extremely hungry a lot of the time, and also very cold. We had no heating of any description, and Shanghai winters are bitter. In the summer we were too hot. In our home, mosquito netting was always put over all windows and doors during the summer, but in camp, though we had mosquito nets over our beds, there was nothing to stop a frightening selection of insects from flying into our rooms. We had to stand to attention at the doors of our rooms during morning and evening roll call, while the guards progressed from building to building to count that we were all still there. I can vividly remember the awful feeling of insects crawling down my back as I stood rooted to the ground, fearing to move so much as a muscle in case a guard spotted me, and beat me (which we had seen happen).

I soon got used to the fact that now, when my father went to work, it was not to his office, but to stoke the boilers at 'Waterloo', the name given to one of the water stations, the others being 'Bubbling Well' and 'Dew Drop Inn'. Likewise my mother went off each day for several hours' 'vegetable duty' – an unpleasant job made worse by lack of water and the fact that the vegetables, and meat or fish when we got them, were usually in a putrid state.

Any idea we children had that we were going to enjoy a long holiday from school soon ended. The Japanese were persuaded to allow a building just outside the camp boundary to be used as a school. Many of the rooms had no glass in the windows, so it was extremely cold in winter. We had no proper text books, exercise books, pens or ink, but we did have marvellous teachers. Lunghwa Academy managed to turn us out at the end of the war able to take our places with our contemporaries in England. Games and sports were organized but these had to be curtailed when it was realized that too much energy was being used up in our undernourished state. Everyone who had brought books into camp donated them to a library. This suited me very well, because I loved reading, and was happy to read everything I could lay my hands on.

Clothing was a real problem. We children were growing taller and thinner all the time, so a clothing exchange was organized. As we grew out of things, they were handed in for someone else to wear. This worked quite well, although I remember that by the end I was having to wear shoes with the toes cut out to make room for my feet.

As well as school we had Guides, Scouts, Cubs and Brownies, Sunday School and Church services. There was drama, opera and revues written by the inmates. We thought the revues were brilliantly funny but the Japanese, who were always invited to attend, did not seem to appreciate the humour.

We were always being cheered by rumours that we were going to be repatriated. But as the months wore on the rumours became more sinister: that we were going to be sent to Japan where we were going to be put in the front line if the Americans invaded. After the war we found out that this had been true. There was at least one shortwave radio operating in the camp but its hiding place was kept a close secret. If it had been found, those responsible for it would have been sentenced to death. But from this source we did know about the progress of the war and we heard about Germany's defeat.

Then the Americans started bombing Shanghai and the airfield near the camp, which meant that anti-aircraft shells were exploding over our buildings and the Chinese village nearby. Fortunately, no one in the camp was injured, but many Chinese were, and they were brought by their families to the camp where they hoped to receive treatment. We had many doctors and nurses among the inmates, but by then virtually nothing in the way of medical supplies, bandages, or dressings.

Early in August 1945 we heard, at first as yet another rumour, that a very powerful bomb had been dropped on Japan – a bomb more terrible than anything known before. As everyone now knows, the dropping of atomic bombs on Hiroshima and Nagasaki, devastating though they were, speedily caused the Japanese to sue for peace, thus sparing countless lives including those of my family and myself and the 1,700 other inmates of Lunghwa Civil Assembly Centre.

Within a month we had returned to our home in Shanghai, and early the following year my mother, sister and I travelled to England. Did our ordeal have any lasting effect on us? Who can tell? Certainly, the day the Japanese bombed Pearl Harbor changed our lives completely.

BERNARD CAMPION

In 1939 I was a radio operator in the 8th Destroyer Flotilla, which was a unit of the formidable China Fleet Britain then boasted.

In the late August my ship – HMS *Delight* – was visiting Weihaiwei when we received an urgent signal to reassemble as a flotilla and to 'proceed with dispatch' to Singapore. During our swift passage south the other eight boats of the flotilla slipped out from their various ports of call to rendezvous with the leader and resume operating as a unit.

We stayed at Singapore just long enough to refuel, and then started across the Indian Ocean towards Ceylon. On Sunday 3 September, we were about halfway across. The weather was vile, and the destroyers were behaving in the manner for which they were renowned whenever the seas were rough. In the cramped and stuffy radio compartment the code-books (lead-covered so that they would sink if jettisoned) were being flung dangerously about by the ship's heavy pitching and rolling. I was reading almost non-stop morse signals, decoding earlier messages, and trying to keep the set tuned in against constant static and 'fading'. From time-to-time I punctuated this versatile performance by sorrowfully bowing my head over the bucket I had prudently lashed to the side of my screwed-down swivel chair . . .

During the course of my dolorous first dog watch (4 p.m. to 6 p.m.) I was desperately counting the minutes to the time I could turn over to my relief – a much older operator who was impervious to the elements – and could gratefully slide down the Messdeck hatch into my waiting hammock. We kept hammocks slung all day in really foul weather, as there was nowhere else the off-watch sailors could survive in comfort.

Towards the end of my watch I started reading a message in 'plain language', which was unusual among so much code and cypher, and the text completely took my mind off my agonizing seasickness for once. Addressed 'To All HM Ships and Establishments at Home and Abroad from Admiralty' it ordered, with Nelsonian simplicity, 'Commence hostilities against Germany forthwith'. I felt I was turning over a page of history as I bawled the message up the voicepipe to the bridge . . .

DOCTOR

PATRICK MOORE

CBE, FRAS

When war was declared, on 3 September 1939, I was lying ill in bed, and had been there for some time – between the ages of seven and sixteen I was in and out of bed; I was sixteen when war was declared.

Not much I could do. I knew I could not pass the medical for the Forces, because I had a crocked heart. So later on, in early 1940, I faked my age and medical, manoeuvred my way into the RAF, and flew as a navigator – and remained in the RAF until the war was over. It was a long time ago now!

ANON

July 1939: schools had closed for the summer holiday – whether they would open again after the holiday, no one knew. I was sixteen and would be seventeen in September. I had just completed my first year in the 6th form at a grammar school studying for Higher Schools Certificate, as it was known then, and hoping to begin at a Teacher Training College in September 1940.

We had already been issued with gas masks and had been told that if war were declared, all schools would remain closed until further notice, and the only way to continue our education would be to be evacuated with our school. None of us wanted to be evacuated but the alternative was to leave school and volunteer for one of the women's services when we were old enough. This was a very attractive thought because we were all keenly patriotic and eager to do our bit for our country. Out of the five girls in the 6th form, four decided to be evacuated and one left school to join the WAAFs when she was old enough. She became a heavy transport driver.

We were all open-minded as to whether war was inevitable or not – we were mostly very optimistic that it would all blow over. I suppose we were really in a fool's paradise and believed that no one was so idiotic as to start a war.

Then on 1 September, we were told to report to school at 11 a.m. with the essentials we had been told to bring. After standing about for hours, we finally left and arrived in Scarborough on the east coast, some forty miles away, five hours later. We four sixth-formers were taken to a boarding house with one Staff, two helpers and fifteen third-formers. We were made to feel very welcome and went to bed quite happy.

On Sunday 3 September we went to church and on arriving back at our billet, assembled in the dining-room and heard that ominous speech: I don't think any of us will ever forget those words 'and consequently this country is at war with Germany'. There was a deathly hush – I think we were all numb.

My immediate thoughts were how would this affect my family and me. I had no brothers, only one sister whose boyfriend was at Cranwell serving in the RAF. I thought the odds were very much against his coming through a war in which air warfare would be so important. He would be among the first to fight: he took part in the dropping of leaflets in German over Germany. These leaflets were just propaganda and I doubt if they did any good. After taking part in several bombing raids in Whitley and Wellington bombers, he was shot down over France. He is buried with his crew, most of them only nineteen years old, in a country churchyard in France. My sister joined the ATS and served in the Signals in the Middle East.

I also thought of the people of Poland being bombed day and night and putting up a tremendous resistance with obsolete planes and weapons. They had no modern tanks to fight the German army; they were still using horses.

During the summer of 1938, our local council had been digging underground shelters in case of air raids. These were useless, as every time it rained they filled with water. I can remember quite clearly seeing worms floating on the top. The scheme was abandoned and we had a brick shelter built in our garden. We equipped it with bunks and other luxuries. I am mentioning all this because I have to say I felt 100 per cent safe in these shelters during an air raid and I never doubted for a moment that I would survive any air raid. I can also say that I never felt frightened during a raid – again the optimism of youth, or perhaps I was just naive.

At this time, I and all my friends believed most strongly that our country could never be beaten in any war by anyone. Our country was absolutely unprepared for war, especially compared with Germany which had been preparing for war for years and had magnificent, modern equipment for warfare on land and sea and in the air. Looking back at our feelings then, it seems ridiculous that we thought like that, but we were young, confident, optimistic and we believed in our country. Throughout the whole of the war, when we stood alone in 1940, when our modern battleships were being sunk by the Japanese in the Pacific in 1941, I can honestly say that never for a moment did I think of defeat. The tide would turn and we would be victorious. I was not alone in this outlook – we young students all thought the same. We believed that right would win and Germany was wrong and doing evil things – they could never win.

J. Northeast

It was on a Saturday night that the bombing of London really started. I lived in a district of London which was called the Isle of Dogs. We were surrounded by docks which the Germans were intent on putting out of action.

I lived with my old mother and came home from work at about 4.30 and she usually had my dinner waiting for me, which she kept by the fire to keep warm as sometimes I was a little late. I came home and she brought out my dinner – then all of a sudden bombs seemed to be dropping everywhere. I told her to go into the coal cupboard which was under the stairs (we lived in a three-storey house) – I went up to the top to look out. It looked as if the whole island was alight: incendiary bombs had been dropped everywhere. I pushed up the window and put my head out. These windows were the old-fashioned type sash windows and I had just got myself leaning out of the window when there was an almighty bang. The window came down – the sash cord had broken – and pinned me underneath. My mother in the coal cupboard could not hear my cries for help. It seemed as if I was stuck there for hours.

When the All Clear siren was sounded, my mother came to look for me and held the window up for me to get out. She was covered from head to toe in coal dust. After we had cleaned ourselves up, she went to get my dinner – it was a nice piece of steak, she said. But it was covered in soot which had been blown down the chimney, so I never had my piece of steak and never had another until the war was over and rationing had finished.

We laughed after it was all over, but the next day we found so many people had been killed: friends, relatives, neighbours. We'd had a funny experience; many people had lost their lives.

L.N. Butler

On the day World War II was declared I can remember quite clearly being at St Andrew's Church, Bexleyheath, Kent, during the morning. As a choirboy of five years of age I was quite the youngest in church at that time. I felt that something was wrong as the number in the congregation was very small indeed – less than five. But elderly Miss Hawes was there – she always was!

Bedonwell Primary School in Bexleyheath was quite different during the war. Many of the younger teachers were with the armed forces which meant that those approaching retirement and not eligible for service stayed in teaching during the war years. Many pupils were evacuated; those who remained still had a strict school routine. Times tables had to be learnt by heart and basic numeracy and literacy were drummed into you even though the Battle of Britain and bombing raids were happening all around.

One morning Mr Russell introduced the class to long

division: 'We are going to divide 7128 by 27' and on the blackboard was chalked 7128 ÷ 27. After the initial introduction the siren went and into the school underground air raid shelters we trooped.

Soon the All Clear sounded and we went back to the sum – 27 into 7, then 27 into 71 and the answer 2 was soon checked. We were taking 54 from 71 when the next 'take cover' went and the air raid shelters beckoned. Mid-morning milk followed by the All Clear soon took us back to lessons.

After some discussion we had arrived at the difficult bit – how many 27s in 172? After some help it was decided that 6 with 10 remaining would do. Before we could answer the last part of how many 27s in 108, the 'take cover' sounded for the third time that morning. Mr Russell gently put the chalk down and said to the class, 'I do not think Mr Hitler wants you to learn long division.'

WING COMMANDER
R. DAUNCEY

My father was a Chartered Accountant, working and living in Antwerp, Belgium. At that time in Antwerp, there was a thriving English 'colony' who, amongst other things, ran a good cricket club. Among their regular opponents was a Dutch team with a pitch and club somewhere near Eindhoven. On 3 September 1939, it was Antwerp Cricket Club's turn to play at Eindhoven and, whilst the match was in progress, some of the spectators listened to Chamberlain's news broadcast about the outbreak of war and the match came to a halt. Silence reigned whilst they listened and for a few minutes afterwards, whereupon the Captain of the Antwerp team said, 'Shall we resume the match?' They did.

G.A. WHITEWAY

Extract from a notebook kept during 1944

TUES. 5.12.44 9.40 P.M. TERRIFIC BANG! WINDOWS & DOORS RATTLE
WHERE WAS IT? AS USUAL. ~~OVER~~ IN THE RIVER.
WED. 6.12.44. ~~7.45~~ 7.15 AM. CRASH!! AT NORTHEND, IN PIT
behind garage. NO CASUALTIES
SAT-SUN. 12-30 AM. BIGGEST BANG OF ALL!! LANDED IN
LOWER ROAD. CEILING CAME DOWN ON HEAD. (IN BED)
SUN. EVENING 6.45 P.M. SIRENS going all round the district
6.55 Flying bomb passes by. Same on Monday.
Tues. 7.15 P.M. Siren going. F.B's " " No V2's.
WED. 7.20 A.M. BANG!! Rocket at WELL HALL.
during day = Worst fog for years! TRAFFIC STOPPED.
SUN. 17-12. 4-00 P.M. ROCKET IN DISTANCE. (FIRST SINCE
4.30 AM. THURSDAY) 2ND V2 at 7 P.M. (GREENWICH)
WED. 20TH. 3.00 A.M. CRASH! ROCKET-BOMB ON
CRAYFORD CENTRAL SCHOOL IRON MILL LANE
VERY thick yellow fog all day & NIGHT
Sat 23rd. Weather cleared at last. Very big bang
at 7.00 P.M. Smaller one at 8-00 P.M. (doodle-bugs in
Quiet Christmas. [VERY THICK FROST] the night)
Tuesday 26TH 9.30. ROCKET IN DISTANCE. (WELLING)
FRIDAY . BIG BANG AT 8-00 P.M. (IN THE RIVER)
P.T.O.

Josef Ertl

WEST GERMAN MINISTER OF AGRICULTURE, 1969–83

I grew up on a farm north of Munich. My memories of 1 September 1939 are quite clear because I was sleeping in the attic and heard the dogs barking wildly at 4.20 in the morning. Soon I heard my father's voice calling out to see who it was. The reply was 'The Postman'. He had brought the call-up orders.

It wasn't much later that my father came to wake me and he told me to get a horse, which we called Hans, ready, fed and groomed as it had to be delivered to the *Wehrmacht* in Munich. After I had prepared the horse I left at seven o'clock and rode the fifteen kilometres to Munich and delivered him there to the barracks.

Later my older brother's call-up papers arrived and my father remarked that he had always said that Hitler, the rogue, would start a war and that it would end in catastrophe for Germany.

When, at midday, I got back to my parents' farm from Munich, I heard Hitler's broadcast from Berlin in which he justified the attack on Poland. It sent a shiver up my spine, especially as my father said, 'I don't know if you or your brother will survive the war.'

During the course of the day we were informed that all foodstuffs were now rationed and that we could sell nothing from the farm without a purchase permit. We also received orders for blackout.

I myself had to tell those customers who came to the farm to fetch milk as well as those that I had to deliver to that these deliveries would have to be suspended since from now on the milk would be taken away from us daily.

I also remember clearly that all our friends and relatives were downcast and full of worry about the future. Nobody I met that day showed any pleasure or enthusiasm about the events. A deep mood of sadness prevailed and everyone was hoping that Hitler would pull back and that it would not come to a great world war.

That's how I remember the first day of September 1939, a beautiful autumn day, and I also recall that in the evening I went to the river for a swim to try to ease the oppression a little, especially concerning my father's pessimistic forecast.

Jorg Kastel

WEST GERMAN AMBASSADOR TO USSR

At seventeen, my first term at law school in Switzerland was just over. In order to go on studying in Germany I had to take part in the harvesting ordered by the government. I helped bring in the hay on my parents' farm in the Bavarian foothills. From sunrise we had been moving the grass, the day labourers, the steward's children in a staggered line and me, clumsily swinging the scythe with my blistered hands. We were all sweating heavily, and the beer which the farmworkers had enjoyed earlier as liquid bread was oozing from every pore.

Suddenly Sepp came running, carrying our snack wrapped in cloth. Breathlessly he called out: 'I've just heard on the radio that our troops have invaded Poland!' We straightened our backs, wiped the sweat from our brows and looked at each other: the boys who would shortly be drafted into the army; the girls, Kathi and Mari; the men, with their grey moustaches and broad-brimmed hats shading their eyes, who had fought in the First World War. 'Well,' was all old Bacher said, he who was able to catch trout with his bare hands and with whom it was very difficult to know if he was joking or not. We ate in silence. Then we started raking the grass.

I was confused. 'So war has been declared,' I thought. Hadn't my father told us so in 1933, just after Hitler came to power? 'Under Hitler there will be war. His policies are leading the Reich into bankruptcy, but he won't allow that to happen. He'd rather enforce his ends with terror!' I remembered my white-haired father who had wanted to teach me to drive a car when I was twelve. He eventually escaped from SS bullets by vaulting over the garden fence and managed to find refuge in London. When, as an exchange student, I visited him in his exile in 1937, he told me about Winston Churchill's warnings of the British appeasement policy. Chamberlain's lack of defiance was going to encourage Hitler to continue his adventures on the continent until the British had no choice but to stop him at the last possible moment.

About that time I met and was influenced by Stephen. The youngest in Margaret's spacious cottage in Sussex, a refuge for Spanish children, Viennese musicians and Anja from Charbin in Manchuria, he was only slightly older than me. He spoke little, and never about politics, but rather smiled in a friendly manner, especially when he took me out in his sailing boat. I had a difficult time with his older brothers: every morning they questioned me about how much I understood of the *Daily Worker*, and they took this boy from Nazi Germany to meetings in Whitechapel where the black communist bass Paul Robeson's 'Ol' Man River' boomed from broad chests.

Stephen's mother had sent him to my boarding school in Germany because she thought he should see the other side of the coin as well. With him I had discussed my personal problems, had been allowed to smoke forbidden cigarettes and had been comforted by his sympathy. What was to become of him? I was convinced that England would soon declare war. Certainly Margaret, a resolute pacifist, would talk Stephen into refusing military service. I thought of Munich in September 1938; my schoolmates and I, integrated into the Hitler Youth by the Youth Law, had been taken to Prinzregentenstrasse in our brown uniforms to cheer Daladier, Mussolini, Hitler and Chamberlain, like all the other people who had been summoned to the occasion. Our cheers for the unexpected and peaceful end of the 'Tchen crisis' were genuine, but my enthusiasm was dampened by my father (who had returned from England) when I came home for the weekend. 'Peace in our time!' he had exclaimed. 'Don't make me laugh! This treaty has made war inevitable; in twelve months at the latest it will be here and we will lose it.'

My thoughts strayed back to the Place St François in Lausanne. A few weeks ago I had met all my friends and the students from various parts of the world whom I hoped would be my future friends. Vociferously we had re-lived our past pleasures and planned new ones: boat trips to Évian in France, hiking tours through the Rhône Valley, a *fondue* in a bistro in Ouchy. What was to become of Tom, the wiry and quick-witted Welshman, of the hard-drinking Dutchmen, of Wanda the sad blonde Polish girl, of beautiful Helen the Dane? And would I ever see Marion from Ascona again? When we had danced for the first time at the students' ball she claimed to be Italian. After the dance fellow German students hissed in my ear, 'That girl is a Jewess from Berlin. You know you'd better be careful.' For me she remained Marion, the Italian girl, even when we kissed for the first time outside her hotel and amid tears she whispered, 'It's true that I come from Berlin.' With her last crumpled letter in my pocket I impatiently awaited the next one.

Beside me Sepp murmured 'That's it. Now we'll have to volunteer or they won't take us. If we don't see to it quickly they'll win the war without us.' Yes, Sepp was right. 'My country right or wrong,' it raced through my mind, as though I was answering my father. Surely he would oppose his youngest son's plans to fight in a war which he regarded as the climax of Hitler's crimes. Was the Fatherland not in need of every man; does the rage of war not turn the adolescent into a real man? I had been told so by many books and marching songs, and this electrified me much more than the permanent doubting of the older generation. Yes, I had to join the army.

In the evening we moved the grass from the cart into the barn. My father, supported by a walking stick, watched me with worried eyes.

One year later I was at last allowed to put on the grey uniform. Five years after that I took it off again before the Americans came to my parents' farm. The turmoil of war had brought me there; not a real man, more a tired one. But I was glad that the nightmare was over. My father's spirits were high again now that we had a future to look forward to.

It was much later that I met Sepp again. He was in a bad state and never talked about his service with the SS. Of the friends in Lausanne I lost all trace. Stephen was killed when his ship was torpedoed in the Mediterranean.

A strange uneasy peace began.

PROFESSOR DOCTOR
TADEUSZ KOSZAROWSKI

It is very difficult for me to speak of the 1939–45 war because of the tragedy of those memories. I can only describe briefly my own tale and that of my closest family.

Around 10 September 1939 I joined a battalion of volunteers in the Eastern Territory of the country. After several encounters I was taken prisoner by Soviet forces on

19 September after an unexpected attack from the east. However, I managed to escape and joined a fresh group of the Polish army that was still fighting. This group then continued to fight on two fronts until 7 October and I was then in German captivity until December 1939. In the meantime my home in Warsaw was destroyed by bombs dropped by the Luftwaffe. My mother and my two sisters were killed.

After leaving the prison camp in December – I was discharged because I was a doctor – I participated in activities of the underground army, the Alliance of Armed Combat – Country's Army.

In 1943/4 for four months I was held in a Gestapo prison. After my release, during the Warsaw Uprising, I was on the right bank of the river Vistula which was taken by Polish and Soviet forces on 14 September 1944.

Later after being demobilized I was organizing hospitals in the free part of the city while fighting was still going on. When all of Warsaw was taken by the Soviet troops it was obvious that the city was in ruins, and amongst them was my second home. My brother was killed and so nobody from my immediate family survived. And that is all.

The description of the horror of German occupation and action in the Polish Resistance is beyond my endurance. I am not able to return to those memories and am not able to write about them. With difficulty I try to understand how it was possible to live through those horrible experiences and I can only wish that no other generation should meet such terrible experiences in their lives.

The story of my family is characteristic of that whole generation; over 15 per cent of the Polish population perished during the Second World War.

BRONYA KLIBANSKI

My experiences are from Eastern Poland. I was born in Grodno which was in north-east Poland (it is now part of the Soviet Union) and this area was occupied by the Russians from 1939 to 1941. At the time I was at school. In the beginning of February 1942 I was asked to move to Bialistock because the Socialist Youth Organisation I was in had its centre there. I left my parents and my family behind. Of course I had to travel illegally because as a Jew I was already in the ghetto of Grodno, and it was not permitted for Jews to travel. I had no documents at all and only relying on the fact that I was young and had no Jewish looks did I succeed in getting safely to Bialistock and entering the ghetto there by a trick.

I was active in the underground movement there which later became very strong. From the Warsaw ghetto the Jewish fighting organization sent Josef Tamarov, one of the organizers, to help us. 'Tamarov' was a false name because he travelled all round Poland organizing the resistance movements in different ghettos, like Vilno, Warsaw, Krakow and many others.

To organize the resistance in Bialistock meant bringing together different groups; there were Communists, Zionists and others that had to prepare together to resist. From the start it was clear to all those living in the ghetto that it would be very difficult to fight because most of the buildings were made of wood and so would not give shelter for fighting. But for Tamarov and for the resistance movement it was clear that Jews should fight in the ghetto if there was no real chance to stay alive. We could not win against the Germans, because after all our numbers were not high and the weapons we had were few and of bad quality, so there was no comparison with the German army. For the purpose of fighting, the ghetto was the territory of the Jews – it would give a Jewish expression of doing something against the Germans, not just to cooperate and go, without any resistance, to the gas chambers and the camps. So this was the only place where we as Jews could fight and die as Jews and take action against the Germans.

Not only did Tamarov head the fighting organization in the Bialistock ghetto, but he also organized underground archives to preserve documents, testimonies, memoirs and so on for future generations, because he was very aware of the efforts the Germans made not to leave any traces of their crimes. Today these archives are very important because they are from 1942 and 1943 before the fighting and the liquidation of the Bialistock ghetto, and show not only how Jews behaved and how the underground movement prepared for fighting, but also the atmosphere, the attitude of the Germans, their tactics and the lies they told to their troops to give them confidence.

I myself was in many dangerous situations. I was sent at the end of 1942 to serve as liaison officer outside the ghetto. This meant I had a passport as a Polish girl and lived outside the ghetto. Of course no one had to know I was working for the underground. I was involved in finding the place to keep the archives, in finding out what the Germans were doing, but the most important was travelling as a Polish girl and looking for arms in the country because there were many peasants who, in 1939, fled the Germans and had left their arms and had many places to hid them. So my task was to find them and buy these arms and transport them by train to Bialistock and then on to the ghetto. I looked for Germans to help me. At the time many Polish girls dealt on the black market, bringing food from the country to the city. This was quite normal. To travel I was working as a servant to three Germans who were guards on the trains, and so when they were working on the line where I wanted to go they let me travel without permission (even Poles needed permission to travel). It was too dangerous to ask, so by working with these people I could always go on their trains and many times they kept my luggage to avoid the Germans searching it. But because I had to travel from the country to the station, sometimes twenty or thirty kilometres, and it was too risky for these people to take me, I used to go on ahead by horse and cart.

One day I was taking my valise and I was going to the station when I saw a German soldier. He was at the station to look out for black marketeers. I went straight up to him and asked him when the train was due. He asked me what I had in the valise. I told him it was bacon, butter and oil and all the things which were forbidden, and asked if I should open it. He said 'No' and actually went with me to the train and told the guard to make sure that no one opened my valise.

I was once denounced by a Polish General. She recognized me and I suppose she didn't really want to harm me, but she couldn't keep such a secret and told the Germans I was Jewish. I wouldn't have known except that one morning I went to work and I saw one of the two Germans whose apartment I was going to clean lying on his bed drunk, and the other one beating him fiercely. I said to one German, 'You go out immediately!' Germans are used to obeying orders so he went, but outside he began to shout, 'She is not even a Pole. She is a Jew.' After this they asked me to leave the city. But I didn't want to flee because I thought that once I ran away I would just continue to run, so I waited to see what would happen. The next day I went to work and one of the Germans, called Kaldenbach, spoke to me in a more familiar way than usual. I spoke Yiddish but my German was not too good, only what I had learned from books in the ghetto, so sometimes I got Jewish words mixed up with the German. He asked me if what I had said was German so I said, 'Herr Kaldenbach, you're right. You know, it could be Yiddish!' He was rather perplexed, but after that everything was all right.

We had small partisan groups in the forest who continued to fight against the Germans. So people fled, escaped from the ghettos and trains and later, after the fighting in the ghettos, my task was to organize their safe escape through the woods. One part of this was to continue to deliver arms to these people. One of our group of five or six girls wanted to help, but she was arrested by the Gestapo and badly wounded when trying to escape.

At the time I had a room in an apartment. I was sharing with a Polish woman and for a week I hid some Jewish girls. The neighbour suspected I was a Jew and the Gestapo came. The officer asked if I was Jewish or a friend of Jews. I looked so German they did not want to believe I was Jewish; it would have upset their stories. I said 'Of course I'm Jewish!' and laughed. He took it as a joke.

We decided that two of the girls who didn't look Jewish would go to the Labour Office and ask for work. They then had to go to the Gestapo for interrogation before being sent to Germany, where they stood a chance of survival. One day a Gestapo officer came and asked if I knew those girls were Jewish. I said I knew they were Polish. He asked to see my papers. I didn't know what to do so I told him I wouldn't show my papers to him, only to a real German Gestapo officer. I don't know if he was, but he left. I wondered whether they would come back or if the German Gestapo would come. I understood why the girls had said I knew they were Jewish: it was to save their own lives, so I couldn't say I didn't know them. I decided to stay because if I had left it would have been proof against me.

By the summer of 1943 I decided it was getting too dangerous and I would have to leave the ghetto. But how? It was unusual for a Polish girl not to live with her family and it would have been suspicious to look for a room; the Germans had all the best rooms anyway.

The husband of the lady in whose apartment I lived was a Polish army officer and he was in captivity. The lady was very nice and helped Secret Service officers. Everyone had to go through my room to reach the other. She was not interested in whether I was a Jew or not and helped me a great deal, but she was sure I was Polish. So one morning I went to where one of her officers was and told the guards I wanted to see him. He was very surprised but he agreed to see me, and was very embarrassed because the Germans did not approve of such friendships. He asked me, not very politely, what I wanted. I told him about everyone passing through my room even when I was in bed, that I didn't like it. I told him I wanted another room, and that all the good rooms with separate entrances were for the Germans. He replied, 'Yes. It should be so!' I told him if I changed it would only be to a better room. He laughed but telephoned to the German office for rooms, the Department for German Housing in the occupied city, and requested a permit for me to have a room reserved for Germans. I found a room; the Polish landlady thought I was collaborating with the Germans, that was the only explanation for getting this room. I thought it was better to be suspected of collaborating than of being a Jew, and I stayed in this room until Liberation.

Afterwards I visited this woman many times. She was very nice but didn't suspect I was a Jew. One day, telling me quite confidentially not to tell anyone, she said, 'You know Maritia Rifelin? She probably was a converted Jewess.' I asked her why she thought that and she told me that at night Maritia was very breathless – it was probably her Jewish soul struggling because she had converted! This is how our people were painted.

JOHN DAVIES

I was then working in the London office of an Italian insurance company which, until Mussolini followed Hitler's policy of anti-Semitism, had also been fundamentally a Jewish business. I think that I was unusually aware of the evil things that were happening in parts of Europe. I had met many members of the staff passing through the London office on their way to begin new lives, many in South America, some in Canada or Australia. Many had fled in turn first from Austria and then from Czechoslovakia. They were people of outstanding ability and amazing resilience. I remember carrying a bag for one man who was on his way to the Brussels office (having left both Vienna and Prague) and his remark, 'Who knows?' Within months, the Germans were in occupation of Belgium. Who knows if he was successful in escaping a third time?

Although I am a critic of the policy of 'appeasement' (and I feel strongly that had firm action been taken, by Britain and France in particular, to check Mussolini's invasion of Abyssinia, Hitler would not have embarked on his policy of expansion), I recall the sense of relief at the Munich Agreement.

For me, 3 September has an added significance as marking an anniversary. Exactly three years later, in 1942, soon after dawn on that date, I was among the crew of a Wellington bomber which crashed in France while returning from a target in Germany. Three of us survived to spend the remainder of the war in Germany. Because I am so conscious of the horrors of the concentration camps I have always felt it right to declare that during a period of two years in a prisoner of war camp in Germany accommodating ten thousand prisoners I neither saw, nor heard any reports of, brutality. Sanitation and many other aspects were bad, however, and it would have been almost intolerable without the weekly food parcels from the Red Cross. Yet these parcels were distributed when the Germans themselves were on minimum rations.

HERMANN BLASCHKO

Let me introduce myself: I was born in Berlin, the then capital of Germany, in the year 1900. Thus, I can remember the beginning of two world wars. In August 1914, as a schoolboy, I stood in a huge crowd outside the Imperial Palace in Berlin and heard the Kaiser make the speech from the balcony that began World War I. It was the jingoism of the crowd that I experienced on that occasion that has forever given me a distaste for mass assemblies.

I started life as a German, and I remained in Germany until 1933. I then left my homeland for good because of my Jewish origin that gave me no hope of a job in Nazi Germany. My emigration to England was made easier by two fortunate circumstances: I had been in England before, as a research student at University College, London for a year from 1929–30 and had made many good friends during my stay. Secondly, my mother had two sisters who had settled in London with their husbands in the 1880s.

I spent one year in London, and in the summer of 1934 I moved to Cambridge, where I earned my living by teaching medical students. I stayed in Cambridge for almost ten years; so I was there at the time of the outbreak of World War II. By that time I had acquired British nationality by naturalization; fortunately my mother had also been able to leave Germany – she had arrived in England on the day Hitler marched into Prague in April 1939. When the bombings started, I was at first not allowed to join the Air Defence activities as an 'Ex-enemy Alien', but this rule was soon rescinded and I then took my part. I was leader of a 'Street Party' in the area where I lived, and also at my place of work where I had to spend about one night a week. I still have, as a momento, the tail end of an incendiary bomb I helped to extinguish near my place of work!

Since many of my younger and more energetic colleagues had moved away, in order to do some work more directly relevant to the war effort, my workload had increased. In a way, I was glad about this. In peacetime I had been given students mainly in order to enable me to earn my living, but now I felt I was really needed. I am glad to say that quite a number of the students I have taught have done extremely well and have made substantial contributions, and I am still friendly with a number of them. I also taught a number of science students, and amongst these are several distinguished scientists, even some Nobel prize winners.

A great number of academic refugees from Germany and Central Europe had arrived in Britain much later than I had, so they were still citizens of their countries of origin. This meant that they were classified as 'Enemy Aliens'. In consequence, they were subjected to a great number of restrictions. Finally, in the summer of 1940, when the war took on more threatening aspects, many of the men were interned and quite a number of them were shipped overseas, to Australia or Canada. As the war progressed and the danger of imminent invasion receded, wiser counsels prevailed! Here was a reservoir of men with a variety of needed abilities that had to be tapped. In consequence, special tribunals were set up, to sort out the people who had been interned. I had many contacts with a voluntary organization that had helped displaced scholars from Central Europe to find suitable places of work in this country and overseas, and had myself been helped by a grant from this body, the 'Society for the Protection of Science and Learning', during my first two years in Cambridge. It is still operating today. The Society had been charged with the task of providing material to the tribunals that had to scrutinize the interned scientists and doctors. I was close at hand and was able to help; it was gratifying to help people to get out of internment, be reunited with their families and enabled to do useful work.

GENERAL CHAIM HERZOG

PRESIDENT OF THE STATE OF ISRAEL

I was a law student at University College in London, to which I had come from my home in Jerusalem. It was a Sunday morning and people carrying their kitbags were rushing about to join their units. I heard Chamberlain's radio address to the nation, announcing the declaration of war against Germany; the world seemed to be coming to an end.

The air raid sirens sounded. The air raid wardens, newly activated, stopped all traffic. I went into a shelter in a public building, into which numbers of people were filing in an orderly British fashion. To my consternation they were all carrying gas masks. In one's mind's eye one foresaw a terrible blitz and poison gas. But the All Clear came soon: it had been a false alarm. Needless to say, the gas mask was never again forgotten!

At the University I was a member of the Officer Cadet Training Unit. When invasion seemed imminent, all the trainees became members of the Defence Forces, linked with the Home Guard in Cambridge. As a resident of Palestine, I was not conscripted. As the Nazi threat to freedom everywhere and the terrible fate facing the Jews became ever clearer, I felt compelled to join the army and volunteered. I was to advance with the British forces invading Europe and freeing not only subject populations but also the pitiful remnants of the Jewish communities.

John Kilyan

I was born in Poland and in 1939 at the start of the war I was 11½ years old and living with a family who had adopted me. (As a baby I had been left on the doorstep of a house in Lvov.) I spent the first twenty-two months of the war in a home in Odessa in Russia, but one night they caught me praying, which wasn't allowed, and so I had to run away. Until 1942, at the outbreak of the German-Russian war, I went back to Poland. To survive there it was necessary to trade in the Jewish ghettos on the black market. While travelling by train to get food with which to trade I was arrested by the Gestapo when the train was impounded, and together with all the other passengers sent to Germany to do forced labour. This happened in May 1943.

I was sent to a place called Baden-Baden where I worked for a year as a forced labourer on a farm, but I was badly treated and decided to escape. When I did manage to get away I went to Regensburg in Bavaria and was taken on by another farmer, but again the treatment was very bad. On one particular occasion, after I had done the milking the farmer wanted to send me into the fields. There was a heavy frost on the ground, and the farmer sent me to work in bare feet. When I asked for shoes he said 'You Polish swine. You can walk barefoot until you die.' I got hold of a fork and hit him. Twenty minutes later the Gestapo arrived and I ended up being sent to Dachau.

After arriving in the back of a lorry I was shaven, given my prisoner's uniform, put in a barracks and put to work. In the beginning we did hard labour, which consisted of rock breaking, ground levelling, road making and building, until we became too weak to work. With the starvation diet this took only two or three months. Breakfast consisted of half a litre of black coffee without sugar and one hundred milligrams of black bread. At midday we had one litre of soup made from flour, boiling water, waste food and scraps. In the evening we had a half-litre of black coffee. The high spot of our week was Wednesday when we had soup made from Red Cross food packages. These packages and parcels had all been confiscated.

Because of the bad food and conditions – generally there were twenty-five people per block in triple bunks, and anywhere between 12,000 and 17,000 in the camp at any one time – disease was rife. Lice and fleas were common. To protest these conditions brought instant punishment which could take any one of many forms. Bad behaviour, stealing and protest were met by an automatic beating and torture which consisted of hanging by the wrists. This was for a minimum of twenty minutes and a maximum of thirty-five. Another form of torture was to pile four or five men on top of each other and place a board over them which the Germans would then use like a see-saw. For bigger punishments people would be put in a three-foot by three-foot room for twenty-four hours, in total darkness, with constantly dripping water. These punishments, although they seem horrific, are just a small part of the things that really went on.

After three months in Dachau I became too weak to work and so I spent my time permanently in the camp. I spent much of my time crawling around amongst the dead bodies searching for crusts. When you had reached this stage of being too weak to walk you were taken to the sick-bay and given injections to make you even weaker in order to prepare you for the ovens.

Fortunately for me, the American army liberated the camp about three weeks before I was due to be burnt. I weighed just over four stones.

Ursula Fischer

I lived with my parents in a small place in East Thuringia, about twelve miles away from the town of Greitz. It was a sunny, warm Sunday and I was sitting at the window eating wonderfully juicy peaches. I was listening to the dance music coming from the café on the opposite side of the street.

Suddenly this music was drowned by the clatter of horses, the rattling of wheels and people marching in step. A long column of soldiers in heavy marching order appeared, wearing uniforms and field packs. They were on their way from our place to Greitz. I remembered the rumour I had heard during the preceding days, that there might be a war started in Poland, and a shudder passed down my spine. But I immediately thought of Hitler who had everything under control. For us, Hitler was like a miracle-worker. Whatever he had got hold of, had always been successful.

Ina Ender-Lautenschlager

At the outbreak of the Second World War fifty years ago I was in Berlin, at the time the capital of Germany. I was twenty-two years old, married and the mother of a three year old son. I was employed at an exclusive fashion house. I liked the job a lot and met many interesting people.

But this was only one side of the coin. The other side was that since 1935 I, my husband and a few friends had been members of an illegal resistance group which fought against Nazi rule in our fatherland. We had been following the political developments of those years with both watchful and alarmed eyes and had experienced the Nazis' terrorist practices ourselves. In 1939 some of my friends and myself had seen the fascist prisons from the inside, but we didn't let them intimidate us. With handbills and other propaganda action we tried to inform people about the barbarous policies being pursued by the Nazis and to shake them into resistance in the pre-war years. In the summer of 1939 we also hoped that England, France and the Soviet Union would put a stop to the aggressive intentions of the Hitler government and so prevent war. Unfortunately England and France behaved quite destructively during negotiations with the USSR. Thus a joint effort of the European great powers against fascist Germany was thwarted. Instead Hitler's government was incited to become more unreasonable in its demands towards Poland to return Danzig to Germany. Their tone became very threatening.

Further events occurred in rapid succession; on Sunday 27 August 1939 food ration cards for September were given out to families all over Germany. At the same time many men in the neighbourhood received their call-up orders from the *Wehrmacht*. Those were alarming signs for an impending armed conflict with neighbouring Poland. Therefore I was not surprised when on the evening of 31 August the Nazis staged a provocation against Gleiwitz radio station which then provided them with the excuse to attack Poland on the following day, Friday 1 September 1939.

For me and many of my countrymen, if they had not already succumbed to the chauvinist Nazi propaganda, this day was known henceforward as 'Black Friday'. I was very worried about my husband who had already been serving in the army for one year. We were naive enough to hope that the Western powers would stop the Nazi aggressor by military force after they had declared war on the Hitler government on Sunday 3 September. But again, like the Sudeten crisis in the autumn of 1938, we were disappointed; Poland, left alone by her allies, was overrun within days and the state of Poland broken.

On the western border of Germany, favoured by the military inactivity of England and France, the so-called 'comic war' began, and nothing really changed for many months. This enabled the Nazis to prepare their next *blitzkrieg*.

For me and my friends the situation gave no grounds for remaining passive. Our attitude was as follows: filled by a boundless hatred of Hitler we were prepared, together with other anti-fascists, to work with all our power for an end to the war and the overthrow of the Nazi regime. Immediately after the declaration of war we intensified our activities, distributing leaflets in Berlin and amongst the soldiers of the 'Westwall' where my husband was. In this way we wanted to demonstrate that the resistance against Hitler was not dead but very much alive.

In the meantime I found other opportunities. Amongst the clientele of the fashion house, for which I was working as a model, were the wives and lady friends of important Nazi officials and top military officers. Eva Braun, Hitler's mistress and later wife, and the wives of Reichsmarshall Goering, of von Ribbentrop the Minister for Foreign Affairs, of Goebbels the Minister of Propaganda, of Field Marshal von Bruachitsch, were among them. Those ladies, whom I was to assist in their selection of garments, were very friendly towards me and chatted openly and affably. The atmosphere was quite intimate. As time went by I managed to associate with them in a rather informal way. They spoke casually of their luxurious life-style and their opinions of the war, both of which contrasted glaringly with the conditions the majority of the population had to suffer during the war years. Very cautiously we used this knowledge for an illegal education campaign amongst the people.

After Germany's attack on the Soviet Union in June 1941 I started cautiously to guide the conversations of these high-ranking, garrulous ladies towards the unconscious disclosure of information concerning the plans of the fascist war lords. Thus I managed to elicit the information that Nazi leaders were planning a celebration of their triumph in Moscow on 7 November. During the late summer the ladies had their appropriate wardrobes made by the fashion house, and Eva Braun, after I had a harmless conversation on fashion, was drawn to make some useful remarks; of course she was totally ignorant of my other identity. For her I was just the popular Frau Ina. All the information that our group managed to gather was radioed to our Russian friends.

As early as 1939 we had been closely connected with the resistance group led by Harro Schulz-Boysen and Arvid Harnack. They coordinated our activities and made the information we assembled available to the Soviet resistance. Our organization later became quite famous as 'The Red Chapel'. In the long run, though, our work could not remain hidden from the *Abwehr*. They began to hunt us down, but not before the summer of 1942 did they manage to trace our resistance group. On the morning of 16 September 1942 I was arrested in my apartment in Berlin by two members of the Gestapo. The Nazis' revenge was terrible. Many friends were sentenced to death or lifelong imprisonment. After months of detention and interrogation I was sent to prison for six years.

On 7 May 1945 I was released by the Red Army. Immediately I and my surviving friends started to help remove the physical and spiritual ruins that twelve years of Hitler's rule and a terrible war had left.

A short afterthought:
After half a century I can objectively relate the activities of my illegal work which more than anything else influenced my youth. How often was I afraid, did my heart beat faster, thoughts rushing through my brain. The feelings, the driving force behind the years of double life, can be easily explained: we were young, eager to live, with strong

opinions about what was happening then; we fought for ourselves, for our children, our families and friends, for a peaceful, just future.

We despised nationalism and racism, but we were forced to witness the infamous and inhuman subjugation of the German people and other nations, the extermination of people who did not share the Nazi ideology, and the provocation of the bloodiest war of all time in order to obtain world domination. This is what we fought against.

REAR ADMIRAL
J.H. ADAMS

At 11.42 a.m. on 3 September I was Second Officer of the Watch in HMS *Walker* carrying out a patrol for the protection of shipping in St George's Channel together with another destroyer, HMS *Walpole*. At that moment a signalman showed me a flash signal, which carried the terse text 'Commence hostilities at once with Germany'. I have a copy of the signal beside me as I write and I can recall the feeling of relief that seemed to go round the bridge as we received the news. The nation, and certainly the Navy, which had mobilized two weeks before and had done the same exercise the year before as well, had been in a state of tension for many months as Hitler had started his annexations in Europe. In a sense it was good to feel that a decision had been made at last and we could start helping the Poles, albeit at a distance, who were under attack on three of their frontiers.

Ten minutes later *Walpole* got a good Asdic contact and carried out what must have been the first depth charge attack of the war. Alas it was only a shoal of fish, which popped to the surface with their bladders forced out through their mouths with the shock of the explosions. We did not stop to pick any up, although at that stage we had not learnt that freshly-killed fish taste differently to fish that have been around for a day or more.

This depth charge attack was to give at least one of our crew a wrong idea within a few hours. We were by then escorting a small cargo vessel, the *Corinthic* of Glasgow. While investigating an Asdic contact, we prepared to carry out a depth charge attack. One of the depth charge crew, who as a reservist had only joined the ship a few days before, fired a depth charge on the preparatory order from the bridge rather than waiting for the order 'FIRE'. The explosion panicked the *Corinthic*'s crew, who lowered the two lifeboats, jumping into them as they went down in erratic jerks to the water line. Someone hoisted the Red Ensign upside-down as a sign of distress while the ship's safety valve to her boilers lifted with a roar of escaping steam. All was chaos and it took us two hours to persuade the crew that there was no submarine about and that they should rejoin their ship and rehoist their boats, which they eventually did with great difficulty. Of such stuff are the many unrecorded incidents of war – except that I kept a journal and my notes vividly recall that day to me now.

When not on watch, I seemed to spend the rest of the day, and night, deciphering the mass of signals coming in – as one would expect on the first day of war. Would that we had had today's technology to help us then, as coding and decoding signals by hand and book took a long, long time.

I recall turning in for a short while before the middle watch that evening, getting into my pyjamas and thence the bunk in my cabin under the torpedo tubes, in a very weary state. Within eight days we and another destroyer, the *Vanquisher*, were to have a head-on collision at speed at night, with fifteen men killed. I was never again to take off all my clothes while at sea until the end of the war, some 5½ years later. You can't be ready for any emergency in pyjamas!

For me the war started 'at once'. I learnt a new lesson every hour. At the gunnery school, HMS *Excellency*, two weeks before, all the Sub-Lieutenants were fallen in and given ships to join from a list read out as an officer went down the ranks. The three on my left were told to join a ship abroad and were killed as their Sunderland flying-boat crashed on take-off the following day. Had I fallen in a few seconds later and been further down the line, I would have been one of those three. I suddenly and naively realized that it did not necessarily require the enemy in order to be killed. Life had suddenly become much more precious and one became more aware of the world about one in an increasingly appreciative manner; and never before had the Boy Scout motto 'Be prepared' seemed more relevant.

Adrianus Cardinal Simonis

ARCHBISHOP OF UTRECHT

I remember the outbreak of World War II very well. Early in the morning my father had received a telephone call informing him that it had happened. It was a beautiful day in spring. I was nine years old and had read in books about 'war'. I had the idea that soldiers would appear in the streets and kill all the 'enemies'. I remember that I went to church straight away, to attend Mass and to make my confession for the last time, as I thought. I was convinced it would be the last day of my life! As the day passed, the sky became more and more blue, my childish ideas of war became more and more realistic, but the contrast between the glorious beauty of nature and the misery that people can inflict on each other became ever greater.

This contrast continued to strike me throughout the war:

God's purpose with men and the world, and the absolute madness that evil people can perpetrate; but also the impotent anger at so much injustice. During the years the war lasted I became increasingly aware of this and my sense grew that all suffering and injustice comes from the Evil One. But I also got a growing awareness of the heroic power of people who resisted the violence of war: the resistance fighters, the Americans, the English, the Canadians, who did their utmost to regain our liberty for us.

To this day I pray that all these sacrifices and all this suffering may not have been in vain, that we may use our liberty, which was regained at the cost of such a fierce struggle, in the service of love and peace, rooted in the truth, which is Christ.

J. JAMIESON

At the outbreak of the war I was twenty years of age, a submariner, and had served in the Royal Navy for the past four years, finding it to be an enjoyable and satisfying life. I had travelled widely, learning something about the ways of other countries, and together with my messmates had socialized with our counterparts in the German and Italian naval forces, finding them to be much the same as ourselves.

In September 1939, I was serving in a submarine based on Malta. On the outbreak of war, the tempo in the Mediterranean changed little, the war at sea being mainly confined to the Atlantic and Northern waters; after a few uneventful patrols we left Malta and were based at Alexandria, where after Italy's declaration of war we sailed for a patrol in the vicinity of the Dodecanese Islands. Apart from one or two small distractions this patrol was uneventful.

Our next patrol was to the Gulf of Taranto, situated at the toe of Italy and on the main enemy convoy route to North

Africa. On 31 July we sighted an enemy convoy and carried out an attack, firing two torpedoes. No hits were registered. We surfaced at midnight on 1 August, and shortly after were rammed by the Italian destroyer *Vivaldi* just aft of the conning tower. She had presumably been searching for us since the attack on the convoy the previous day. We were still at 'Diving Stations' in the fore-ends and did not know what had happened until the word was passed forward to 'Abandon Ship', and we left through the forehatch. I remember vividly that as she went down and sank below the surface the light from the tube-space was still shining.

After some hours in the sea, the survivors were picked up by the destroyer's boats, and we were landed early next morning at the naval base at Taranto. We were well treated here and quartered in the naval hospital staffed by a religious order. The following day we were interviewed by a rather smooth character, a naval intelligence officer who had apparently at some stage in his career been a schoolmaster domiciled in Hull. He was very liberal with the cigarettes and coffee, but as the Geneva Convention requires that a POW need only state his name, rank and official number, I do not think that he learned anything of value. Mind you, a few of the more imaginative amongst us did volunteer the somewhat spurious information that our engines had been manufactured by Messrs. Crosse & Blackwell and that our torpedoes were Type 57 Heinz Mark Fives. We were then kitted up with a fairly comprehensive outfit of clothing, the main item being Italian naval overalls with a large 'P.G.' in red stitched on the back and on one leg, denoting that we were POWs.

We stayed in Taranto for about a fortnight and adapted to our new environment. On the whole we were well treated, although we found the change of diet hard to stomach. Eventually we were entrained under a strong guard and embarked on an eighteen-hour journey to Venice, where our final destination was a small island in Venice lagoon called Poveglia. Over the years it had fulfilled many purposes. A religious order had once lived there, but more recently it had been a sanitorium for the tubercular. It was sparsely furnished with three-tiered bunk beds and stone floors, and we were issued with Italian rations: pasta, olive oil, puree, rice and similar items of Italian cuisine. The results, as we prepared them, were pretty unpalatable, but we soon learned.

We were guarded by about fifty soldiers from a fascist regiment who quickly became housetrained. Unfortunately, there were also a dozen carabinieri, distinctly unfriendly and quite willing to demonstrate the fact. Our compound was surrounded by a high wire fence, and the dead ground to the beach boasted three rows of barbed wire. The distance to the mainland was three miles or so. We were permitted a limited amount of freedom outside the compound, and usually two of us would pay a daily visit to the Italian administrative block under guard, ostensibly to enquire about mail or any other excuse, but in reality to steal anything we could lay our hands on with an eye to future usefulness. Our prize acquisition was a pair of secateurs stolen from the gardener. We also manufactured our own compass, a relatively simple matter.

By this time, after six weeks of captivity during which time Italian hospitality had begun to pall, I and my friends Stan Dryer, Spike Hunt and Jack Tooes agreed that it was time we went home. We were fully confident that we would have no difficulty in leaving the island, our main problem being that geographically Italy is an extremely difficult place from which to escape. Surrounded by sea on three sides, the only alternative is north over the mountain route to Switzerland. Bearing in mind our sparse resources this was not considered to be a viable option.

We decided, therefore, that if possible we would steal a boat and make our way to Yugoslavia, which at that time was neutral. Meanwhile we cultivated those guards who were English speaking, and gleaned from them as much local information as possible. Our few remaining personal possessions were bartered for Italian chocolate and other items. Finally on a Saturday evening, chosen because the guards would be more relaxed at the weekend, we unstitched the 'P.G.' from our overalls and shortly after dark arranged a diversion. A huge metal store cupboard was overturned on to the stone floor, the resulting noise reverberating throughout the building. A willing volunteer was inserted under it and proceeded to issue the most blood-curdling screams. As the duty guards rushed through the main gate and the front door, we left by the back door.

We scaled the wire fence, cut through a succession of barbed wire fences, and on reaching the beach tossed the secateurs into the lagoon. Lacing our boots together round our necks we then swam fully-clothed towards the mainland, some five kilometres distant. We landed on the causeway leading directly to Venice, one side bordering the lagoon and the other the Adriatic. We headed north towards Venice, keeping our eyes open for any boat that might be suitable for the purpose. Shortly after, a carabiniere came cycling towards us on the other side of the road, carbine slung over his shoulder. As he neared us he waved and shouted something in Italian. We waved back and shouted *Buona notte* and he cycled on. We had thus exhausted two of the six words from our Italian vocabulary.

After about four miles, we realized that our search for a boat was futile, and decided to skirt Venice and head east towards Trieste and the border. Soon we began to encounter a few civilians and entered Venice itself. There was no blackout, and the city was thronged with people enjoying their Saturday evening. We split into pairs and mingled with them as they left a cinema, with no one giving us a second glance.

Passing the Lido, we struck off towards the east, reaching the shoreline once again (now a well known holiday resort) at about midnight, and just before dawn turned inland. The countryside was mainly agricultural, and there were few people about. We found a quiet place to rest, eat and review the situation. With hindsight, we were wrongly dressed for a long journey, poorly provisioned, and of course at that time we had little knowledge of the language. We were recaptured four days later, spent the night in the local police station, and thence to Venice naval base. We were placed in separate cells but were otherwise well treated, except that all requests for a wash were greeted with the reply '*Domani, domani*,' a word that we were to become very familiar with in the years to come. Actually, we must have looked pretty villainous, as we hadn't bathed or shaved for almost a week. An Italian sailor did give me a bottle of scent, but it smelled worse than I did, so I gave it to Spike. I hope he didn't drink it.

The following morning we were taken before the Italian Naval C-in-C, no less. He was a dear old thing in a most splendid uniform, and much bemedalled. He told us through an interpreter that he had fought with the British in World War I, that he was very sorry to see us here, and that we were very brave young men.

We agreed. Loudly. *Si, si*. We were rapidly becoming bilingual.

He went on to say that we had been very naughty, we had tied up hundreds of men for nearly a week searching for us, and that we must be punished.

We disagreed. Silently.

I felt sorry for him, for the next day three of our officers were to disappear, to be searched for all over northern Italy. They were discovered seven days later, having spent the time in the loft immediately over the *Commandante*'s office. Sadly, they weren't as fortunate as us and were treated rather badly when discovered.

The following day, we were manacled and escorted by eighteen armed guards, six carabinieris and one lieutenant and entrained for our journey south.

Our destination was Fonti di Amore, which struck us as being a rather quaint name for a prison camp. It was situated in the Abruzzi Mountains in the province of Aquilla. We were told by our escort that escape would be impossible from there. Once the train got under way, the soldiers took off their jackets and boots, and immediately went to sleep. The carabinieris kept awake, and we never saw the officer for the rest of the journey. We did however manage to toss one of the soldiers' boots out of the window. It was an eighteen-hour journey and although we were given something to eat, our manacles were not removed for the whole of that time. On arrival there was some delay as the *tenente* was understandably cross at noticing one of his escort marching along at the rear with only one boot. Actually, the laugh was on us as we were marched to the cells, given a moth-eaten, smelly blanket, and there we stayed for the next thirty days.

No fountain.

No love.

Conditions were appalling. There were no sanitary or washing facilities, and we saw no one except at noon every day when our rations were handed through the door. On the eighteenth day we were visited by a young Italian officer to whom we protested strongly about the conditions and told him that his jail wasn't fit for pigs. He countered by saying that it was good enough for Italian troops. There wasn't a diplomatic reply to that, so we pointed out that Italy was a signatory to the Geneva Convention and should abide by it, and so on, *ad int*. Spike, forever the humorist, said he would write to the council. In the event, from then on we were given two hours of exercise daily, which was a relief in more ways than one.

On the thirtieth day we were released and taken under escort to the main compound where we were welcomed back by our messmates, although it was noticeable that they tended to keep a little upwind of us. However, after countless buckets of cold water, a change of borrowed clothing and a shave, we were as good as new. For my sins, I would later spend two more periods in this home-from-home, although due to the influence of the Red Cross and the protecting powers it was to become slightly more comfortable. Not a lot.

We have all seen prison camps depicted on TV and film. This one was no exception. Long huts accommodating eighty men in wooden bunk beds. Acres of barbed wire and floodlit watchtowers by night. As the fighting escalated in North Africa, a trickle of allied prisoners began to arrive, together with the odd RAF bomber crew, until eventually the compound was full to capacity by midsummer 1941: just under a thousand men.

Mail from home started to arrive, and the Red Cross parcels to augment our meagre Italian rations. These were issued fortnightly, one between two, a wise decision on the part of the Senior British Officer, for the supply was uncertain and the winter in that area was cold and hard. A few words about these parcels: each contained ten pounds of staple foods, i.e. porridge, tea, sugar, meat, margarine, milk powder, chocolate, dried fruit, oxo, etc. – and soap. Each parcel was different and this resulted in much swapping. Porridge was the favourite as it was most filling. As each was issued between two men, virtually everyone paired off during their stay in the camp, leading to some unlikely combinations and to friendships that were sustained long after the war ended.

Day-to-day life in the camp would have made an interesting study for a student of sociology, for with the introduction of conscription the Armed Forces at that time consisted of men from all walks of life. Our population therefore was made up of all strata of society. They integrated well, possibly because all were equal. Every trade and profession was represented. There were tailors, bank managers, actors, musicians, accountants, teachers, farm workers and even a locksmith and a wig-maker. Also among them were many brilliant men who after the war went on to become well-known personalities in their chosen spheres.

It would not be unusual to see a former stevedore carefully cutting razor-thin slices of bread, scrupulously apportioned, whilst his chum, a former accountant, would be outside coaxing a flame from a fire built with a broken bedboard, busily brewing tea. I like to think that both these men, and many others like them, totally different in many respects, learned much from each other.

We gradually became organized. Books sent from home were, after reading, donated to the camp library. Classes were formed, for there were men both qualified and willing to pass their knowledge on to others.

By agreement with our respective governments we were paid one lira per day, the equivalent today of one new penny. This was not spent on riotous living, but was paid in camp currency and could only be spent with the Italians. It was deducted from our pay on return to the UK. Unfortunately, the Italians didn't exactly have a lot to offer, resulting in some strange purchases. For instance, on one occasion we were offered a load of chestnuts and for the next few weeks we enjoyed Chestnut Soup: grated chestnuts boiled with the addition of Red Cross oxo; Chestnut Porridge: grated chestnuts boiled together with Red Cross milk powder; Chestnut Duff: grated chestnuts with Red Cross raisins and a little bread baked over an open fire. And so on.

Many of the guards could be corrupted, usually with English cigarettes or soap, and in return we would receive either information or materials likely to be of value in an escape attempt. Even the visiting priest was not averse to a little black marketeering. We stole everything from the Italians that wasn't screwed down. If it was, we took the screws as well.

From time to time a hut would be searched, but such was

our intelligence that we usually knew which hut was to be turned over and at what time, and it was seldom that anything was found.

There were many attempts to escape. This was not particularly heroic, it simply stemmed from a desire to return home, frustration, boredom, and a feeling of satisfaction at having put one over on the Italians. The rules were quite simple. If discovered whilst breaking out of the camp, one could be shot if not surrendering when challenged. This was legitimate. A calculated risk. Having successfully overcome this hurdle it was important not to get caught stealing or assaulting a civilian. This carried a long civilian gaol sentence. All that one had to do then was to find a way out of the country and go home. In point of fact, this was rarely achieved until the Allies landed in Italy.

It was also important to remember that in general the Italians are a most excitable race, and in the event of the escapee being recaptured by a crowd of Italian peasants, each of them is likely to want to relate to his grandson in the years to come that he singlehandedly overpowered a huge desperate eight foot tall English brigand. This usually results in a very bruised escapee.

Hitherto, this narrative has been written in a somewhat lighthearted vein. It wasn't quite like that.

Unlike a normal gaol sentence, which is a fixed term, ours was indeterminate in that we did not know if and when we would be returning home. In some instances, men would receive letters from home revealing that their wives and children had been killed in a bombing raid. Others would learn that a similar fate had befallen other members of the family. This news would arrive months after the actual occurrence, and he would be worried about not receiving any mail. This news would have been bad enough at home, but for a prisoner it would have been devastating. Others would learn that their wives had been unfaithful. Personally, I lost my mother and ultimately my home. My brother was shot down over Germany, fortunately surviving. There was nothing one could do but mourn.

Medical attention was inadequate, and some died who with proper care would have survived. There were cases of ill-treatment, and on one occasion two carabinieris in a drunken brawl shot dead two of our fellows for no reason at all.

Above all, we were hungry. And in the long winter, cold and hungry.

Added to this, although they did not yet know it, many would spend a further two years as prisoners in Germany. And yet, despite all this, I cannot recall anyone ever expressing their doubts as to the outcome of the war.

As for my partners in crime in Venice, we later became separated, but Jack crossed the border into Switzerland, was interned for a time, and returned home. Spike escaped and lived with an Italian family, before being betrayed to the Germans, and spent the rest of the war in Germany. He returned home in 1945, broken in health. Stan and myself reached the UK in the latter part of 1943 and returned to service in submarines.

I do not bear any ill-will towards the Italians. They are a warm and happy people, and theirs is a beautiful country with a fascinating history and a musical language, with their art, architecture and music being rightly renowned throughout the world.

LIEUTENANT-COLONEL PEDER KLEPSVIK

But why a small rowing boat? Why not a larger vessel, preferably a motor or steamboat? The answer was simple: there was no larger boat in our possession on the island.

The island – Lindøy in Finnås-Bomlø, approximately three

miles long and one mile wide – housed my parents, five sisters, four cows, one horse, one pig, a couple of dozen sheep, some hens, all tied into a happy combination of a small farmer-fisherman's way of family life. Not much to live on, you might say. Perhaps so. However, thinking back, we were content and reasonably happy, all of us helping to make ends meet.

I had already had an experience of war, having been detained by the Russians in Archangel in November/December 1939, bound for the UK with timber. However, we were eventually released and made our way to Hull early in 1940. Returning to Norway, I signed off, having been called up to serve in the Navy from May 1940. At the age of twenty I was, in my own opinion, an experienced sailor.

And so came 9 April 1940. What a day! Our defence having been totally neglected, we had no chance whatsoever and, what is more, we had been spared from wars for almost 130 years. I hurried to report to our local county sheriff, whose duty it was to direct the local mobilization. Since I had no previous military training, I was ordered to return home and await further instructions.

Then came 16 April. The western part of Norway was overrun and surrendered to the enemy. There was still fighting going on in the north, but it was evident that a surrender was inevitable there also.

One evening, a friend of the family, Mr Johannes Baldersheim, came to our island. Johannes had already been to the local sheriff protesting the surrender. In his opinion this was in opposition to the Norwegian Constitution. He suggested an escape to the UK and, as I said before, since we possessed only small rowing boats, we soon agreed to use one of those rather than 'borrow' (steal) a larger vessel. Our country was at war. We had some knowledge of what kind of enemy we were up against. There was no hesitation – our duty was clear. My brother Olav, a steward on a Norwegian ship, was already in the service of the Allies. Preparations began the following morning.

We needed a sail. This we bought from a neighbour. (He suggested that coffins should be included in our supplies.) We found another neighbour who possessed an old lifeboat compass. We found some cork and nailed it underneath the seats of our rowing boat in order to float in the event of holes and leakage due to machine-gunning. Then the most important life-preserving item: water! My father had a couple of small old wooden kegs. Being rather dry after some thirty years in storage, they were sunk into a well to swell the wood to make them watertight. They simply fell apart.

Then came the time to visit Sheriff Henrik Robberstad. He was well aware of our intention. (Later he became one of the key men of the local resistance movement.) He issued a pro forma hand-written passport to Johannes and put his official stamp on my already valid passport, which had been stamped recently in the UK.

The next item was food. Mr Skimmeland, who ran the local general shop, offered tinned fishballs, meatballs and various other consumables, insisting on post war payment. (Post war came, and he insisted on payment post mortem.)

Finally, departure, late in the evening of 16 May 1940. My parents, sisters and the pig constituted the farewell party. My mother cried, blessed us and prayed for a safe journey and a welcome back to a liberated Norway.

So off we went. We had previously planned a course, heading for Kinnairds Head, the nearest point on the Scottish coast, some 300 nautical miles away.

The Norwegian day of liberty, 17 May, found us outside Norwegian territorial waters. Symbolically we enjoyed perfect freedom of the same kind as our forefathers had obtained on 17 May 1814 after 400 years of Danish domination.

Oh yes, the weather. Perfectly calm North Sea. Just like a mirror. We had both been rowing all the time. Beautiful, yes, but not so beautiful were all those Heinkels, Dorniers, etc. filling the sky above our heads. They were all heading north, a nasty-looking swastika on their tails. I often wonder if they observed us. However, they seemed to ignore the little nutshell below.

So we continued to row our four-oared little boat, keeping a steady course towards 'Blighty'. The following day the coastline of Norway was no longer visible, but the mountain 'Sigjo' could be seen for well over twenty-four hours. On the second night we observed some lights, but not knowing whether they were friends or enemies, we did not dare to attract their attention. The same night we passed a lot of horn mines and a floating life raft.

On the third day the weather started to change and a slight wind from the northwest became increasingly uncomfortable. Any kind of rest or sleep was out of the question. During the day the north-westerly wind increased to a gale and we had to reduce sail to a little triangle. The rest of the journey was not only strenuous, it was a battle for life with the sea and the wind. Observing that the direction of the current was the opposite of the wind direction, we decided to change to a more southerly course. Three times we did this; in all, almost thirty degrees.

The waves breaking over the boat destroyed our water and bread. We had no time to open tins or get anything to eat, and there was nothing to drink. These conditions lasted for about thirty hours all-told. At the end we became so tired that the mind seemed to stop working – we continued sailing, rowing and bailing automatically.

Eventually, on the fifth morning, the wind calmed down and misty rain set in, but the sea was very heavy. Suddenly, we heard the fog signal – it later turned out to be exactly the one for which we had been heading – Kinnairds Head, only one or two nautical miles away. Then out of the mist loomed a grey shape. Johannes saw the ship's flag – he first thought it was a swastika. As we drew nearer we realized we were being approached by a British ship flying the White Ensign. We had a small Norwegian flag which was promptly hoisted on our own mast. As ship and rowing boat passed each other, a hard Scottish voice shouted down, 'Where do you come from?' I shouted back, 'We are coming from Norway.' Nothing was said after that until the ship turned round and came back and, closing, we heard the same voice shout, 'Where to hell do you say you came from?'

Then things started happening very quickly. The ship, *Lord Plender*, an armed trawler, commanded by skipper Lieutenant John Brebner from Aberdeen, came alongside and, before we knew where we were, half a dozen hands dragged us over the rail and on to the deck of the trawler. Our boat was taken in tow. The skipper offered us a drink. Baldersheim, being a teetotaller, refused. I took a drink of whisky and was just about knocked out by it. We were then treated as admirals, everybody trying to be of service. We were fed and put into bunks to sleep. Then came the real trouble – cramp. My limbs were not functioning normally: it took more than three hours to get to sleep as a result.

Escorting a convoy, the trawler took us to Kirkwall where we were accommodated in a home for old people. After staying there for two days, we joined a Norwegian merchant vessel and I sailed the Atlantic for a year, signing off in London at the end of May 1941 to join the Air Force, and was trained in Canada as a Wireless Operator Mechanic. Johannes Baldersheim sailed the entire war in the merchant navy after making a personal promise not to take a day off as long as the war lasted. He kept his promise.

LIEUTENANT-COLONEL
EGIL JOHANSEN

'23 December 1942. Darkness, hopelessness, anxiety for the future lay oppressively over town and hamlet in our conquered country. The German war machine rolled mercilessly onward and it appeared that nothing could stop it. People bowed under the yoke and whispered with tired voices in the darkness: How long will it last? It was a painful and oppressive time when even the message of Christmas failed to penetrate one's heart. Then appeared a gleam of light from heaven.'

That was how sixteen-year-old Ola Grøttland began a school essay in 1946.

But on 23 December 1942 the twelve-year-old Ola was feeling happy and excited as, clutching his parcels tightly, he ran homeward after a visit to his grandmother. Even if the parcels contained only ersatz soap, toothbrushes, hand-knitted mittens and thick woollen socks, they were all very acceptable in those days.

It was a fine, calm day. Suddenly Ola caught sight of an aircraft which came in low and began to circle. People were not unused to aircraft in those days – the German air traffic between south and north Norway went over Vega – but this aircraft did not act in the way that aircraft did usually. It flew very low, banked and flew with one wing low for long periods. Ola could see people inside the aircraft and thought that they were waving. Then he saw something thrown out of the aircraft. He stiffened: anxiety hammered in his breast. Were they bombs? But there was no explosion and the aircraft disappeared.

Just after Ola reached home, a man came cycling at top speed yelling that an 'Englishman' had thrown out sacks of coffee and tobacco and greetings from King Haakon and Prime Minister Nygårdsvold. Ola hurried out again. He ran as fast as his legs would carry him, but arrived too late. The sacks had fallen into a densely populated area and the old saying about 'first to the mill' once again proved its validity. Ola was out of luck, but his friends had arrived in time to get hold of the empty sacks – attractively decorated in red, white and blue. The adults had made sure of the contents.

There was great excitement: people laughed and cried. The youngsters, not normally very enthusiastic about cod liver oil, swallowed the cod liver oil capsules as if they were sweets. And English chewing tobacco was consumed with great relish. Ola had his first smoke that day and ambled around proudly with a cigarette in the corner of his mouth. The lovely smell of newly brewed coffee hung over the whole town.

It was an unforgettable day. For a little while war was forgotten. The adults smiled and enjoyed themselves enormously. 'Just think, the Englishmen have been here with Christmas presents and greetings from the King and Government.' They had not been forgotten up there in far away Norway. The light of hope shone in the darkness of Advent.

Then came the Germans, many of them, armed to the teeth. They learned that sacks had fallen from the skies – two had even fallen on the church steps. They hunted back and forth, but the results were as lean as could be. They sniffed the aroma of coffee and noticed that people looked suspiciously pleased – they did not usually look like that when the *herrenvolk* came to visit – but they found nothing.

In one place a sack fell on the roof of a house and broke a tile. The owner of the house contacted the mayor and claimed compensation. The result of the claim is unknown, but rumour has it that the mayor seized the sack and its contents.

As late as spring 1943 the youngsters continued to receive

cod liver oil capsules and the adults had real coffee and cigarettes on special occasions. But the most important thing about the incident was that it cheered people up. They felt closer to each other and patriotic feelings blossomed as never before. It was truly a light in the darkness which gave new strength and new faith during gloomy times.

About forty years later Ola, by then Lieutenant-Colonel Grøttland of the RNOAF, was talking about the incident. One of those present, Lieutenant-Colonel Egil Johansen, exclaimed 'Then we have met before!': he was one of the crew of the *Catalina* from which the Christmas presents had been dropped.

CAPTAIN
LEON KOTLOWSKI

I was born in Warsaw on 27 April 1927 and lived with my family in the Jewish quarter of the city. My father was a tailor, a good tailor, and we lived at 9 Stafsky Street. At that time Warsaw was the city with the largest Jewish population: maybe 600,000 people were Jewish out of a total population of about 1,300,000 people.

In September 1939 the German forces attacked Poland and this was the beginning of the war. On the first day my father was mobilized into the Polish Cavalry as a Corporal. I stayed at home with my mother, one sister and two brothers. I was the eldest. We stayed in Warsaw. I remember the first bombing by German planes over the city. I couldn't believe it when the German planes bombed the civilian buildings in the Jewish quarter. I could hear the bombs falling and they destroyed many buildings. It was on a Wednesday and I saw many friends and neighbours killed on the street. My mother took us and we went to a very big shelter in a German beer factory called Haberbusch and

Schiele in Warsaw. There were hundreds of people there, Polish and Jewish, and we all slept together on the floor, hundreds of people together.

The Germans bombed Warsaw during the night. The President of Warsaw, Starjinsky, broadcast over the radio telling the Polish people not to capitulate to the Germans. All the government went away to Romania and the German army occupied all Poland around Warsaw. They used planes and ground artillery to attack Warsaw.

My family stayed in the shelter in the beer factory. We were all hungry and had no food at all. Somebody told us that there was a bakers in the Cherniakow quarter where we could buy bread and so my mother sent me there. There was a huge queue of people, and all the while the Germans were bombing. I saw many people killed and there was much blood in the streets, but we were so hungry that I stayed in the queue and managed to buy bread for my family. I took the bread home, but I was so hungry that I was nibbling at it all the way. I was 12½ years old.

After three or four weeks the Germans occupied Warsaw and there were big parades in the streets. The first time the Germans came into Warsaw they threw bread to the people. Because I was the oldest child I was sent to get some of the black bread but I was small and the crowds of people jostled so much that I thought I was going to suffocate, and I had to go home without any bread that day.

Not far from our home the Germans opened a military kitchen at Platz Bronie. Every day there they gave soup out. I had to take a bowl to collect the soup. I stood in the queue all night, from ten o'clock in the evening. The kitchen was opened at eight in the morning and began giving out soup to the people. When I got as near as twenty to twenty-five people ahead of me in the line I was very excited because I would be able to take soup to my family, but then one Polish woman told the Germans that I was Jewish. The Germans couldn't tell who was Jewish but the Polish people told them. The German soldier kicked me and I fell over. I got no soup and I cried very much.

Two months later my father came back home. He told us that his regiment had hidden in a forest near a city called Kutnow. The Germans surrounded them, captured them and took the whole regiment to prison. The Jewish soldiers were separated from the Polish soldiers who were put into passenger carriages. The Jewish soldiers were put in wooden freight wagons but they were engineers and carried small handsaws with them so they cut a hole in the floor of the wagon. When they next stopped at a small station they all escaped through the hole in the floor and my father came home.

The SS and SD came to Warsaw. They began to shave the beards of the Jewish men and hit them. My father said we must escape to the Russian side to live. He took my brother to the Russian side but at this time the Germans had marked Warsaw into a sort of grid and systematically bombed each section in rotation. They put all the Jewish people to do this work, and after taking my brother away my father was put to this work.

One day my father came home in the evening from this work and in the morning of the next day they tried to take him. Then we came to the Russian side, to the River Bug. We stayed in Bialistock where there were hundreds of thousands of people who had escaped from the German side. Because my father had been a very good tailor he began to work in the Russian Army Tailoring Unit. He made the uniforms for Russian officers while we lived in one room of a Jewish family home. One day in Bialistock my father met his brother-in-law and he gave him some money and sent him back to Warsaw to bring the rest of the family. It was a very difficult mission because the Germans shot people crossing the river. They tried five or six times before they managed to cross safely.

After some time the Russian government contracted

people to do work in Russia. My father and my mother told us we couldn't stay there any longer and that we had to get away further away from the Germans. So they signed on for one year's building work in Berezniki in Siberia. We travelled for three weeks on a freight train. It was wintertime, December 1939 or January 1940, and there was ice hanging from the roof of the wagon.

After the year's contract finished we moved to a big textile centre called Ivanover. My father worked in his own trade of tailor and I went to the professional school to learn mechanics.

During 1941 the German army attacked the Russian front and in the winter of that year my father was mobilized into the Russian army and I didn't see him again until he left. He finished the war in Budapest in Hungary. Mother was left with her five children (another sister had been born in Russia). It was a hard life, always hungry.

In 1942 I was mobilized into the Russian army. We had to go to Tambov so one night I left home without telling my family where I was going, and with Alik, my Russian friend, went to the train. At Tambov we went to the recruitment centre where officers came to select the men for their regiments. The next day Alik was taken to the artillery. I didn't see him again. His family told me he went to the Japanese front. The Commander then told me I was too young and to go home. He said that maybe by the time I was old enough to be mobilized the war would be over. They gave me two more years, but I still wanted to fight against the Germans. After nine days a tank major came and took people into his regiment. I went to this major and asked him if he would take me. I told him I had been to the professional school and I was a mechanic and I could do the work. So he took me as a messenger for the tank division as I was so young. He took me to Stalingrad. Near Stalingrad, in a large village called Shirokoe on the River Volga, there had been a very hard fight with the Germans. I began as a messenger and then was given the job of carrying the ammunition to the guns. After that I became a tank driver (a T34 tank) and then I worked a radio machine-gun.

My happiest moment came when our two armies surrounded the Germans. It had been a hard fight and in the winter of 1943 the 22nd Army capitulated. I was very satisfied when I saw all the German prisoners being taken. I saw Field Marshall von Powells, the commander of the 22nd Army, in an open-top car and I saw him sign the surrender document.

After the Stalingrad battle we went behind the lines and our army organized a course for tank commanders. I was very fit and had a good record so my regiment sent me to the training course. It was held in a village called Pitomnk where there was a military airport. In three months we did the whole programme which normally takes three years to complete. It was very hard work and we didn't get much sleep. All the work was done in the field. At the end of the course I was 2nd-Lieutenant at the age of seventeen and became a front-line tank commander. I was wounded near Woroniez. After I left hospital I was in the second Ukrainian front, first of all as a tank commander and then a tank company commander.

I saw what the Germans did to the Jews when I was staying in Dharnitza and went to Babi Yar, a town in the forest near Kiev. I saw hundreds and thousands of bodies. Later I went to Schepetovka, Chernovitz. This was the first city we went to and the Jewish people were so friendly. We went to the synagogue and they invited us into their homes. From there we went to Petrom Ploestt to a very very hard battle against both the Romanian and German armies. The artillery hit my tank and I was very badly wounded and spent two weeks in hospital before I was able to get up. I didn't know what had happened. From the hospital the Russian commander sent me to the Polish army and I chose to go to tank school in the Ukraine to teach Polish tankists about radio. I had been a 2nd-Lieutenant and then a full Lieutenant. But I could not stay there, I had to be in the action. I sent one report after another saying that I'd like to fight the Germans and so they sent me to a Polish regiment called 13 PAS. I went with them first to the Maidanek concentration camp. What I saw there really shook me. I do not need to describe it. Everyone knows how terrible those places were.

At Zmerinka (the biggest railway centre in the Ukraine with 150 tracks) we had a very hard fight with the Germans. We advanced and so did the Germans, and when we broke through the German lines we went all ways. Every officer had a map and the map showed the way we must go forward and where we must stop for petrol. After stopping in the forest near Tishkowka to get fuel and ammunition we stopped next at a little town called Proskurov about 15 km from Tishkowka. We had two days to rest and to clean the tanks, which we parked widely spaced out so that if we were bombed the tanks would not all be immobilized at once. I had four tanks under my control. When we stopped I left the tanks to go for a walk and get some fresh air. It was 14 March 1944, and it had been the Jewish festival of Purim. I was seventeen years old. As I walked through the forest I thought I could hear voices. I searched around and found a heap of snow and ice that didn't look natural. I brushed it aside and found a dugout shelter, not a natural one. There was a family in it: a woman of maybe fifty-two or fifty-three years old, her husband of sixty or a little older, and three little girls. They were very hungry and crying and their clothes were ragged and dirty. On the ground was straw which smelled terrible. They had apparently lived there for three years because the place had been occupied by the Germans. When the family saw me they were afraid and huddled together, and afterwards they told me it was because in 1941 when the Germans had come, the Soviet army had not been wearing badges on their shoulders, only on the collar. Afer that, before Stalingrad, the Russian government gave them shoulder badges, but these people didn't know whether I was German or Russian. They were also afraid because the Germans had a Ukrainian army under the command of Blassov (after the war he was hanged). They were even worse than the SS. They were murderers. So when this family saw me they thought I was from the Blassov army and that it was the end of their lives.

I went into the shelter and my heart was pounding. I spoke to the people in Russian and told them not to be afraid as I was an officer with the Red Army and I was bringing them freedom: this was the end of their fears. I asked them what had happened in the town. They told me that the Jews had been murdered. We cried together and I told them I was Jewish and that they needn't be afraid. This was the first Jewish civilian family I met. The father said, 'Today is Purim.'

They told me that before the Russians had been attacked in June 1941 they stayed in a big city called Winnica. They had had friends there before the war from a good Urkainian family. They had been together in business and when the Nazis occupied the Ukraine and began to kill Jews the Ukrainians had dug the shelter for this family during the nights. They gave them food even though they didn't have enough for themselves. For three years they had stayed in that dugout. At this time anybody who was caught helping Jews was killed by the Germans.

I went to see my regimental commander, Vice-Colonel Woroncow, to see if he would come with me to visit the family. I pleaded with him to grant me two days' leave because I wanted to help this family. We took food and a military overcoat to them. I stayed, with my ordnance officer, not far from there near a small town (I don't remember its name). Some Ukrainians who had lived there were taken to prison by the Nazis and murdered, so I took the Jewish family to an empty apartment that had belonged to one of these Ukrainian families. We got a horse and cart and I took the family into the town and organized beds, tables, everything I could.

When my leave was over I had to go back to my regiment. The mother cooked a Ukrainian meal for me and she always called me 'my child'. When I left she gave me a photo and asked if I had a photograph of myself she could have so she could pray to God for my safety. I gave her a photo I had in my pocket of myself and my friend on the first day we had our Russian uniforms. This made her very happy. After that I sent clothes and other things from Germany to the family, and to the family that had helped them.

After the war I taught Polish tankists at the tankists' school because I was wounded and a war invalid. I was demobbed in 1946 and went home to my family who were still in Ivanover in Russia. For the first time in five years I saw my father. He had also been demobbed and the whole family returned to Poland.

In April 1957 the whole family went to Israel and in August 1958 I was taken into the Israeli Military Reserve. I fought again in the Six Day War and afterwards the Soviet Union and the other communist countries broke off diplomatic relations with Israel. All the veterans from the Iron Curtain block returned their medals and orders to their respective governments because of this.

Four generations of my family have fought in wars. My grandfather in World War I from 1914 to 1916 when he was killed in the army. My father served in the Polish army in 1939 and from 1941 to 1945 in the Russian Army. I was in the Soviet, Polish and Israeli armies, my children in the Israeli army. I think that this is enough. There must be peace. This cannot be right when one man in uniform kills another man in uniform, because somewhere there is a mother and a father, maybe a wife and children, and they will cry when their loved one is killed.

FRAU EMMI BONHOEFFER

In 1933, when Hitler became *Reichskanzler*, it was clear that he would go to war. He had written in his book *Mein Kampf*: 'Each generation needs its war. I shall take care that ours will get one'.

During the following six years political propaganda worked successfully in stirring up a passionate nationalism by exploiting the feelings of humiliation, resulting from those tremendous economic burdens loaded upon the entire nation through the Treaty of Versailles which ended World War I. One of Hitler's first visible political acts was to lower unemployment by instituting a new road-building programme, which eased life immediately for many families. He then boosted the steel industry and started producing arms. All this was accompanied by a style of propaganda which catered for the inferior instincts of revenge.

We saw the catastrophy coming nearer and hoped that somebody from the army would kill Hitler, or that the Western Allies would be determined and strong enough to stop him. Neither happened. So when Hitler invaded Poland, the shock was enormous. On 3 September when my husband came home with the news that the Western Allies had declared war on Germany, both of us felt hopeful and despondent at the same time: hopeful that this was the moment when the military would refuse to follow Hitler's provocative aggression, but rather would assassinate him; desperate because we realized that if he was not stopped, death and misery would be the inevitable outcome throughout Europe. I remember that I was trembling so much I was unable to feed my baby. Tragically enough it turned out that Hitler fought successfully at first (he was well prepared!).

The old historical evidence proved itself once again; as

long as the army fights successfully, nationalism becomes blind and stronger than morality, reason or sense of justice.

This was what I felt, as did my family, whose members worked in the Resistance from 1930. All of them were sentenced to death and executed.

COUNT WOLF VON BAUDISSIN

As a child I had already experienced the First World War which initially aroused great national enthusiasm in Germany, only then to have people becoming more and more introspective in view of the sacrifices and destruction.

As an adult I was deeply concerned that Hitler would let loose the Second World War. I experienced the beginning of the war as a General Staff Officer of a division which was positioned on the western border to defend against possible French and British attacks. It wasn't easy to define military and political responsibility, to balance responsibility for the lives of German soldiers against the certainty that a German victory would have made it impossible to remove Hitler from power.

So I wish for all in the West and the East that the memory of the Second World War will help us to become more peace-loving, that is to be ready to settle conflicts between states without force and according to agreed proceedings.

HENRY METELMANN

I was not seventeen years old when the war started. I lived with my parents in Hamburg, Germany. The propaganda, especially against Poland, had blared for months. Now, of course, I know that it all was propaganda, but in those days I believed it all. I thought that governments don't lie, at least not mine. That's where I made my first mistake.

I was still in bed when my mother told me that we were at war with Poland. She was very sad about it; like my father, she hated war. They both were sure that wars come because the financially powerful people in all capitalist countries make much profit from war, from the killing of the innocent. I with my Hitler Youth ideas thought it was all great. On the radio was much military music. There were plenty of speeches from the top Nazis, many statements were repeated all day long. I think it was later in the day that Hitler made his 'great' speech to the Reichstag. He shouted and bawled and accused the Poles of having provoked us for weeks. You mustn't forget, he was a very self-centred man, would not listen to anyone, thought he was right and clever and even great. I clearly remember what he said, and the mad shouts of excitement that followed: *heil, heil, heil* – ! A nation going mad! On that same evening we had to go to a Hitler Youth meeting. We were told about glory and greatness and the wisdom of our Führer and such rubbish. We felt, I think, as many British people felt when a task force was sent to the Falklands. I was a fool, I believed it all, all that incredible rubbish, and I was concerned that I was too young to take part in all the 'great' things, that it all would be over by the time I was eighteen and old enough to become a soldier.

Two days later, the radio blared again. It was a beautiful warm late summer's day. The news this time was that the perfidious British under Chamberlain had dared to send us an ultimatum to pull out our troops from Poland. It was pointed out that the British should keep their noses out of it as they had invaded many countries themselves and had made many countries part of their Empire against the will of the people living in them. Of course, our 'wise' Führer did not allow our good country Germany to be blackmailed by the crafty British. So we were at war with Britain. But they had declared it on us, not we on them. And now we will show them, wipe the floor with them. That was our attitude! Now, half a century later, I have a job to understand how I could have been such a fool. I walked in the town with my friends in the warm sunshine. There was military music and radio speeches and statements to be heard everywhere. But the mood of the older people was subdued: there was no hurrah-shouting, and only we youngsters walked around with proudly smiling faces.

There were no abrupt changes. For several months butter had already been rationed but now slowly more food scarcities appeared. My parents pointed out to me that people with money could buy everything they wanted, it was only us poor working people who had to suffer shortages. By then I was a locksmith apprentice with the railways in Hamburg. Within days we were engaged in making light excluders for train headlights.

After I was eighteen I was called up to the army. I was still full of myself and believed in our righteousness and had no doubt in our eventual victory. I was thoroughly trained in barracks in Germany, was sent as an occupation soldier to France and then went with a Panzer Division to Russia where I stayed for several years, took part in many battles, got wounded several times and slowly became disillusioned. But that's another story.

H.T. FITZSIMMONS

Having had many close shaves during the Blitz in London and Portsmouth I suddenly found myself on board HMS *Prince of Wales* serving as telegraphist on the C-in-C's staff. We arrived in Singapore about 1 December 1941 after much secrecy about our movements, and we thought we were on to a good thing, we'd struck lucky: no war, plenty of sunshine, plenty of food, drink, everything. We definitely thought our luck was in.

At 4 a.m. on 8 December I had just relieved my opposite number in the wireless office when I began to receive an emergency message, in plain language, announcing the declaration of war with Japan. Other operators were also receiving this signal on other frequencies, and whilst this was going on the anti-aircraft batteries were engaged in action against enemy aircraft making a surprise attack on Singapore.

Some hours later we cleared away for sea in company with HMS *Repulse* and the destroyers HMS *Electra*, HMS *Express*, HMS *Vampire* and HMS *Tenedos*. This was Force 2. But we had no aircraft carrier and no air cover. We steamed north to locate and engage the enemy invasion fleets now landing there. At approximately 11 a.m. on 10 December 1941 we were attacked by a very large force of enemy aircraft – about twenty-eight aircraft were deployed to engage us – all highly trained and especially selected crews for the job. Having no air cover to break up the formations our anti-aircraft defence was split by high and low level attacks by very determined pilots. Having survived considerable numbers of torpedoes launched against us, one finally found its mark, immediately destroying all power, propulsion and steering. Unable to steer and unable to train the guns, we were a helpless sitting duck. Realizing this the enemy turned and concentrated their fury on HMS *Repulse* which was trying to defend us. The attack was fierce and finally *Repulse* was overcome and sunk. The aircraft now renewed their attack on the *Prince of Wales* and, no longer able to defend herself, she finally sank at 1.20 p.m. In a very brave attempt to save lives, the Captain of the *Express* took his destroyer alongside the sinking ship to evacuate the wounded, but the ship began to roll over and only by superb seamanship did the Captain of the *Express* manage to avoid his ship being dragged down with her.

Once in the water I soon found myself separated from the other survivors and my main concern was to try to keep some sense of bearing from the sun, in order that I might attempt to swim towards the coast. I soon realized that once it became dark I would have very little chance of survival; sharks and exhaustion would see to that.

After swimming for four to five hours I began to feel very exhausted. I had swallowed a considerable amount of oil fuel and, due to an injury to my upper back by bomb blast, I found I had very little strength to use my arms. I had now given up hope and was lying on my back when I spotted two silver specks in the sky which began a long swooping dive towards me. Fearing that I was about to be machine gunned by enemy aircraft, I duck-dived and swam underwater as deep as possible. After several attempts at this I found I could not carry on and I just lay on my back waiting for the end. Then I realized the aircraft were friendly RAAF planes spotting for the destroyers, who were picking up survivors. The *Electra*, guided by the planes, finally came to pick me up – 'You're bloody lucky! We're about to turn back. You must be one of the last.' I was told the destroyer was packed solid with survivors below and on deck. I was given quite a number of mugs of neat rum to help fortify me, but it had very little effect.

Some time after midnight we arrived in Singapore Naval Base where we were given hot soup, more rum and some food. Then we were given piles of cotton waste to try to remove the oil fuel from our bodies. After a long scrub in the shower I finally collapsed completely exhausted on a pile of blankets and slept, dead to the world, until the next day.

Over 800 men died that day and many of the survivors were later to lose their lives in other ships in the Java Sea battle, and many more from their treatment as Japanese prisoners of war.

Just one day in the life of a very ordinary seaman. . . .

Top: *British Aircraft Carrier with Eastern Fleet during Sigli raid, July 1944*

Bottom: *Beaufighters of RAF Coastal Command attacking enemy convoy off Heligoland, July 1944*

(Photographs: *Imperial War Museum*)

Peace: a short-lived hope in September 1938 . . .

. . . but it came at last

(Photograph: Colonel Hammond, WRAC)

SIDNEY LAWRENCE

Extract courtesy of Department of Sound Records, Imperial War Museum

I heard on the radio that we had gone to war with Germany, but we all knew really that it was coming. We almost felt a sense of relief and just thanked God that something was at last being done to stop Hitler.

At the time I was working as an optician but as I was already a volunteer reservist in my spare time I went straight into the RAF, where I was trained first at Cardington in Bedfordshire and then at RAF Cranwell as an Instrument Engineer, before being stationed at RAF Finningley in Yorkshire where I stayed until 1941. My posting then was to Singapore.

In December of that year I was at Kota Bahru in the north of Malaya when, in common with the American fleet at Pearl Harbor, we suffered the first surprise attack by the Japanese. This was on 8 December 1941. It was in the early hours of the morning and I was coming back from having a shower and only had a towel around me. Most people were in bed. Just as I got back into the hut I heard a series of tremendous explosions. I had no ieda what was happening. Then the tannoy system came on: 'Pay attention! Pay attention! All station personnel take action war stations immediately!' Next thing I realized was that Japanese planes were flying over us and we were being strafed. I fell on to my bed and to this day I can still hear the bullets ripping through the wooden walls of my hut. I managed to put on my shirt and shorts and ran down to the aerodrome to see if there was anything I could do. By daylight we could actually see the Japanese fleet and our planes were just being armed, taking off, flying in a short circle, dropping their bombs or torpedoes and returning to land and re-arm. This went on until there was nothing left.

What few planes were left after this were taken away by their pilots and we were simply left behind.

I realized that there was nothing left for us except to escape through the jungle so I went back to my hut and found a water bottle which I filled. Unfortunately I had no carrier for the bottle so I fixed it to my belt, although as it stuck out at an angle it was rather uncomfortable. I looked around for other personnel to see what I could do and I ended up with soldiers of the Indian Army. I was given a Vickers machine gun and fought to resist the Japanese landings. I was about a quarter of a mile from the beach in a ditch and we were mowing the Japanese down as they came forward, but they just kept coming in swarms. Where there were dead bodies they just climbed over them. It was like trying to keep back a swarm of ants. I personally must have hit hundreds of them. Nearby where there was a small river it literally ran red with blood. Our ammunition though was running out, and we were given the order to pull back. I jumped out of my ditch and was running back, terrified, covered in perspiration, when I suddenly felt a terrific jerking movement and a wetness down my left side. I fell flat on my face allowing the bullets to go over my head. I had a sort of temporary blackout and with my eyes half closed, I felt wet down one side and thought the whole of my side had been shot away. Slowly I put my hand down to my side. I could not get up. When I brought my hand up and opened my eyes to look at it I realized that it was water that had made me wet, not blood. As soon as I realized this, my brain seemed to start working again and I was up like a shot, but until that moment I could not have moved. My water bottle was peppered with holes like a colander but I was untouched. Not one bullet had even touched me.

We got into the jungle and found our way to a road where natives had trucks and we were taken southwards with refugees of all nationalities. What particularly struck me was the hundreds of crying, abandoned native children. Either their parents had been killed or they had simply run away and left their children. It was a most heart-rending experience to pick up a little child, dirty, blood stained, crying, and having them hug me while I tried to reassure them. Eventually, though, we got back to Singapore although the Japanese were not all that far behind us.

Singapore was in chaos. It had been bombed at about the same time as we had been attacked at Kota Bahru and the impregnable fortress of Singapore was in a state of dreadful chaos. By February we were given orders to leave for Sumatra. At the harbour were thousands of people trying to get away but, I am sad to say, the people to get permits to leave were European, while the Asiatics were just pushed away. This was organized by high ranking officials of the Singapore administration and army officers as well. Every so often the Japanese flew over and bombed us and we stood there, literally getting spattered with people's blood, and then we witnessed what could only be a typically British scene. Trestle tables flying in the air with bodies, papers all over the place, and then when the raid was over the same men who had been sitting there putting the trestle tables back, collecting up papers, sitting down and starting all over again to issue their permits. I was put on the gang plank of a ship and told to allow only those with permits to go aboard. It was heart-breaking when native people, hugging children, came and looked at me so pathetically. Permits? I knew they had no permits. When I could I turned my back and told them, 'Don't be here when I turn back', and when I did turn back they were gone. I knew where. The ship I left left on, the *Perak*, was so overloaded that they had to put men in the crow's nest with megaphones pleading with the people to move to port or starboard to prevent us actually turning over.

At Palembang in Sumatra we had two make-shift aerodromes, but they didn't last long as the Japanese sent parachutists and they dropped in swarms and took the two airfields. So we had to get out of there as fast as we could. We managed to get away by train with people packed inside and covering the roof and sides as well, and we made our way to the southern tip of Sumatra and crossed the Sunda Straits to Java.

After much to-ing and fro-ing we ended up on a hastily made aerodrome in the mountains with just a few aircraft. Most of the military had been evacuated to India or Australia and there were just about 600 British personnel dotted about throughout the island, and some Dutch. Eventually the Japanese again sent parachutists to try and take our airfield. We had with us a small contingent of about thirty Gurkhas and they attacked hundreds of Japanese. Roaring and shouting, wielding their special Gurkha knives, I actually saw them lop heads straight off, laughing while they did it. The memory of it has never left me. Their morale was so high. They then came back to me smiling, many of them covered in blood. I have no idea how many bodies they left behind. 'Come along. Come with us. You'll be safe,' and I did feel safe, too.

Finally, though, in March 1942 the Dutch surrendered and we were ordered to lay down our arms. We were herded together and put into camps. I was sent to Khalidjati. The intention was to make us work on an aerodrome filling in the potholes which we had actually made during the fighting. We were lined up and a Japanese officer with a soldier with him went down the line. Stopping at the first man he said 'You will promise to work for the holy land of Japan.' This man said, in the foulest language possible, 'You know what you can do with that! If you think I'm going to work for Japan you've made a big mistake!' The butt of the soldier's rifle smashed at his head, the fellow fell; he put his bayonet through him and then beat his head in with the rifle butt. The officer then moved on to the second man, asked the same question and was given the same answer. They did exactly the same to him. I was about the sixth one in the line and I can remember to this day standing to attention as we were supposed to be, saying my prayers. 'Dear God. Give me the strength to do exactly the same as these fellows are doing. Give me the strength to say no. I don't want to be the first one to say yes.' The officer came to the third man and asked him and with great relief I heard him say 'Yes'. When my turn came, I too said yes, and from then we worked for what they called 'the holy land of Japan'.

The Japanese despised us for having allowed ourselves to be taken prisoner. We should have committed suicide rather than be captured was what they thought. They had not signed the Geneva Convention and so we had no real defence at all against their treatment. They could treat us as they liked. They wanted to degrade us and to treat us as less than the dregs of the earth. Food was appalling and we were beaten. They made a point of making sure we witnessed any punishments and if you turned away or didn't watch, you were badly beaten. In one case we were forced to watch the mass rape of about twelve Dutch women in a field by dozens of soldiers. The helplessness and pity I felt at having to watch was unbearable. Some women survived and some died, but I do not know how many as we were moved away while they were all still lying on the ground. The worst punishment I received was when I was caught trying to slip food to a prisoner in a sort of solitary confinement. He had been locked away in a dark hut, and when they caught me he was taken out and I was put in and tied up by my wrists to the ceiling with my feet about a foot or two off the floor. I was left like this for nearly two days without any relief whatsoever. When they finally came in the light was blinding. They cut me down and I dropped on to the floor and I put my arms down. The agony was something appalling. I had actually got used to hanging by my arms and after the first few hours I didn't feel any pain. Another punishment was to choose two prisoners, give each a club and then make them beat one another.

From March until October 1942 I was held in Java and then we were taken by ship – the *Shonan Maru* – via

Singapore and Vietnam to Moji in Japan. The voyage was hell. Of over 2000 on the ship only 288 survived. We were kept battened down and allowed out very rarely, and dysentary very quickly spread. What food there was was appalling. When men died they just took the bodies and threw them over the side.

In Japan I was made to work in a variety of camps doing all sorts of jobs from loading ships, working in a copper refinery and coal mining and in January 1945 I was moved to Nagasaki. I can remember there all of us being called together for the camp commandant to inform us that the war in Europe was over. Japan, though, would fight on 'for ever!' We would never be allowed to be released as prisoners of war, but if Japan were to be invaded we were to be killed. The rumour in our camp was that we would be driven into a tunnel that we had been forced to dig in a nearby hillside and the whole lot would be blown in. That was how we were to die.

In Nagasaki I worked in the engineering yards of the Mitsubishi company. Quite often we saw American aircraft and there was quite a lot of bombing. When this happened we were often sent out to clear rubble.

On this particular day, 9 August 1945, it was a hot summer's day. At about eleven o'clock in the morning I was working outside with others shifting rubble into heaps. A plane came over and, looking up, I could see something glistening and I thought, 'Oh, they've opened the bomb door and I've caught the reflection in the sun.' I was by a rather large mound of rubble and I stood looking at that plane. Quite suddenly there was the most vivid, the most awful flash, a terrible booming noise and a feeling of hot wind and air. I can remember the flash being sufficiently vivid for me, for some reason or other, to cover my left eye and I shut tight my right eye. The next thing I realized was a sort of sucking noise and seeing black smoke, or what I thought was black smoke, rising in the usual spiral and then the mushroom cloud which seemed to get bigger and bigger and seemed to be blotting out the sun. And yet I was still standing there and looking at all this not knowing what it was.

The soldier who was near me said in Japanese, 'What's that?' I replied, 'I don't know, Mr Soldier'. To my amazement he left his rifle and turned and ran back towards the camp. I looked around me. Everyone was dead and I didn't have a scratch on me. I had actually been protected by the mound of rubble – the epicentre of the blast was only just over a mile away.

When I moved back to the camp in a daze the camp and its perimeter fence had gone. Everything was quiet. I thought, because of the smoke, that an oil dump had been hit at the shipyards. I knew nothing about atomic bombs and I had heard nothing of Hiroshima.

There were trees which on one side were dead white, the foliage gone, the trunks and the branches dead white; and the other side was all intact with foliage. There were small hills and it was as though someone had whitewashed one side in a straight line and left the grass to grow on the other side. I crossed a little bridge and there were shadows of people actually emblazoned in the concrete. No people, just the shadows. It was obvious that someone had been sitting and standing there, and there in the concrete, was the shadow of a sitting person and the shadow of a standing person. Everyone left alive was in a complete and utter daze.

There was a dreadful smell of burned flesh and bone and there were bodies that looked like they had come from a slaughter house – raw meat, slices of meat dripping blood. Some people, to my astonishment, were ripped, their flesh was ripped raw from head to toe, but only on one side. Yet they seem intact on the other side. It obviously depended on which way they happened to be facing at that particular time.

The Japanese asked us to help and see if there were any people left alive, and I came across a little girl. One side of her was burned completely and the other side was untouched. All she did was sit there whimpering. Just whimpering. Not crying in agony, just sitting there whimpering. I picked her up and carried her to the soldiers, who now carried no rifles, and she was put on to a truck. I remember saying to a soldier, 'What have we done to you?' and, tears rolling down his face, he said, 'What have we done to each other?' From that moment I felt at one with them. All the misery and starvation, all the three and a half years of what I'd been through seemed to vanish and I felt that they were the same as me and I was the same as them.